Bombs *for* Breakfast

A REAL LIFE STORY

GARY GREEN

Michael Terence
Publishing

First published in paperback by
Michael Terence Publishing in 2018
www.mtp.agency

ISBN 9781912639045

There are a lot of people that deserve this.

My choice though is simple, my Nan, Margery Green

23rd May 1935 – 27th July 2017.

My biggest regret is that you never got to read my book Nan. You saw the worst of me, I just hope you know how much I love and miss you.

Gramp, thank you for being my Dad when I never had one.

Bombs *for* Breakfast

A REAL LIFE STORY

GARY GREEN

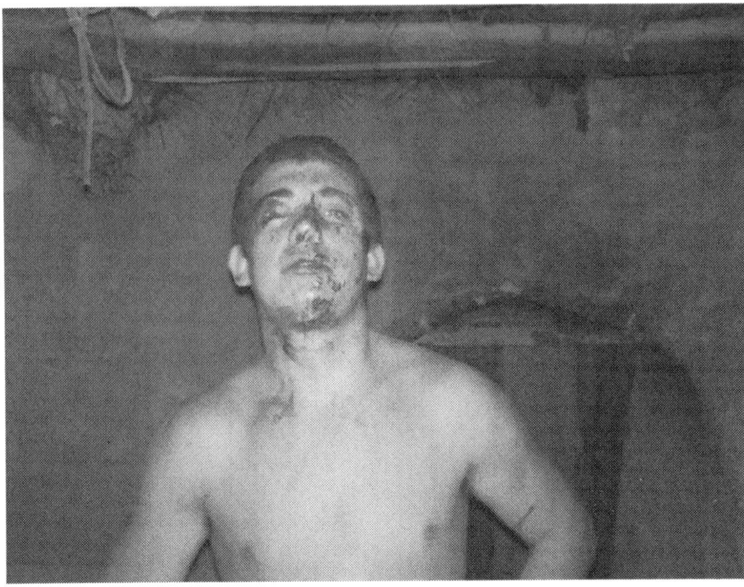

Bombs for Breakfast - 15 minutes after injury in PB Parang,
21st August 2009.

Chapter 1
Bombs for Breakfast

The most frequent question I am asked, and I think all veterans that have been where I have been, are asked the same question.

"Have you ever killed anyone?"

This is not a question I give credence to. However, this book is about being absolutely honest, so as a contractual agreement to being honest, I will answer that question now.

"I don't know."

That is the honest answer, I could have killed no one, I could have killed one hundred people, where we were, we could never confirm a kill as we never came face to face with the enemy. The closest I came to knowing that I killed someone was on sentry position two with a 7.62 general purpose machine gun. We were in contact from compound four. I saw the enemy fire from the door way next to a sloping roof. The compound was two hundred meters away, I pulled the trigger and fired into the door way and the firing stopped. To me this was my kill, I will never know. That is the most honest answer I can give, and the rest of the book will follow the same suit. I am no war criminal, I am no thug, I am a human being that was in a non-human situation please remember that as you turn through these pages.

While writing this book, I have flickered through about one million different emotions had one hundred thousand negative thoughts. Ejaculated ten thousand times, been to the toilet eight thousand times, had one thousand hours of sleep, one hundred very different and contradicting personalities. I have spent three weeks in therapy and finally had one prominent and chronic thought in my head. This feeling was pure, to keep it simple, a simple idea in which would set this writing apart from all the other literature you read about war. This book is not a war book, it's insight, it's a journey into the belly of the beast, and this mission will be an honest walk through the life of a soldier, the difficulties of adjusting afterwards and the real harsh realities with each reason behind them. I shall not glorify any of the stories. I would not insult your intelligence by lying about these experiences, I shall merely educate and enlighten you on what goes on behind closed doors. I will give you a sense of realism to which is usually portrayed by the media and gaming industry as something it is not.

The story is my life and what I have been through and how each part has affected my life. Step by step you'll read about the development of my mind and how it was rewired and evolved into a tool for the Army to be utilised on the battlefield as an efficient killing machine, to then being thrown aside into the foreign world of civilian life. Life in which I struggled to adjust. To be able to understand how and why I took the paths I have, you have to follow my footsteps. From the council house I grew up in, the father I never knew, the firefights in Afghanistan to the places I spent nights taking cocaine in and how I dragged myself out of the cycle to try to live a healthy life with PTSD.

Today is just another day, I wake up feeling like shit! I feel empty, something in my life is missing. Living as a hollow shell of who and what I used to be. I was once trained and carved into a devastating instrument to be used at the British Army's disposal is now at war with no other enemy than its self. I am that instrument, or should I say I was that instrument. So I beg of you, remember that fact. For reading this book without remembering my past, would give you a misguided perspective of which I am. I am not a bad person, but my actions and reactions to my situation can quite easily give that impression, for I have done some terrible things. The world I am allowing you access to is not a world you are familiar with; it's a world I have grown up in, a world I live in, this world is my escape, my enemy, my best friend and above all it is my mind. My mind is like no other yet similar to thousands; it's a mind twisted by depression and PTSD.

My body is scarred and filled with metal, but it operates in almost the same way as it once did. The only mark that instantly stands out is the eyelid and eyebrow that surrounds my right eye, what was once a peach tone landmark upon my face, is now blushed continuously and scarred, the twisted reminder of my time served in hell. Though this I can live with, in my own right it makes me a legend, a talking point in the smoking areas of the bars and clubs I once frequented. It lent itself to a promiscuous lifestyle, yet this was not my disability. My disability was and is inside, unseen, manifesting itself through my actions. Whether that is upon someone who just happened to be in the wrong place, at the wrong time, as my pain and anger erupted from a mind consumed and misguided with alcohol, or at night when I can't sleep due to the torturous memories and thoughts that swim around my head 24/7. My disability had cost me my relationship, my career, and my home. The pain I hid inside slowly corroded me like a poisonous acid bubbling inside, leading me down all the wrong paths, forcing me to make bad decisions, in turn hurting the ones I love most. This went on and on until finally, I exploded and completely self-destructed and the venom from my condition was fired upon everyone around me. This was it. Undoubtedly this was rock bottom. I had finally hit the place where everyone said I would, the site I denied existed, a place I had hidden, a place I believed I could control. But no, this was not rock bottom, for me exploding was merely the tip of the iceberg.

My journey through Afghanistan and the struggle to bottle my feelings up was only the start of my condition, what I had given birth to was just the start of a battle, that even as I am writing this now, I am still battling. The sleepless nights, the constant thinking, the inability to switch off. This book is a form of therapy, a catalogue of my thoughts and emotions. Though sometimes I can barely think, as Robbie Williams puts it "I contemplate thinking about thinking" then I think of something else, a million thoughts race around my head every second as if I refuse to let my brain rest. There is one way in which I used to be able to control this, but it's not the right way, and it is very ill-advised, it's my party piece, my escape from the mind. It used to be my mistress away from my thoughts, and for around fourteen pounds ninety-nine pence this litre bottle of medicine will give you a nights distraction from the reality of life. A medication I very much over indulged myself with that comes with its own set of problematic side effects. These will be very much apparent later on.

As my story will reveal my situation and thought process tends to wander, my mind is a playground and I spend most of my time playing cat and mouse with myself. To stop and think about one situation, one problem for longer than 5 minutes never seems to happen. The smallest seed planted into my mind will be a mile-long beanstalk in less than 20 seconds, from a short opportunity I will plan my whole life and genuinely believe that this is the life I will lead. My theory on this is that I am continually searching for something to fill the void inside me. I am continually craving that sense of self-worth that I have not felt since I left the Army. Losing that status is part of the crippling factor of my mental state, I used to be full of pride, I thought I was invincible and stood a thousand feet high, I was Rifleman Green, I felt like I belonged. The army was not just a job for me, it was a lifestyle, it was the meaning of my existence, and I was good at it. I thought nothing would ever take me away from it when it did, that's when my life changed, and I would never be the same person again.

Now you may have a small understanding of how my mind works, and as you continue, it might give you some explanation as to why I have acted the way I have. The actions I have taken have always been acted out with an unclear mind. I will now take you through a violent and unfair journey and reveal the path I have taken that has left me the precarious character I am today. At no better fitting point is there to begin this travel through my timeline, than that of the act of fate that would change my life forever.

The following only includes nicknames, apart from my name. I would not want to put any of my brothers at risk from any backlash. This includes the latter part of my book where I will talk about drugs. My confession is therapy and sobriety. Others have the prerogative of full confidentiality and immunity.

The date is 21st August 2009, the time is 05:00, most people would still be in bed dreaming, some may already be getting up for work. Drowsily filling up their kettle for a morning refreshment to accompany a half-hearted buttered slice of toast. But I have had sausage and beans boiled and consumed in a perfectly designed foiled bag. This small packet is pumped with the right amount of fuel for me to be able to operate without feeling faint, my body has been fed. I then consume a bottle of water, I am not thirsty, but I have long been taught the lesson that a dehydrated body is ineffective, and I do not wish to face those consequences. My feet have been powdered so to stop infection; my feet are taped up to provide an extra barrier between my blistered feet and the ground. My boots are tied tight at the bottom to support my ankle but slightly loose at the top to allow my feet to breathe. In my bottom left pocket of my combat trouser is an FFD (first field dressing) with a tourniquet attached. I am trained as a team medic to provide life-saving first aid to any one of my comrades should the worst happen, with each section having two team medics. Our dog tags have two pieces, one attached to our boot and one around our neck in case either become detached from our bodies. We even mark up our trousers and arms both sides, each limb has its owners' details much like a license plate on a car, but in Afghanistan, you need one on every panel!

My pre-patrol administration is complete, next is my weapon.

For this patrol I have been appointed LMG (light machine gun) Gunner, I inspect my gun, it is stripped down. Stripping a weapon is like stripping a woman, remove the top cover, pop the clips and you're into the working parts. The movement becomes second nature, your weapon is your life, your companion, your protector, you look after your weapon, and your weapon will look after you. The working parts of my gun are clean, so it is brushed down, oiled and reassembled. My role within the section is usually the lead man of the patrol, my kit usually has three speedball pouches to allow me to quickly reload my rifle when its hungry for another magazine of twenty-eight 5.56 rounds, this needs to be changed. I replace them with a different pouch capable of holding a belt of one hundred 5.56 linked rounds. I will carry one hundred and fifty loaded and wrapped around my weapon, another three hundred and fifty in my day sack. Weapons, ammunition, water, rations, medical kit, it's all carried on your person, so it's consolidated, organised and appropriately placed in a position to be readily accessible when needed. I am a Rifleman. This is my craft, my speciality, my living, it is what I am trained to do. My kit can be taken anywhere in the world with me, and I will close with and kill our countries enemies using this equipment, with each pouch I place, is placed in accordance to my specific needs and will all count towards my effectiveness on the battlefield.

If you're wondering why I am taking these measures, it is because I am at war, ripped away from society, trained to kill, thrown into combat, forced to kill, all the clichés that follow the stature of an infantryman. This infantryman, 30037006 Rifleman Green, as I am now known to the Army, Gary Christopher Peter Green as I'm known to my Family and Greeny, Gazza, Greendog as I'm known to the men that surround me, Is in PB (patrol base) Parang. Our PB is situated on the southern line of Helmand Provinces FLET (forward line of enemy troops). We are told that to the south of us is 'Bandit Country,' and the only barrier between our enemy and us is the two rows of sand-filled Hesco blocks, dug out of the ground of Afghanistan itself. There's a slight irony in manipulating the ground to defend us from the enemy that occupy it. The small area we live and fight out of is smaller than a football pitch, a protected fishbowl, viewed and spectated upon by the Taliban and Afghan people, we have no way to distinguish between either party until there's a weapon in their hand.

The Platoon Commander 'Boss' is briefing the section commanders, going over the fine points of the patrol even though the orders have already been given, when there are lives at stake at every second it never hurts to go over the finer points. In conjunction with this the Platoon Sergeant 'Pratty' is handing out the platoons ammunition for the patrol, the task is handed to the sections 2ic's (second in command) who then split it between the Riflemen in each section. Each piece of ammunition is counted along the way, who has been given what, by keeping this 'Ammo State,' the re-supply chain can run effectively. Pratty is also handing out other Platoon equipment, such as ECM (Electronic Counter Measures) there are three ECM packs for each section, each gives out a different signal and provide a safety bubble against I.E.D's detonated by electronic signals. They are each worn on the back of a Rifleman and add around 50 extra pounds in weight to a Rifleman's kit, it is not a very popular choice. You also have to carry two spare batteries, which would be split down between the section, more weight! Together with this kit, there is night vision, medical pack, stretcher, grenades (smoke, phosphorus, and fragmentation) LASM (light anti-structure missile) spare radio batteries, ladders and this all has to be carried on our backs. Each piece of kit needs a new space often making you bulky, heavy and feeling uncomfortable. We are Riflemen by name and by trade, and it is our responsibility to adapt and overcome.

Each Rifleman packs their kit specific to their needs and begins the process of attaching the kit to their bodies. Every single item, down to the smallest lace and strap has its place. Some of the kit is so heavy that a buddy-buddy system has to be used to lift the day sacks onto the backs of other Rifleman. We check each other's equipment, last minute details. Those last critical imperfections get corrected so that while we're on the ground, we'll be as comfortable as we can be. Whether that is loosening the straps on your day sack, so the weight of it isn't constricting the blood flow to your arms or pulling your collar up so your body armour isn't rubbing against your neck. All these little things can make a huge difference in your performance and mental wellbeing. After all, with the threat of imminent death hanging over you at every step you take you don't want your attention redirected to a scratch or pinch, no, your life and the life of the men fighting beside you rely on your full care and professionalism. You sort your kit, you do your job, for a mere second of distraction can quickly become the difference in everyone coming back safe from patrol and a chaotic bloodbath.

We line up in our order, the actual order of the patrol eludes me these days, but from the puzzle box that is my mind I remember that our section (2 section) was last to leave the Patrol Base. The patrol was followed by one of the two Mastiff's that we had in our Patrol Base as fire support. I was the last man of the section, which is unusual as I'm usually front man of the patrol searching for I.E.D's (Improvised Explosive Devises) or second man in the patrol acting as Cope's cover man. But for this patrol, I was supposed to be part of the rear party and fall into the sentry rotation, but that's not the kind of Rifleman I was, I wanted to be a part of everything. Me and 'old man', a TA attachment to our Platoon chose to swap roles. He took up my position on sentry duty and I took up his LMG and attached myself to the back of the section. Being on sentry/stag was not my idea of fighting, most, if not all, rifleman will tell you it's one of the worst parts of warfare albeit, an essential part. I always found it hard to stay focused and alert. When you're so fatigued it's easy to switch off when performing a mundane task for a prolonged period, so, you either end up masturbating or thinking about home. Don't get me wrong, we were professional Rifleman, and we fought hard, harder than most during our tour but human nature is human nature and boys will be boys.

My kit is ready. I'm excited about taking the LMG on patrol and can't wait to get some rounds down. The human in me wants to be compassionate, I think you need it in a place like Afghanistan, it's what separates us from the enemy. But the Rifleman in me, the killer, the soldier, wants to get on the ground and start 'brassing up' the enemy (a term that implies to shoot the enemy that derives from the brass casings that are expelled from your weapon after the shot is fired) for what I have seen them do. It's a strange feeling wanting to kill someone, not in the fantasist view of wanting to kill someone because you're angry, this is not what I'm feeling, what I am feeling is a joyous excitement. I want to kill the enemy because they are my enemy, I want the bragging rights, the glory in destroying my country's enemies. These people have not directly hurt me, but I have come to their country to kill them. It reminds me of a quote I once read.

"Each Warrior wants to leave the mark of his will, his signature, on important acts he touches. This is not the voice of ego but the human spirit, rising and declaring that it has something to contribute to the solution of the hardest problems, no matter how vexing!" – Pat Riley

I don't quite understand why, but I am here, I chose this profession because I enjoyed playing video games and watching movies and decided that's 'what I want to do, I want to kill.' This may seem like an immature decision, but it's what I chose, and it's what I was good at. Now I'm waiting to go on the ground for the hundredth time to prove my hand in combat. As I stand at the rear of the patrol waiting to leave the gate, I look around at the men who once again I'm about to go and fight side by side with. Staring at their faces, all I see is a group of young men, a group of young men that have followed a series of different paths that have lead us all to the same place. The average age of the men I stand amongst is between 18 and 20, and I am only 20 at this point in my life. These young men are from many different places, we have many diverse backgrounds, but as I look around us all, we are family, a band of brothers. We have been given the nickname Spartan 7, due to the fact we are a small group of Riflemen defending a small position on the FLET (Forward Line of Enemy Troops). In our AO (Area of Operations) we were outnumbered by Taliban, so there's the similarity of Leonidas and his 300 Spartans and us being 7 Platoon is where that name came. I can see why we earned that title. Every time we were on the ground, young men were executing the most demanding tasks day in, day out in the most extreme of circumstances. Young men that bare the marks and burden of great responsibilities upon their bodies, boys if you will, that if it were not for the paths they have undertaken, would maybe have dirty knees from playing football. Instead they have blood upon their bodies from the many injured comrades they have tended to and that of their enemies, we have each, in turn, earned the name of Spartan 7 in combat and some paid for that title with their blood.

Pratty is the man in front of me. He signifies to me that he is about to leave the gate with a simple nod of the head, I, in turn, nod back to let him know I have understood. I position myself against the Hesco cover to watch him leave, and he never goes from my sight as I grant him the five-meter distance that each rifleman leaves between the other. We do not exceed this gap, each step, each movement, each distance from here on out, is controlled and drilled into us. We move across the ground as one, eight separate limbs of the section moving together in sync. I follow Pratty out the of the Patrol Base, the patrol is moving in a 'herringbone' formation, spread out on both sides of the track. The first two Riflemen at the front of each side of the patrol are carrying a Valom metal detector. It is their responsibility to search the ground for concealed I.E.D's, while on patrol it is imperative to stay focused, you have to keep your wits about you. You have to watch the footsteps of the person in front of you as they will be following the footsteps of the person in front of them, right up to the first man with the Valom. The path they are clearing with the metal detector is the only safe lane and stepping out of that safe lane is dicing with death. Many a limb has been lost due to the sake of one misplaced footstep. It's a scary concept that one step can mean the difference between life and death.

As I step out of the patrol base my focus is straight away to the south, my LMG is up in the shoulder, my glance is cold and focused above the aperture of my weapon, scanning the ground intensely for a target to fire upon. At this moment my eyes and gun are the rear protection for the patrol, although this close to the Patrol Base we are still covered by the Sentry. Sangar one is to my forward left as I'm covering down to the south and I know whoever is in there will be ready to react to any contact we receive in a split second, yet still, I do not avert my gaze, I keep watch.

We move forward ten to fifteen meters, then the signal is given to go firm, and at that precise second, the patrol stands still. Each Rifleman turns to face the outside of the patrol and goes down on one knee, being on one knee gives the Rifleman a more stable firing position and makes a smaller target for the enemy. When you're static on the battlefield, you want to be as invisible as you can, as you never know who has you in their sights. I take a knee and face out from the rear of the patrol searching into likely enemy positions, anything from a hole in the wall, a doorway, a tree line anything where you might suspect the enemy to appear.

While the patrol has all-around protection Pratty directs the Mastiff out of the gate, and it joins the back of patrol.

The Mastiff is a heavily armoured Protected Patrol Vehicle, capable of fixing a 50cal Machine Gun or Grenade Machine Gun on the top to offer fire support, for this patrol we had a sniper, 'Doris,' on top cover with his .338 Sniper Rifle giving over watch for the patrol. Stants a potential Sniper working alongside Doris is in the back of the Mastiff with Jock (one of the other fire support attachments to our platoon) driving the vehicle.

With the vehicle now at the back of the patrol, we slowly start to move off, we are moving slowly and get another ten meters before we are told to go firm again. This time with the Mastiff to my rear I face out to the left of the patrol down a small alleyway in-between to compound walls. I'm searching over the top of my sights with my LMG on my shoulder, I see nothing but the rural environment I have become accustomed to, nothing stands out. Pratty after speaking to Jock in the Mastiff gives the signal, and the patrol continues to move on, as the last man I am the last to move off before the Mastiff. I stand and take one step forward with my left leg, the next few moments are a muffled memory from my senses reacting to the most significant shock my body has ever felt. Firstly, I remember the feeling, the shock wave of the explosion going off, it was an immense power that seemed to rip through me and had sent my LMG flying out of my hands and somersaulted me into the middle of the track, parallel to this was the feeling of the debris smashing into me. The only way I can describe the feeling is it's how I imagine it would feel like to be hit by a truck. It's almost as if I felt each piece of the wall hit me individually, for the second that it must have lasted the rock that exploded from the wall smashed against my body like waves crashing against a rock face. The dull feeling of stones pelting your face and body while you head to the ground is over so quickly that it's almost as if it never happened. The next sense I remember I had, was sight, what I could see, as I opened my eyes I realised I was on the floor, disorientated I looked around, what a second ago was the familiar rural surroundings of the track towards Kalshaw Kallay was now nothing more than a cloud of brown dust. I was engulfed in a brown swarm of dust particles that had been kicked up by the explosion, I see nothing but brown. The last sense to register with me, is the sound, to this day I can't remember hearing the explosion I can only remember the deep ringing that came after it.

Nothing was explicit, for the split second as I lay there I believed I was dead, my body was paralysed. Once that second had passed I knew I had to move, I had to get myself together. My body was raging with adrenaline, from the force that had just hit seemed like a blow of wind. I sat up, and that's when my first clear thought came to my head, CHECK YOUR LEGS, I looked down, they were still there, so were my arms. I patted them down just to make sure there was nothing I couldn't see, but for my relief, my limbs were all intact, I was fine!! I scrambled to my feet and realised that my weapon was missing, I was trying to scan the floor to search for my gun, that's when I caught a glimpse of something falling to the floor. As I looked down, I could just about make out what it was, and it was a stream of blood falling from my face to the floor. 'How had I forgot to check my head.' I raised my hand to my right eye which seemed to be the source of the blood, all I could feel from my eye was the sensation that I had something in there that made me uncomfortable. As I removed my hand and looked, all I could see was a hand covered in blood.

What had been a mind that was relatively calm about the situation was now consumed with panic. "It's me," I screamed. "I'm the casualty." This wasn't the first explosion I had witnessed, but it was the first one In which I had been injured. I was panicking, I had never felt so alone in my whole life, it made me feel like a lost child in a supermarket searching the aisles for my Mum. My whole mind went blank, and suddenly the whole situation had closed in on me. I wasn't fine, and my face started to feel like fire. I couldn't control the pain and itching in my eye. "It's me," I screamed again.

"Greeny, Greeny," I heard a familiar voice call. It was Jonesy, my section commander, his figure and face appeared through the confusion and chaos from the swarm of dust that still concealed the incident point.

"Greeny, are you ok?" Jonesy asked as he reached me, I was still stood up wandering in the dust.

"Sit down mate, are you hurt?" At this point he had sat me down and was checking me over. "MEDIC!" He screamed as he continued.

"It's just my eye, is it fucked... Is it fucked?" I asked knowing the answer, but I had to ask. He replies in a reassuring voice. "It's fine, you're going to be alright mate." But I can tell from the way he was acting that he did not believe what he was saying, but as is the nature of the beast I would've said the same thing.

Jonesy starts to send messages back to the Patrol base to let them know what was going on, how many casualties, the severity of injuries, what type of contact, the time, location and specific information that is crucial to Operational Intelligence. While this is going on, there are so many procedures running side by side to add to the fluency of each drill. This is why our forces are so productive, this is why we are the best in the world.

As I sat there waiting to be told how my extraction would happen, I couldn't help feeling as if I was in a movie. When you're in such situations as this, it almost becomes surreal. I didn't see my life flash before my eyes, but I did feel the sensation that I was watching what was happening at the cinema, that I wasn't there. I was just playing the lead role in my own life, and I was already watching this back. I could see myself, the hero, what was only about 30 seconds, was beginning to feel like a lifetime. Perhaps what my mind was doing was taking me away from the situation, from the reality of the chaos that surrounded me, I was forced to think back to the start. What had lead me here? What was I doing here? How did this quiet boy from a small town in England, end up halfway across the world with half of his face blown off? I started to go all the way back and dictate my journey.

Me and my sister Kylie, every child is born innocent.

Chapter 2
The past before the past

Looking back on my life, it's safe to say I haven't always been a violent alcoholic with a mental disposition. Like every other single person on this planet, I was born an innocent child.

I was born Gary Christopher Tomlin at 21:00hrs on the 5th of June 1989, weighing 8lb 4.5oz. I was born into a happy family. We lived in a 3-bedroomed council house on an estate in Banbury. The idyll of a happy family was short-lived, however, although the events of those early years are suppressed somewhere in my head, and my mum, for reasons of her own, doesn't wish to tell me the full story. I can only give you an account of what I can remember, and what I have learned from other family members and friends, as I grew up. Whatever the story is, led to my parents' divorce, and my Mums' consequent alcoholism. During the divorce proceedings, we moved to my nan's house, and my Dad looked for a place of his own. Nevertheless, families are strong. We pulled together. I have a large family, on my mum's side alone, and everyone chipped in, cleaning up the old house and redecorating it for us. We moved back in at a later date, but it wasn't the same.

Whatever happened had taken its toll on mum. She became a very heavy drinker and couldn't cope. One night it became too much. We were all in the kitchen, sat huddled together in the corner next to the cooker. Mum was holding onto us both, crying, saying she was sorry, over and over again. I was too young to understand. I didn't know what was happening. There was a rolled-up towel laid on the kitchen floor that served to block the draft that habitually blew in through the small gap between the kitchen door and the cold kitchen flooring. The windows were closed and sealed up. No fresh air was allowed access into the kitchen, and gas was hissing forth from all four of the cooker's rings and the open oven door. It would take several minutes for the effects to kick in, but they would manifest themselves, and soon. I began to cough. I was struggling to catch my breath, and so was my sister. We didn't understand why we couldn't breathe properly, but we were scared, holding onto mum, who was still crying. I looked into her eyes and began to sob, coughing more incessantly as it became harder to breathe. There must have been something in my eyes that impacted on mum's state of mind, because, suddenly, the outcome changed utterly. It's like a light came into her eyes, and she knew, no matter what, she had to stay strong. From setting up her suicide and the infanticide of her two young children, my Mum had wholly changed tack. She had looked into my eyes and suddenly known that I needed her strength now, just as I had when I was born. A few years passed, and things got better for my family. My Dad had left us for good. My Mum battled for us through the courts without much resistance from Dad, who had agreed to sign a letter that stipulated no contact between him and us and to allow us to have our surname changed. We were now all, Green. Shortly afterward, we moved to the family home (where my Mum remains today), a new home and a fresh start. It was still a council house, but it honestly did, and still does, feel like our home. We were mostly very happy. But I would spend every Fathers' Day, writing cards to my Gramp. At school, I felt so left out. We would all be making Fathers' Day cards. Everyone would be writing cards for their dads, except me. I would be writing mine to my Gramp. It's hard, growing up without a dad in your life. Mum had to be both mum and dad. She took me to football practice, wiped the blood from my scraped knees and did her very best to make sure we never missed out.

I started school when I was five. Some of the friends I made in those early years are still my friends today. My behaviour throughout education tended to repeat itself through my entire life. Each term report read almost the same: 'Gary is an intelligent pupil although easily distracted by others. He grasps concepts quickly but seems happier playing the class clown.' To be honest not much has changed.

As human beings, we are social creatures. Maybe it's just that I was, perhaps, more sociable than most. As a young boy, my imagination flourished. I loved being outside! For me, half an hour in the back garden was a fairy-tale. I could create entire landscapes and play within them, with just a single thought. Every trip outside was a new adventure. Sometimes I would accompany mum on shopping trips. It was a case of Gary Green and the battle with the monster in the bread aisle. See what I mean? I could look at the simplest of objects, and they would manifest into monsters before my very eyes!

There were five other lads on our street. We all became good mates, and the minute we got back from school, we would hang out together. In an age where mobile phones didn't exist, and being too skint to have a house phone, meant that we would have to go out and knock for each other. There was always something somewhat daunting about hitting on a mate's door. We would spend all our spare time in those streets, exploring every road, every shortcut, field, and park. The number of times we would meet up with other lads, play football, then end up in a bit of a scrap! Looking back at our age now, the fights were somewhat brutal, but that's just part and parcel of growing up as a lad.

When we were about eleven, Bren and I would stay over at each other's houses, and wait up until 4 am, when everyone else was sleeping. We used to 'borrow' his older brothers' camouflage jackets, that would swamp us in the same way my mum's nighty did when I was five. We would creep downstairs, tiptoe over to the living room window, and begin, very carefully, removing the ornaments from the windowsill, hiding them behind the sofa. We would quietly open the window, and, one after the other, we would climb out and leg it to the hedge, where we believed we were invisible. The last one through would pull the curtain closed again, and push the window shut, so our tracks were covered and nobody could tell it had been opened in the first place. With no small degree of stealth, we would move from car to car, all the way up the street, as if we were WW2 soldiers moving through occupied France. There was a house at the end of the street with a row of tall conifer trees that we could hide. We would lie in wait for our 'enemy' the target being the poor, unsuspecting milkman and his milk float of treasure. We could hear the familiar buzz of his milk float from two streets away. We could hear him getting closer; this was it! He'd reach our street, and we would watch him, like lions stalking their prey through long grass. He'd disembark from the milk float, carrying customers' milk to their doors, depositing it on the doorsteps with the familiar chink of glass bottles. We never moved a single muscle as we watched him drive away. We'd look at each other and say the same words, "Next time we'll get it," and we would jointly manoeuvre, completely undetected, all the way home again. Another failed mission against the infamous milk float!

One of my closest friends as a child was also my cousin, Dan. He and I would spend every weekend at each other's houses. When I stayed at his, we would go to Salt Way. This is a mile-long track between Banbury Secondary School and the rural outskirts of town. We spent endless hours running away from dinosaurs in that area. Countless conflicts with 'enemy soldiers', with nothing more to defend ourselves with than sticks that vaguely resembled rifles in shape. We always managed to survive. The only real, live beast we ever saw (not counting the odd wandering cat or dog on the leash), was a fox. To our inexperienced and untrained eyes, this fox was a vast and vicious predator, that was going to kill and eat us! We got home in record time, I can tell you!

As I got older, my love for the outdoors remained untarnished. My days at school were long and depressing, apart from that lunch break, when we could get outside and play football, run about, or suchlike. Whatever it was, I didn't care, as long as I had that freedom to roam the playing fields. As soon as we were called back inside, I'd never been able to concentrate or apply myself. I would fill my time by joking around with my friends, or back-chatting the teachers, to make everyone laugh. When 3 pm came around, and I was free from the clutches of the education system, I would run home. I'd be in the house for about five minutes before I'd be off outside, ready to kick a football about with my mates, and win the World Cup, even if only in my mind. It's clear, what sort of path I was heading towards. I had no interest in learning, which I regret now. I was capable of doing the work and rarely came a cropper when a teacher put me on the spot by asking me a question when I had been messing about instead of listening. Instead, I would spend entire lessons creating stories or drawing pictures in the back of my notebook. Although very artistic with a pen in my hand, my attention span was less than five minutes when it came to anything more academic.

I remember being nervous when starting at secondary school. Moving held a lot of fear for me because, as I saw it, I was leaving a safe place. I was happy being the big fish in a small pond, but that was about to change, and I was to be a tiny fish in a vast lagoon. My childhood thus far had made me quite a rough-and-tumble, boisterous young lad; very confident and cock-sure of myself. However, this new educational stage was to wreak an enormous change in me. Exit, the happy-go-lucky urchin; enter, an insecure, timider young man. My school wasn't rough. In fact, it was instead the opposite, and the change in pace hit me hard. I suppose I found it difficult because, the higher up the school you go, the more your school life revolves around image and popularity. Everyone had a brand-new school uniform. It was navy blue. Everyone sported trendy hairdos, cut to the correct length and with the front sticking up. I, on the other hand, wore my sister's hand-me-down jumpers to school; these were the old versions, with a purplish tinge to them. The sleeves were loose at the ends where they had been worn before. My own hair was overgrown, over my ears and neck. I still wanted to fit in, though, so I'd mess it upwards at the front with some of that cheap 39p hair gel you can get from the local chemist. It would start to wilt soon after application, and by the time lunch break came around, it would be curled over, dropping into my eyes. Every Christmas, my sister and I would both get provident vouchers; one hundred pounds' worth. We would rush into town to get new school bags from Argos - Nike ones if the price was right; or I would get some new football trainers from JJB sports. At least I would look the part for the January term.

I was reasonably timid as a teenager as well, although still very cheeky; a comedian around my friends, even towards my teachers. I was never on the streets, or getting into trouble with a lot of others. Outside of school, I kept myself to myself. The rough young lad I had once been, wasn't there anymore. All I was interested in was playing football and being a clown. By the time I took my GCSEs, I had spent very little time studying. So, faced with black-printed questions on my exam paper that I had no hope of answering; this meant only one thing: leaving school with no real grades. I got my results, and they were no real surprise. Although it was my choice not to study, and to be a clown instead, I still felt disappointed. They ranged from a U in resistant materials to my highest grade, D, in science. I received an E in English, so it's kind of ironic that I'm writing a book. A council estate boy with no education, taking a grasp of literature! It's almost enough to restore faith in the underprivileged youth of society!

My later teen life involved staying in as much as possible. At 16 I was studying mechanics at the Oxford and Cherwell Valley College. It was okay. I applied myself and learned what I could, but I did not feel fulfilled. Much the same as my time at school, I had the answers but would spend my time drawing modified cars and daydreaming about the Fast and the Furious. I was always thinking twenty years ahead of myself. I had a weekend job at Littlewoods. Customers saw me as a cheeky little chap, folding up their clothes, and smiling back politely as I made small talk, wishing them a lovely rest of the day. Meanwhile, in my mind, I wanted for something more. Something to take away the monotony of this lifestyle. I am polite, but at the same time, it's hard to keep smiling on top of false happiness. I wasn't happy.

I was over halfway through my first year at college. I had flown through the assessments which we had been given. I found it easy. There was no challenge. There wasn't much variance in work; spark plug, oil filter, same old, same old. I needed something new. Something to ignite my mind and get my engine running, not the customers'. I couldn't see myself in overalls, stretched out underneath a car, fixing the same problems for the rest of my life. It wasn't that I never enjoyed it because I did. I guess it was just the fear of monotony. The fear of having no greater purpose, that grabbed me. I needed more. And by chance, and as the laws of fate would have it, one door closes, and another one opens. I was working at Littlewoods, and the company had gone into administration, so we were all going to be made redundant. A charismatic gentleman had come into the shop to buy some of the store's mannequins. He had asked me to help him load them into his van. I was my usual, polite and helpful self. And as long ago as it was, I can only remember exchanging some small talk with him, but he seemed to have nevertheless taken a shine to me. We finished loading the mannequins into his van. I bid him farewell and made my way back to the store. He followed me back in and asked for a quick word. He said he had an opportunity for me. He produced his card and told me to meet him the following Saturday at his motorbike shop. To this day, this was one of the best possible testimonials to my character.

That Saturday, I made the trip to the motorbike shop. I was excited, though part of me was nervous. After all, I had accepted an invitation from a charismatic, middle-aged man to meet him in a motorbike shop, in the middle of an industrial estate. I know this sounds like the beginning of a generic horror movie involving the sodomy of a pubescent teenager. There was my imagination, putting the situation out of proportion again. In my mind, a prospective job interview had turned into me possibly being the latest gang rape victim of the Hells Angels in the undercover grease shop of horrors! As I approached the store, it seemed rather small, but the bikes were fascinating, especially the sports bikes, they seemed to exude excitement, speed, and freedom. When you look at a machine of such calibre, you tend not to look at it, but rather the possibilities of where it can take you. With an imagination like mine, I was instantly transported to Top Gun. Had I got a pair of aviator-style sunglasses to hand at that precise moment, I would have ridden that bike off into the sunset.

Jim, the charismatic middle-aged man, came out to meet me. He was not the member of a Hells Angels gang rape ring, and my sphincter was safe. He took me to his desk and began to talk to me, but my mind was overcrowded with bikes, helmets, gloves and leather jackets. In my eyes, I had just stepped into a new world of possibilities. I took few words in, and I was sold. From what I can remember, Jim had explained that my personality had been a significant factor that had led to the interview. I suppose I should thank my Mum for raising me right, or maybe I was that rare breed – a young man with good manners! Either way, the opportunity he offered was a lifetime skill in sales. He would teach me all he knew on a probationary basis, and I would sell motorbikes for him and earn a commission. To a seventeen-year-old lad, money, motorcycles and the overall cocksure life of a salesman is almost irresistible.

I took Jim up on his offer and started work at the motorbike shop. I loved the working life. At the tender age of seventeen, I was earning a full-time wage. The most money I had ever had in my pocket was on average £150 a month from my

Littlewoods job, and that was like Christmas to me. Growing up, we never had money. We always struggled to get by. Don't get me wrong, we never went hungry, but we would have to scrape by when other children wore the Nike trainers to school or the Adidas tracksuit. I would be wearing the Umbro trainers and the two-stripe tracksuit bottoms, but it does make you appreciate good quality items when you can get them. I remember on holiday, my Mum bought me an Adidas jacket, and I got it a size too big so that it would last longer. I was so proud of that coat. I must have worn it solidly for about three years. Whenever the rent man came to the door, we would have to perform the 'nobody at home' drill, and hide behind the sofa with the TV turned off. So, having a full month's money in my pocket made me feel like a millionaire.

I was doing well. I was learning all the sales techniques they had to offer, and I was frequently winning 'salesman of the month,' but my wages were not reflecting the work effort. My basic salary was one thing, but the commission seemed far below my expectations. Say I sold £50,000 worth of motorbikes, my salary would still rarely exceed £1,000, and to me, this seemed very unfair and gave me a narrowed view of what I was doing. This was my first begrudging thought about consumerism and the way the world works. My favourite part of the day was talking to customers; finding out what they did for a living, and then daydreaming about doing that, rather than focusing on what I was doing in the here and now. I also found out that the bikes were marked three hundred and fifty pounds over their recommended retail prices. The theory was, if they paid for the bike in full there and then, we would make more money. And if we offered three hundred and fifty pounds off, they thought we were giving them a good deal, when we were still making full whack. With my ethical stance, I became disillusioned and unhappy with what I was doing. I would look in with the mechanics and spend most of my time talking to them, taking an interest in what they were doing. They were making more money than I was and seemed happier. I had a meeting with Jim as he could tell I was unhappy. He said that I needed to separate myself from the mechanics and focus on what I was doing because my sale record was slipping. I tried taking his points on board, but I found myself drifting and becoming unstimulated. Financial incentive meant little to me. I needed something more fulfilling. A few weeks passed, then I handed in my notice. I thanked him for what he had taught me, and for the opportunity, but my career as a salesman was over.

I signed back up for college and finished my first year. Starting all over again wasn't a good feeling, but something about not completing that year had stuck in my head. I had to know that I could do it, and I did. There was a tutor on the course. A Scottish bloke. I only remember his first name: James. He had served in the Royal Electrical and Mechanical Engineers in the British Army and had told us many stories, getting us all fired up. A lot of people talked about signing up, but no one went ahead with it, except me. I finished my year, declined to sign up for the second year, and went to the careers office.

Sitting there in the careers office, I was sure I was going to join the REME or the Royal Engineers. I spoke to a Sgt Taylor who was a Royal Green Jacket. I told him about my level one mechanics grade, and that I wanted to join the Engineers. He showed me the recruitment video with all the career options, and the first one that came up was the Infantry. I was amazed. It was everything I had been looking for since I was a little boy. The excitement. The fieldcraft. The aggression. Everything that followed that, seemed the second rate. From watching Band of Brothers to Ultimate Force it was evident that this is what I wanted to do. I was ready to pick up that rifle-shaped stick and join the troops again.

SGT Taylor came up to me and asked what I wanted to do. I looked at him in this life-changing moment and said, "I want to be a Royal Green Jacket". He explained that a new regiment was forming with the Royal Green Jackets, and this regiment was going to be named, 'The Rifles'. I was booked in to do my BARB test, which is a simple aptitude test, to see which branch of the Armed Forces you would be suited for. No matter the score I got, I was going to be a rifleman. I flew through my BARB test and I was sent away to ADSC, (Army Development and Selection Centre) in Purbright.

Receiving my instructions for ADSC was exhilarating, I was sent my travel warrant for the train, a packing list of what I would need to take, and directions of where I would need to go, and who I would need to meet. Packing for ADSC made me feel like I was packing to go to war. It was the first independent step I had ever really taken. I had never even been on the train on my own before. My kit was packed, and I was ready to go. I was nervous because I hadn't even trained for it. I had done no running, no press-ups, and no sit-ups. I had been to the gym occasionally, but that was as far as I had gone with it. I never slept a wink that night. In the morning I had my breakfast, kissed my mum goodbye and left. I was walking like I was ten men all rolled into one. I produced my travel warrant at the station with a cocky arrogance. I wanted everyone to know where I was going. Eighteen-year-old chubby virgin Gary Green was joining the Army! However, my new-found pride was in short supply when it came to the train journey itself. I must have asked one hundred times if I was heading to the right station, and each time I was reassured.

I got off at Pirbright station. Outside, there were about fifteen nervous faces, all with suitcases. I figured we were all going to the same place, so we made small talk, debating on what events would ensue. A minibus turned up, and a tall man jumped out: "If you're here for ADSC, jump in!" We approached nervously, taking it in turns to move forward when he yelled: "No fucking about, jump on!" That was enough for our collective good manners to fly out of the window. We all dived on as quickly as we could.

The weekend passed without incident, just a series of different leadership and teamwork challenges, which I completed with no difficulty. We took part in a grenade lesson, where we were tested on the information we had been told, just to ensure we could take in, and pass on, information. Again, I passed with flying colours. The final day was for the tests on physical ability. The mile-and-a-half run was the one challenge I had been dreading, as I hadn't ran that far before. I finished somewhere in the middle of the group. Some of the fitter lads had already ended, and we were on the last two hundred meters. I had one lad on my tail, we were trying to sprint the last bit when some female sergeant shouted at the lad behind me: "Come on! Get past him! He's a fat cunt!" I didn't let him beat me to the end. Although the words had hurt me, and I would have loved to have punched her straight in the face, those words stayed with me, and perhaps it's why, from then on, I pushed myself hard and excelled in PT.

I had my final interview with the officer commanding ADSC, and I had passed. He said I was a 'grey man'. Meaning: I met every standard, but because I wasn't arrogant, I would naturally blend in better, and wouldn't be so noticeable in a crowd. He said this was an excellent quality to have since being noticed for good or ill attributes could have negative consequences. He shook my hand and wished me luck. On the train back, the few of us heading in the same direction were buzzing and talking about what we were going to do. We all wished each other luck and, although we said we would, we never kept in touch. I got home and told all my family the good news. From that day, I walked around with a different stride. A more confident and purposeful one. So many people thought I would fail at the first hurdle, and now I was on my way to proving them wrong.

I got the phone call: "Hi Gary. It's Sgt Tay. I'm pleased to inform you that you have passed selection. You are now 30037006 Rifleman Green. Pop into us on the 6th September to do your oath of allegiance, then just keep up your fitness and you will be off to ITC (Infantry Training Centre) Catterick on the 18th November 2007." I never forgot that number. 30037006 was imprinted on my brain forever.

The Oath of Allegiance

"I, Gary Christopher Peter Green, swear by Almighty God, that I will be faithful and bear true allegiance to Her Majesty Queen Elizabeth II, Her Heirs, and Successors. And that I will, as in duty bound, honestly and faithfully defend Her Majesty, Her Heirs, and Successors, in person, crown, and dignity. Against all enemies and will observe and obey all orders of Her Majesty, Her Heirs and Successors, and of the Generals and Officers set over me."

Week Two of training with my famous number 2 hair cut and Rifles track suit.

Chapter 3
You are now Rifleman Green

How much sleep can you expect to get the day before you leave to join the Army? The steps leading up to it are in theory the most natural parts, like a long early drive to work as the passenger in a work van. The sleep beforehand, the calm before the storm, the precious moments of freedom I had left. They seemed little like freedom, not at all calm, instead they were filled with doubt and anxiety. My head filled with prayers of escape, not by choice but by a freak accident, a train crash, a snowstorm, a broken leg, anything where I could retain dignity yet not have to face the 26-week gruelling transformation I had in store. It wasn't that I was scared of hard work, it was just the idea of it was far more appealing than departing on a life-changing journey, like placing a bet without having to lose my money.

There wasn't even a snowman's testicle on the ground outside as I awoke, there was only a cold yet peaceful morning. As my leg was not broken either I decided to get out of bed. As detailed on my joining instructions I was to wear a suit upon arrival. Mine was navy blue, I had worn it to two job interviews, my prom, and a wedding. My shoes were scuffed, worn, and in fact, I had worn them for nearly a year as work shoes. My things were packed, a visual representation of my efforts to prepare myself, I certainly wasn't going to win a prize for best dressed, but I was wearing a suit, and I had no money for anything else so this is how they would have me.

As a sensitive eighteen-year-old that had never spent longer than maybe a night away from his mother, saying goodbye was not going to be easy. The last conversation I had with my family escapes my memory, I know I didn't cry, it would not have been in my nature to be dramatic. I would like to think I told my mum that I loved her, that I would always be her little boy, that I looked at my little brother, told him he was to be the man of the house now and that he was to look after his mum and his sister. That I told him I loved him, that I was proud of what an intelligent young boy he was. To my sister I would say that she has become a beautiful young lady and I will always look up to her. That if anyone ever broke her heart, I would hurt them. These are the message's I would like to have said. Unfortunately, my reaction to most situations is to use humour. I had no idea of the consequences of my actions, or the gravity of the situation I was putting myself and my family in.

The journey with my Mum and uncle to the train station was more relaxed. As we arrived two lads that I met during our Oath of Allegiance who I had recognised from my secondary school were already waiting, we had arranged to travel up together. They were twins, both in smart suits, clean shaven and sharp haircuts, practically ready-made soldiers who had spent all their lives in cadets. The relief of not having to travel on my own and having a friendly face to see during the next six months was insurmountable, we had our tickets, we waved goodbye, and we headed to our platform.

The train journey was one filled with intense mystery and contemplation, the three of us were pondering each eventuality and sharing with one another our predicted outcomes. We were on our way to a new life, an alien environment to which none of us could genuinely guess the calibre, we remained engaged in that conversation as we travelled further north than I had ever been in my life. The sting of the journey was removed by the conversing amongst the three of us, and it gave me a mental break from the pessimistic voice inside. The excitement grew the more we talked and the further we travelled. There was no mention of families and how much we would miss them, the comradeship was already increasing, we were each other's support network building each other's confidence as a way to combat the fear. Without even knowing, a strange emotion arises when you're out of your comfort zone. An almost funny feeling, you look at them and they look at you, and you both know you're about to enter the shit, and at that moment you realise you both have to do it, so, you smile.

The train was closing into Darlington, the nearest train station ITC Catterick, it must have been somewhat late as I remember a dark sky, this very much added to the atmosphere. We nervously left the train station where we were greeted (if that can be used as the correct term in this context) by a tall figure in combat uniform "you Rifles?" He asked as we approached him. "Yes sir," I said, trying to be respectful.

"Sir? Do I look like a fucking officer? No, I work for a living, now you three cunts throw your kit under there (gesturing to the undercarriage to one of the three coaches) and jump on the fucking wagon.... Don't just fucking stand there then hurry the fuck up, get a bit of urgency you fucking crow bags."

I didn't understand many of the references but by the sound of his voice I wasn't about to question the abuse, we threw our kit under the coach and jumped aboard, I don't think I've ever sat in so much silence as I did for that entire coach journey.

We pulled into camp, and I glanced down at the guard on the gate who was in combat gear and carrying an SA80 assault rifle, it was like I was watching myself in Jarhead, from that second I absorbed every single moment!! I fucking loved it; I loved being shouted at, I loved orders, in my head everything I went through was carving me into a killer, a stronger person than I was before, a defender of the country. 'Fucking throw it at me' that's what was going through my head.

We were taken off the coach and straight into the cookhouse. We lined up for our food and sat down. I was looking around at everyone that had been on my coach, judging their faces, their build, their attitude trying to figure everyone out. I had been sat down no longer than a minute when the figure who had got us on and off the coach shouted.

"Two fucking minutes be lined up on the road with your kit, don't be fucking late or I'll beast you cunts." No one ate one more mouthful of food, we were lined up on the road with our kit talking amongst our selves "SHUT THE FUCK UP" shouted the figure as he came out of the cookhouse, "get in the fucking press-up position, who told you cunts you could talk? You've got a lot to fucking learn, you're the worst bunch of cunts we've had come through here now get your fucking noses to the floor" 2 minutes of press-ups to the command "lower" or "raise," and it was over.

"Back on your fucking feet.... Now turn to your right. You fucking mongs can't march yet, so we're doubling back to the block.... Follow me and stay in fucking line you cunts."

He jogged off slowly, and we scrambled with bulky amounts of kit to keep up with him. Welcome to the Infantry, eat fast, do as your told and shut the fuck up. Follow orders before you know them, punch yourself if told to hit yourself, if you're smacked in the nuts while standing still you carry on holding still, run when told to run, fight when told to fight. No questions asked you do as you're told, and you thank them for it. It's drilled into you from week one day one. If you hesitate, your friends will die, it is directly your fault whatever happens. If your weapon fails, it is your fault for not maintaining your weapon, if your kit breaks you did not fit it correctly, you are responsible for everything you do and the result of everything you do.

First night in the block we had to hand in our ID to find out which of the four Corporals sections we were going to be in, I was in 'One Section' along with one of the twins, for which I was grateful. Our section commander was a tall well built Fijian, who I would later serve with, in Afghanistan. We were shown our section rooms in which my bed space was not located due to space restrictions, so I along with two other blokes were put into a four-man spare room. That first night I laid in bed and cried silently into my pillow, I don't think it was nerves or fear which forced the tears from my eyes, I believe it was just more the realisation of the whole situation, I wanted to be home!

Apart from the ill-received welcome and the crying on the first night of our journey here at ITC Catterick one of my initial memories that would shape my character was an incident I wasn't even involved in. I just happened to be in the wrong place at the wrong time. The person who was the focus of this incident appeared on a Panorama documentary in 2008 due to the bullying that went on within ITC. An undercover reporter posed as a recruit and secretly filmed the harassment and the process that we needed to undertake to fight effectively on the front line in Afghanistan. Whether his actions were right or wrong, they were displayed to the whole world.

The incident took place in the first week of being there. I hadn't even received my Rifles tracksuit or got my infamous number two all over haircut. I was still the eighteen-year-old virgin mummy's boy. Two other young lads that were part of my training platoon, went for a cigarette, I, not even a smoker (then), went with them just to talk and be social. Unaware there was a designated smoking area, we were stood outside a side door discussing the mysteries that awaited us and speculating what was about to come. What did come through the door was the Corporal who had not yet been caught out for his bullying, what he saw was three recruits smoking outside a British Army building disregarding the nonsmoking rule. He was not happy, never before have I been so intimidated and so frightened.

"Who the fuck do you think you are?" He screamed at us. The three of us white with fear had no reply, had no lifeline, had just to stand and take the onslaught he bestowed on us. "You fucking Cunts" he spat as he slapped me hard on the side of my face. He grabbed one of the other lads around the throat and threatened to smash his face in. I remember wanting to burst into tears. Fear paralysed me to the spot, and I was rooted to the ground. He grabbed us individually, pushing us against the wall, slapping us as he repeatedly screamed at us, we knew our place, we took it, and we knew we were best to shut up. "Get on your fucking faces" he screamed, we all instantly laid face first on the ground ready to do press ups, he put his foot on the back of my head and pushed it into the floor.

"If I catch you fucking cunts smoking out here again I'll smash the fucking lot of ya." He ordered us to do press-ups until we could no longer see him as he walked away. I have never felt so helpless as I did in those few minutes, needless to say, no one smoked in that doorway again.

Before we had our uniform given to us there was a week of administration, signing our rights and lives away, the overall theme from what I could understand and what I can remember was that if we were to be injured or to die it would not be the Army's fault. If the Army told us to jump off a cliff and we were to harm ourselves, it would not be the Army's fault. The training process is designed to be tough. It's designed to turn you into a robust infantryman ready to fight and kill on the front line in the hardest of environments. It's one of the most mentally and physically demanding jobs in the world. Thus, the training must prepare you for it. The risk of injury and the risk of people self-harming or committing suicide is higher than that of an ordinary job. The Army apparently wants no responsibility for this, so we signed our rights away.

During this week of administration, we needed to be in some sort of uniform, this is the British Army after all and uniformity is critical. The Army won't just hand out a full kit list to a platoon worth of recruits until they had signed their life away. So, we were given, 'given' not the correct word as we had to pay for it, but without that in mind, we were 'given' a Rifles tracksuit so that after a fashion we matched. Side by side we stood with a tracksuit embroiled with the insignia of our regiment, 'The Rifles.' We were indeed uniformed and regimented, well at least that's how we felt. The hair on our heads was deemed unacceptable by the standards of her Majesty's Armed Forces, so it needed sorting. On camp was a barber, we had to pay ten pounds for a number two all over haircut. The same haircut I had growing up as a child, courtesy of my auntie, only this time I had to pay ten pounds for it. I came out looking like I once did on a Monday morning at school, unhappy.

A bitter November morning breeze swept across the open parade ground. The breeze made the temperature sore far below the frosty degree it already was. My outer shell was a wool jumper, layered underneath was an Army issued green shirt, and underneath that I wore a thermal under layer. Which would seem sufficient for a British winter morning. However, this place always had an amplified chill. It pierced through my clothes and gripped my skin as if it was forcing me to shudder under its icy grasp. I want to shiver, I want a second of freedom from this statue prison I am locked in, I want to run back to my room and hide under my sheets with a hot water bottle. I want one of my mums' hot chocolates to take away this freeze from me. None of these that sat so high on my wish list at that moment in time are available for me right now. This parade ground is not my home, I am a prisoner here, and 'Sgt Frenchie' is the warden. FYI, I call him Frenchie in this book and I would call him by this if I saw him now. If I had called him Frenchie at that moment, he would have wrapped his Cain straight around my face until my teeth fell out.

I have been stood to attention for forty-five minutes since 07:30hrs, we have all been held here, the heels of our feet struck together and the toe cap of our polished boots facing out at a forty-five-degree angle. Our legs and back rigid strait as if we were pressed against a wall, fat or skinny you suck your gut in and push your chest out as if you're being pumped up like a flat tire. Our chin is so far up that our nose points toward the sky, yet our eye line remains dead ahead of us. At this point a topless marching band could drift to the right or left of us offering free blowjobs, and our eyes would stay forever forward. Our arms strapped and pinned to our sides with our thumbs following the seem of our trousers as if they had been stitched into them. This is how we learned discipline.

The whole platoon stood in a circle frozen to the spot, Sgt Frenchie was in the centre observing to make sure not even an eyelid moved a fraction from the position we had been left in. Our section commanders patrolled the inner circle ready to strike anyone that coughed, sneezed, farted, itched or blinked. There was not a good enough reason in this world that you could move for, nothing but fear and pride kept you routed to that spot.

If you asked me at the time, I would say that our training team were the most horrible people in the world, but on reflection, they were the best people in the world. They took thirty young boys and against the odds trained and moulded us into exactly what the Army needed us to be, what we needed us to be and above all else what the men who we fought beside required us to be. Although each member of the training team had different styles of teaching, communicating, fitness and personalities, as is often familiar with the Army they were all similar. Above all else they had the responsibility to make sure we were up to standard because in six months' time, their lives could depend on us. We were not just in a summer camp learning how to put a weapon together because it was interesting. We were not doing fitness so we looked good in a mirror. We were training our bodies and minds so that we could become killers on the front line.

One of the things you quickly realise and prepare for is the beasting in fitness, no matter what it said on detail. 'Four-mile steady state run,' for example, was not going to be a four-mile steady state run. What it meant was, a four-mile steady state run with forty minutes of additional beasting. This can come in many shapes and sizes. One example, the traditional racing to and from different reference points. 'Pays to be a winner,' meaning if you weren't in the top 10 you had to go again and again until only the last few were left. This forced you to put 100% effort into each race. A command that regularly comes out in these exercises is 'GRENADE!' Screamed in a manner that was projected so violently, that you thought a grenade had gone off. As soon as you heard this, you threw your body to the ground as fast as you could and crawled with every part of your body in the direction you were first moving while being screamed at, 'GET YOUR FUCKING ASS DOWN.' Or, 'IF THAT WERE A REAL GRENADE YOU WOULD BE DEAD BY NOW YOU USELESS CUNT.' You were always being pushed, all you can do at moments like these is look at the man suffering next to you and smile. We had three of these PT (Physical Training) sessions a week, each had different goals and aims', each was progressive. Some runs were conducted in trainers, some were conducted in boots and some were conducted in your full kit. Every aspect was engineered to develop you into a military tool, the littlest thing could provide the most significant lesson.

We were always learning to adapt. You don't just watch something and learn. You live it, and you learn to apply it and replicate it into different situations. Something as simple as learning how to pack your kit. It wasn't just the lesson of what goes where, it was the importance of why. In the Infantry the kit on your back is your life, it's what you live from, it's what you fight from. If you are on a Reconnaissance patrol, which entails you to be close to the enemy, the last thing you want is something rattling in your day sack. We would pack our kit, put it on then jump up and down. If there was any noise or rattling, you would need to repack it. Much of these small lessons and habits that you learn within training stay with you for the rest of your life. Timekeeping and sense of urgency are two prime examples, you can tell ex-squaddies because they will always seem in a rush. There were many ways they would drill this into us, one way was showering. We would come back from PT covered in mud and sweat at let's say 09:52 and start a map lesson at 10:00. As we get outside the block, we would get instructions such as.

“Right you've got three minutes to get in there get showered and be back outside on the road in three ranks. If any of you are fucking late I’ll beast you round block until your eyes bleed...... Well get running you cunts.”

Then came the onslaught of 30 plus blokes running towards four showers bollock naked. The way we got around this was a system of, one man gets wet, leaves the shower and starts soaping himself up while his replacement gets wet. Once lathered up they change back and said bloke washes soap off then runs to his room to get dressed. There was a lot of men soaped up running around naked in those days. You made sure you washed quickly held your meat and two veg and got to your towel sharpish. One false move and through no one's fault, you could have bumped uglies. We had long since gotten over any embarrassment of being naked around each other though, there’s not much choice when forty blokes are taught how to wash correctly. Including how to pull your foreskin back and clean, in the words of one of our corporals.

"Pull your foreskin back and make sure you properly clean all around your bell end, I know what some of you scruffy little grot bags are like."

One thing was for sure though, at the end of that three minutes you were back on that road and ready to be marched to the next destination. After time you were subconsciously quicker in completing tasks, your mind starts to work quicker, you actively look to make up time and find smarter ways of doing things. You begin to see that sense of urgency, which on the battlefield is of utmost importance, when you need to reload an empty weapon or fix a stoppage. But this presents problems at home when you're waiting for your partner to get ready and your itching to leave. They have not been installed with the same discipline. You find yourself fighting the urge to shout at them, 'get a fucking grip of yourself, where's your sense of urgency?' All the things that are second nature to you, the little things that never leave.

The first six weeks of training you are treated like filth, you are nothing but civilians being sifted through, finding your weaknesses and trying to break you, only the strong were to remain. One lad whose name I cannot mention had taken a fork, of all things, from the cookhouse and tried to cut his wrists in the shower block. He was sent straight to the mental health team and subsequently discharged. The process of training promotes violence and aggression in a controlled manner, some people cannot recognise this or are too weak to handle the pressure. In the process of the transformation from civilian to killer, some are mentally broken. Another incident, about a lad who was no doubt mentally damaged from the process. 'Milky Bar Kid' a very skinny young lad, who was bullied from day one and I have to admit I played parts in this. He was one of those characters that just made life so hard for himself. He was regularly back chatting and asking stupid questions, forgetting things and never learned. He was holding the group back, so as is the nature of the beast he was singled out and bullied. This kangaroo court culture would usually encourage the person to improve and develop to fit in, but Milky Bar Kid was just not cut out for it, and in the later weeks we found him crying his eyes out on his bed. There was nothing that would stop him crying, and he was sent to the mental health team and put on suicide watch. Everyone had to take a look in the mirror that night. This kid was maybe one or two episodes away from killing himself and becoming another tragic story, as a team, we failed him.

By week five we were ready for our week six 'beret' parade, this is usually performed on week six, but we had a week less due to our start date and the Christmas leave period. The parade is only a short demonstration of drill and the culmination of some of the basic soldiering skills, a short field exercise, basic PFA (personal fitness assessment) and weapons handling test on the SA80 Assault Rifle. The day before the parade was the parent's day where the families are invited to come and watch the parade along with other military-themed activities such as ration tasting. There was a demonstration on the digital range and a look at how we live in the field, a minimal insight to what happens but it's still good for the families to have some idea and see their shiny boy soldiers. Most families came up with a car, just mums and dads, etc. Not my family, no, my family came up like the Dingles, about twelve of them by minibus. I do love having a big family though, and it was lovely to have the support. I was very proud for them to be there and to see me in uniform, especially my Mum, I had missed her so much.

After the beret test, I felt more like a soldier, I was now allowed to wear my regimental headdress and cap badge around camp rather than the military caps. They are known as 'Crow Caps' because everyone knew if you were wearing them you were in the first six-week period of training. Once we had finished the parade, we were given our first period of leave which was two weeks back home. We were lucky because our slot was over the Christmas period which meant we got to spend Christmas at home with our families, a bonus to a well-deserved two-week break. I remember when I got home after my first five weeks away, it was the first time I had been out of camp. Military lifestyle was already drummed into me, and I walked with a swagger. I was used to being marched everywhere as a group to the command of the corporals shouting 'left, right, left, right.' Everywhere I walked my hands were naturally swinging, my back was straight, and my head was up. I felt like superman without my cape, like I was hiding my identity that I wasn't just a regular person, I was a Rifleman!

The time I spent at home was a novelty, it was nice to not be under the scrutiny of the training team, to have freedom, but, I was itching, I was itching for the punishment, the feeling of having to fight to be the best. Something had been born inside of me, a desire to want to be all I could be, a desire to fight and I loved it. The time at home dragged, I enjoyed seeing my family, don't get me wrong, but it wasn't the same. I wanted to go back, some things you just take to, it becomes you, and this was me, I was the Army, and the Army was me.

Before I knew it I was at the train station, my kit was packed and slung over my shoulder in my oversized issued black grip bag. I wanted people to know I was in the Army, I was proud of that fact, it never left me, if I could I would have worn my uniform everywhere. I met with the twins on the platform, as our train pulled away our families were stood at the fence waving. At the time I was embarrassed but looking back with a bit more life experience, it's those little moments, the going the extra mile that makes a lot of difference and is indeed the difference between someone who tries to care and someone who truly does, my family genuinely care.

The train journey as usual on the way to Catterick was long and tiring, very mentally tiring as well. The conversation frequently revolved around what to expect and explored the worst-case scenarios. The most frightening thing is that the worst-case scenarios we could come up with were not far from the truth, in fact sometimes the reality was far harder to believe. The first six weeks were just a taste of what was about to come, a mere starting block before we started to train to be infantrymen. That is when our metal would be tested, that's when boys become men, that's when the strong would succeed, and the weak would fall. Anyone can be pushed to run for five miles, but only some are robust enough to be awoken at three in the morning, piss wet through, in below minus temperatures to the sound of explosives and gunfire. Only the strong can decide to pack their kit in the systematic manner that's been drilled into them, no matter how tired, how cold or how confused you are. You follow the correct drills, in a matter of seconds your kit is packed and in front of you. You're in the prone position on the right-hand side of your kit with your rifle made ready to fire pointing in the general direction of the enemy. Waiting to shoot like a coiled viper about to bite and release venom into the blood of its prey. Only the strong can ignore natures basic instinct to curl up in a ball and hide. You ignore the cold, wet clothes that are wrapped around your body, and you ignore the sting of the chill that strikes your fingers as they brush against the damp ground on which you are lying. You ignore this because you know that the only way to get some comfort is to fight for it, so you await the fight and the inevitable three hours of patrolling that will follow it. You embrace it because you know that once you get that hour uninterrupted sleep in your dirty sleeping bag that you will have earned it. That is the best kind of rest. That is what we were heading for, and we didn't even know it.

Back in the block there was not much talk about what we had got for Christmas or what we got up to except the odd story about girls that the lads had been with back home. As a virgin at that point, it wasn't like I had much to boast about, but I played along and made up a few one-night stand stories to keep my head above water. One thing I learned very quickly is that the environment we were in, allows for no weakness. It was time to sleep, as in the morning the two-week break was about to get knocked out of us, and the hell continued.

Every lesson has a purpose, you should take knowledge from experience. A smart person doesn't just do what he's taught, he questions it. He asks why he has to do something. I ask, I ask every time. Anyone can follow instruction, you can show a monkey how to fire an AK-47. What you can't do is teach a monkey to change his magazine while moving from one piece of cover to another. Release the working parts of his rifle, allowing the bolt to push a round into the empty chamber in time to adopt a stable kneeling position and return appropriate and an accurate rate of fire towards the enemy. So, I ask, I gain every single piece of knowledge to make me the most useful Rifleman I can be.

Everything the Army does is to turn you into a competent killer, and they will bring out every single piece of anger that's inside you and teach you how to use it effectively. The Army doesn't need blind rage, what the Army needs is controlled aggression. What controlled aggression is, is being able to use all aggression that is deep down in the belly for a split second. Zero to 100 in the blink of an eye. Everyone has this inside them, it just needs to be unleashed, for some this is easier than others. You fight every fight as if someone is about to harm your family. You wouldn't just pull them away or ask them to stop, you scream in their face, you hit, you strike, and you punch them until they die. You fix your sword to your rifle and you go, you scream in the face of the enemy as you charge him. You stare him in the eyes as you precisely strike the end of your sword into his body. You aim for his ribs, you twist your sword inside of his rib cage to break the bone, so he bleeds internally before he dies, and also so your sword doesn't get stuck inside his dying body. If necessary, you're ready to smile and do it again. If that fails, stick it in their face, stick it in their neck, do whatever it takes to kill that person. That is what you are taught, that is what they need, they need you to be able to do it in a split second. That controlled aggression needs to be reachable at the flick of a switch. One second you can be smiling at your child, the next second you need to be able to stick the enemy in the neck with a blade.

From how you tie your shoelaces to how you shit, piss and drink your water, even down to how you breathe is a valuable lesson. If one thing is wrong or out of place you become less efficient. Simple tasks that can be perceived as pointless or redundant can have the most meaning or the most significant repercussions if executed incorrectly. Questionable and harsh lessons are learned every day, each rolls from one to another.

There is a moral in punishment. Punishment is necessary because it makes you more robust, it moulds your mind-set into someone who can take, take, take and then take even more shit and after taking all that shit can stand up and say give me some more. When the chips are down you don't fold, you still need be able to operate, no matter how worn down you have become, how many miles you have had to go, no matter how much sweat has run down your face and collected in your helmet strap. You keep pushing. If your rounds have run out you charge the enemy with your sword, when your sword snaps you beat the enemy with your rifle. When the butt of your rifle breaks you stomp the enemy, when the leather on your boots break you hit them with your hands, when your knuckles are cracked you bite them with your teeth. You never stop.

Chapter 4
"What makes the grass grow?"

It's 05:45, we are up, dressed and doing our block jobs, the same routine as before but after two weeks off it was just a little harder. There were floors to hoover, toilets to clean, beds to be made, floors to be swept, floors to be mopped and breakfast to be eaten, all before 06:45. And if all was not complete and up to scratch then it was going to be a bad start to the day.

Various lessons were undertaken, from map reading to section attacks. We learned how to pick out contour lines on a map so we could avoid high ground while depicting our route, we learned how to use this against our enemy. We could choose high points next to enemy position to give a significant amount of covering fire, while a lead section could move alongside a natural water feature and get close enough to launch an attack. It was fascinating to see how all the pieces of what seems like a bunch of men running about with guns, actually comes together and forms a precise, tactical manoeuvre. This meant a lot of time spent in the field, and hours spent looking at hills, following tree lines and working out bearings on reference points.

We march back to the block "left, right, left, right, left, right." You can guarantee a few things in the Army, and one of those things is that someone will always lose the step.

"Get the shagging step.... Right you cunts get in the fucking press-up position, you're supposed to be week six Riflemen by now, and you can't even get the fucking step. You shit cunt excuse of a platoon. You're supposed to be a body of men. You're marching around like a bunch of fucking civvies, if you can't even march together how the fuck are you going to fight together? Now when I say up, you cunts have got ten seconds to get back to the block and be outside ready for PT in two fucking minutes or I'm going to smash the fucking lot of you until eleven o'clock tonight, stand by you fucking mongs.... UP!! Ten, nine, eight".

As I said previously, this was a very regular occurrence, it's mainly because in the field nothing is guaranteed and possibly a little bit that the training team got frustrated with us. Either way by the time he finished his count you were in that block getting changed. As usual and as the law of physics state, we were about one minute late which meant we were going to get beasted all day by our PTI and all night by our training team, just another day at ITC Catterick.

As the hours go by there is not much that keeps you going, I suppose that part of it is the fact that you can't say no. So many times I have had to look far beneath my exterior body and inside that place that says, "no, don't give up." Whether that was face down in a puddle waiting for an attack in sub-zero temperatures, or as I get beasted outside my room. It's our fifth change parade. I lie in the press up position wearing my dark green matching thermal jumper and long johns. My sleeping bag hood is over my head, the bag travels down my back and comes back up through my legs with the handle at the bottom wrapped around my neck, we are parading as turtles. I look at my arms. I can see them physically shaking as I struggle to hold the position, too scared to let go and yet also exhausted trying to keep the exercise up. This is the make or break point, you either find that place or you give up. After being run around the block, god knows how many times, after more press-ups than Charles Bronson and enough wardrobe changes to facilitate a cabaret show we were sent to bed. The process of how I prepared for sleep that night is far gone from my memory, but I'm sure for that period I slept like a baby, that period was cut very short!

Some point between 04:30 and 05:00 hours that morning our door came crashing through, my eyes snapped wide open with my heart in my throat, poised somewhere between full alert and half asleep. A thought popped into my head, perhaps my Mums come crashing through the door to surprise me with a cup of tea and a bacon sandwich, how cute of her.

"Get out of bed Green you fat lazy cunt" I can't believe my Mum is speaking to me like that, all of a sudden I'm on the floor, dragged from my cocoon of warmth and comfort.

"Get the fucking block jobs done then go and get some fucking scoff, sword training today, outside the back of the block 07:00 in full CFO (Combat Fighting Order) don't be fucking late you cunts". Just like that he was gone as quick as he had come. All the rumours and horrific speculation was about to be unveiled, were we going to have to stab a pig? Were we going to have to fight each other? Were we going to have to stick each other? All the gossip was going to be ironed out, but first, scoff.

We stood uniformed, green and black, helmets fitted to our heads, webbing and daysacks tight to our bodies, weapons held in the right hand and supported by the left, we marched along as a body of men. We were heading out of camp onto the training area, I had butterflies floating in my stomach although at the minute it felt like there was ten thousand of them raving. Whenever I had this feeling I had a genuine desire to give up, to call it quits and throw in the towel. A million voices would think of excuses not to do it, but, that one voice always told me to stay and I always did. "Prepare to double," that was the delayed order I had been waiting for, those first few minutes of fitness were always the worst, not because they were the hardest it's just that getting into it. I still remember just wanting it to be delayed as long as possible, one more minute of walking and I would be happy. 'I hope we take ages at the armoury, I hope the gates locked to the back area so we have to wait for a couple of minutes.' It was passed that point now, and we were in full swing of things, thirty young boys running to face this sword training we had heard so much about. "DOUBLE MARCH."

A few miles of running in full kit and we were pulled over to the side, "split into groups of four, standby... GO!!" we quickly flapped and grouped in a cluster fuck of who goes where. Here it comes, I thought to myself.

"Right you stupid fucking cunts, you can't even follow a simple fucking instruction."

He started grabbing us and throwing us into corners, "one two three four, one two three four" he barked as we were huddled like sheep being thrown into separate pens, sheep about to get lead to the slaughter.

"You lot twenty-five meters that way, and you lot, twenty-five meters the other way, fucking move."

We dispersed in the directions as ordered.

Now anyone that knows anything about the Army and first fire and manoeuvre will know the saying, 'I'm up, he's seen me, I'm down.' To educate those who may not know what this is I'll explain. It is a basic principle to use while under fire from the enemy. So for example, you are on patrol in let's say Russia. (Russia as this is a principle to be used in conventional warfare, not in the deserts of Afghanistan because as you will find out stepping into even a centre meter of ground that hasn't been checked can have life-ending effects). Moving through the rural landscape, you come under fire. The first instinct is to fire back, RTR (return fire – take cover – return appropriate fire). To keep things simple you are attacked from the front, two hundred meters ahead in a small-fortified position. So you return fire, two rounds in the general direction of the enemy, this is to discourage the enemy from carrying on the attack in the first instance. They may even take cover due to the volley of rounds that are now coming toward them. That will give you time to assess the situation and locate the enemy, if not already done. Second instinct, take cover, so you hit the deck and get as low to the ground as you can, perhaps behind a rock, wall or an original piece of raised ground. Now you have taken cover, it's time to return appropriate fire and suppress or kill the enemy, if you're lucky.

This is where 'I'm up, he's seen me, I'm down' comes in. Now the enemy is suppressed you can now look to manoeuvre towards them and launching an assault on their position. Let's say your section of men on this patrol consists of eight men, so we split that down into two fire teams of four men. One fire team provides covering fire for the other while they move towards the enemy. The theory is that you should be moving forward (in a zig-zag motion) for as long as it takes you to say. 'I'm up, he's seen me, I'm down' in your head. This way the enemy should not be able to get a clean shot on you moving before you're back on the floor and firing back at them.

Now that is explained, I will put into a context of how this life-saving tactic made our lives hell for the next hour. Fifty meters apart we stood in a line and practised over and over and over again, the 'I'm up, he's seen me, I'm down' drill. We ran towards each other shouting out the drill and then hurled ourselves on the ground and began crawling through the wet and frosty grass, knees red raw, chest burning from gasping in the cold air. "Check magazine, check pouches, MOVING" you would scream as you jumped up and begun sprinting side to side. If you didn't check your kit correctly and something fell out, your magazine fell as you were crawling or even your pouch just came undone. Then amongst the panting for the January air and the weak knees you had, you would also have a member of the training team screaming insults in your face. Kicking you, punching you or sending you crawling up a hill to learn your lesson.

"WHY CAN'T YOU DO A POUCH UP."

"WHY THE FUCK WAS YOU PUT IN MY PLATOON?".

"GET A FUCKING GRIP GREENY, ARE YOU A FUCKING RETARD?".

Just a few small examples of what might be hurled in your face as they thrust a boot in your side. This lasted for, as I stated previously, around an hour. The hard thing was we knew this wasn't sword training. This was just something to piss us off before we even got there. You quickly learn to try and anticipate what was next and gauge the length of time things were going to last. We hadn't started sword training yet, and we were already tired, wet and pissed off. This was going to be a long morning, probably a long day and night too.

We were tabbing through the back area of Catterick, sweat pouring down our faces yet practically freezing before it drips from the chinstraps that held the heavy helmet in place. We break through a small woodblock. The area in front of us is dark and misty, the smell of pyrotechnics burned the nostrils and the crack of smoke grenades igniting hit our eardrums as a sheet of white hides even our most immediate of surroundings. Through the smokescreen comes the ear piercing crack and thuds of rounds being fired into the air. Rifles explode as the trigger releases the hammer which knocks the firing pin, the tip of the firing pin strikes the percussion cap of the round that sits in the chamber. This causes the gunpowder inside the brass casing to explode, forcing the gas of the blank cartridge to shoot down the barrel and smash against the blank firing attachment. The sound is similar to that of a small bomb going off, followed by a sledge-hammer crashing against glass finished off by the sound of the brass flying out of the ejection opening and the bolt and it's carrier being pushed back by the recoil spring where it sits ready to repeat the process.

A dark figure advances through the thick clouds that blind us, the advance is aggressive and the character begins screaming but the words seem less than whispers amongst the weapons that drown out all else. A face painted with green, brown and black stripes beame clear. The tall figure is in our faces within seconds with his rifle just above our heads and begins firing. We are gripped up and propelled toward an open space where the smoke has cleared slightly, the air is still misty and the sky dull. We're away from each other in a rectangle formation, each man an arms' length from the man to his left and four steps back from the man to his front. We march on the spot, each time our right foot hits the floor we scream "Kill." There's a chorus spreading throughout the rural landscape. We bang our black issued boots against the floor as if we were trapped and it was our only way out. The thud echoes as we strike the ground in harmony and the noise spreads like a drum beat with screams of bloodthirsty recruits. It sounds like the chant of football fans on match day, "kill, kill, kill." We march on the spot tirelessly, yelling the command we have been given, until our throats are sore, until we could no longer talk, if that's what it had taken. The man covered in green and brown camouflage paint occasionally grabs one of us by the throat and tells us to scream louder, standing in front of you until he's happy that he can feel the anger in the breath that beats across his face with every scream.

"Now when I ask, 'what makes the grass grow?' you cunts scream blood, blood, blood as loud as you can every time your right foot hits the floor, you fucking hear me?"

"YES CORPORAL" we respond in perfect unison.

"Ok, then what makes the fucking grass grow?"

Perhaps I should put everything said by one of the training team in capital letters, with exclamation marks at the end of the sentence and an emoji of a yelling face. Or hopefully you've grasped the intensity of the situation, and you can gather that everything they say to us and tell us to do was conveyed in the manner that you would expect to get transferred to you if you had just punched someone's baby in the face.

"BLOOD, BLOOD, BLOOD" we respond at the top of our

voices.

We huddled into a pen, a pen made from four metal spikes in the ground and with three of the sides cordoned off with red tape leaving one side open. We sat like school kids in an assembly. School kids with green, brown and black war paint covering our faces, school kids in green combats that were worn down and discoloured from continuous use and school kids that were learning how to violently kill someone with a steel blade. Our swords are explained to us, you may know them as bayonets, but as Riflemen, we know this steel blade that fixes onto the end of our rifles as a sword. This is because the founding fathers of the regiment were the first infantrymen to use a rifle, they were the first sharpshooters of their kind. The Baker Rifle they used was shorter than the French musket so to compensate in close quarter battle; riflemen had their baker rifle equipped with an extended blade (sword). They could shoot you from further away and they could kill you up close as well. The sword is a weapon only to be used as a last resort.

From our seated position our eyes were directed to a tree roughly three hundred meters away, (approximately three football pitches in length, not to make you think too hard). This reference point was called heaven, when we were told to go to heaven, we were to leave our weapons on the ground, run to the tree, run around it, and run back. Our eyes were then directed to the left, where there was a downward slope. Roughly one hundred meters away, (approximately one football pitch in case your maths is rusty). At the bottom of the hill is a tree and on the other side of the tree is a stream. When we were told to go to hell, we would run to the tree, jump into the stream, crawl through the water on our belt buckles, climb up the muddy, slippery bank and run back to our pen to remain seated. For as long as I live the term Heaven and Hell will only ever have those two meanings. Just to make sure we understood these instructions we were sent to hell, about thirty men sent running, racing each other. Crawling through the cold water, the skin of the elbows and knees bashing against the stones that rested beneath the shallow water. Scrambling around and over one another to overcome the steep bank. Racing back to the pen with boots full of water and knees smothered with thick mud and little else. But we had not yet learned about heaven, so before we had fully grasped our false sense of security in being able to sit and catch our breath, we were sent to heaven. Legs heavy and weighed down by the water of hell, our hundred percent effort produced little more than a fast jog. As our inferior faces passed each other along what seemed a colossal journey, I noticed, and it wasn't the first time, that no expression was exchanged, not a smile, not even a nod of acknowledgement, just determination and focus on getting back. Boots crash the ground, body's fall and slip in the effort to carry on. "GRENADE!" Comes the unwanted, loud soul-destroying command from the training team. We crawl on our belt buckles, mustering the energy to move the body parts required to plod forward, "UP!" As we near the target, a surge of energy is seen in the whole platoon, the spur comes from competition and fear as the counting down from ten begins to echo through the Smokey air that fills our lungs. We all knew that if you were not one of the ones back in that pen before the number zero was called, you would be going again. At these moments you see people give everything they have, they may only produce the slightest of improvement, but it is visually honest as much as they can provide and that if they give more, they would probably collapse. These people are usually the ones that don't make it, and although they have nearly died trying to reach the target within those ten agonising seconds, they are sent to do all it again. The lucky ones, usually myself included, smugly get to watch and do press-ups. Wet, sweating, cold and tired we are removed from our pen and placed back in formation, facing our enemies, which at this point we couldn't decide whether it was our training team or the sandbag dummies that opposed us.

In our rectangle formation, we stand on the spot ready to

mimic the training instructors' drills. The Army's way of teaching, apart from screaming in your face or punching you until you get it right, is EDIP (Explain, Demonstrate, Imitate, Practice). So, the drill is explained to us, then we are shown, then we copy the exercise, and then we practice it, simple? Surely? The skill we learnt was to scream, "EN GARDE" at the top of our lungs while holding our rifles at the hip with the barrel end of the weapon facing toward the enemy. Walk towards the enemy brandishing your war face. Your war face is the face you make when killing the enemy. It is you screaming as loud and as aggressively as you can.

"SHOW ME YOUR FUCKING WAR FACES!"

A flurry of screaming erupted. No matter how hard you would scream, how emphasised your cry and how tense your face was, the response would be something along the lines. "I said your fucking war face not your cum face," or "you're supposed to strike fear into the hearts of the enemy, not make them fucking laugh." Following your advance to the enemy while screaming, we thrust our sword into the gut of the dummy, twist left and right so it doesn't get stuck. Scream, "check sword" at the top of your lungs, whilst physically grabbing the handle to ensure it hasn't come loose. Scream, "HIGH PORT" at the top of your lungs. Then, a stroll down to hell or up to heaven and back while waiting for your turn to repeat and of course not forgetting the chant of, 'kill, kill, kill'.

One of the best feelings, tabbing back to camp, knowing that every footstep I took now, was taking me away from sword training and closer to a shower and closer to my bed. Muscles I never even knew I had in my body were aching. Each time my leg had to take the weight of my exhausted body and the kit that was attached to me, felt like a mammoth task. It's quite amazing how quick your exterior being can forget about pain and exhaustion once your interior person is ignited. My legs, although they hurt were able to carry on because in my head I knew I was close to salvation. Perhaps that's how it works for monks, they know it's temporary, their reward is of course enlightenment, and my award was going to be a hot shower and lying in my fucking bed.

Sword training in the grand scheme of things was like learning to reverse park before a driving test, and there was still a lot more to learn. To be a qualified infantryman, (for lack of a better phrase) you had to be competent in a wide range of areas, there were milestones throughout the course. None in perspective was more important than the other. As a rifleman, I suppose one of the essential skills in a conflict situation was marksmanship and weapon handling. It had started in the first few weeks. Lesson one was the simple process of getting familiar with the rifle. The SA80 assault rifle was the primary weapon used by the British Army. It's known for its iconic appearance as the magazine sit's behind the trigger grip of the firearm, the SA80 fires 5.56 rounds designed to maim and kill the enemy, the 5.56 rounds are designed that when impacted upon the enemy, will ricochet around the bones rendering the enemy out of action. We learnt al ofl this, we learnt to name each part of the weapon, then we learnt how to strip the weapon, how to load the magazine, how to clean the weapon, how to take the weapon apart with your eyes closed, how to react when a weapon stops firing, the drills necessary to get the weapon firing again. Finally we had to take a test, the APWHT (Annual Personal Weapons Handling Test) this consisted of loading a magazine of thirty rounds in thirty seconds, making the weapon ready to fire, conducting the stoppage drills, unloading the weapon and making the weapon safe. Then and only then we qualified to fire the weapon with live rounds. You quickly learn that firing a weapon in real life is nothing like it is in the movies or on a video game. It's a lot harder than it looks. For a start your body posture has to be correct. You see all those films where Arnold Schwarzenegger is firing a machine gun from the hip. It's complete bullshit. I hate to break the news, but if you shoot a weapon from the hip, you wouldn't be able to hit a barn door from five meters away. Another quick thing whilst we're on the subject, a pistol, only accurate up to twenty-five meters and firing with one hand is entirely out of the question, if all these gangsters that go running around the streets knew how to use them then the world would be in trouble. A rifle becomes a part of your body, an extended limb that once mastered, indeed becomes a lifelong partner. You become more comfortable with the butt buried into your shoulder and your cheek resting into the cheek piece than you do hugging your mother.

It's quite an experience the first time you fire a rifle, it's quite terrifying knowing the ability to kill someone is literally in your hands, the devastation that this tool in your hands could cause is something to be embraced. There must only be a small link between the mind of a serial killer and that of a 'normal' person. I had thoughts as much as everyone else. 'I wonder what would happen if I shot someone in the leg' or 'imagine if I just shot myself in the face now' there's only a small part of your brain that stops you carrying out these thoughts. The sound of a rifle being fired quickly snaps you back into reality, a piercing noise similar to that of a firework. The first time you hear it in your ear as you gently squeeze the trigger deafens you, for a split second, then after a few more times it just becomes normal, you become hungry for it. You enjoy the recoil shock that your body cushions as the bullet sores true, towards the target. The first time you begin firing live rounds your ears are protected by the issued green ear defenders. Of course, these make you look like an idiot, and you don't want to wear them. Like all humans the instant you are given something you 'must' wear, you want to take it off.

For some reason every time we went to the ranges in Catterick, it pissed it down, the heavens would open for us. Thirty young men sat in the rain, shivering, scoffing down range stew served in mess tins. Range stew was nothing more than all the shit that was left over from the cookhouse, thrown into a pot and delivered to the ranges for cold, wet and hungry rifleman to pour down their throats. There was, of course, one experience that toppled every experience of being sat in the damp grass with bitter winds smashing icy rain droplets in my face. And that was the first and only time I didn't complete my drills correctly. I had become cocky, completing my weapon drills fast as I knew them like the back of my hand. I neglected to check my change leaver, readied my weapon and faced it down range ready to brass up the first target that lifted above the grass bank ahead. As the target rose, I slowed my breathing, slightly pulled the trigger back, held my breath, eyed my mark straight down the middle and squeezed. Instead of the single shot I had prepared for, a burst of rounds flew from the barrel of my rifle. At that moment my heart sank deep in my stomach, it was the same feeling that you get when your teacher has caught you bunking from school, I knew I had done something wrong, I knew I was in trouble. The full screw next to me ran straight behind me and swung back his leg, propelling his black combat assault boot straight between my legs, the pain was so intense I thought I was going to be sick right where I laid. His hand came over my helmet and pulled it back over my head, choking me with the chin strap that had become tight across my neck. "Green, you stupid fucking cunt that's why you do you for fucking checks" my head was thrown forward into the ground "pay attention you little prick." At that moment I tried so hard to hold back the tears as I looked through my sight, I could feel them start to roll down my face as I decided to be a man and take the punishment on the chin. Be the rifleman I was training to be, but I couldn't be, I felt like I was out of my league, not in my comfort zone. I hid my feelings and carried on as if everything was normal except the fact that I felt if I coughed too hard my bollocks would pop out of my mouth.

Every time my barrel pointed down range, from the instant my sights aligned with the centre of the figure eleven target and each moment I gently squeezed that trigger, my mind imagined that instead of the mark, there was, in fact, the enemy. Everyone else was firing at wooden targets, but me, I was shooting metal slugs towards Terry Taliban in the name of the

Sovereign Lady, Our Majesty, The Queen.

It's strange, as I sit writing this, all I'm doing is remembering things, I'm reliving a story that I feel isn't mine. I'm not doing it now. It isn't a current diary recording my aggressive pursuit to kill someone. I'm trying to look back and think, so, what part of this fucked me up the most then. Why am I sat in Costa now, with my red headband matching my oversized red chequered shirt, why the fuck am I wearing a headband? My hair is quite long, but more of the 'I should probably get a haircut' stage, rather than the 'I better wear a headband to stop my hair falling in my face while I'm eating' stage. I hope that somewhere along this journey, the people and myself reading this, form a bond and that together we can find a solution and a realisation that something needs to be done. War is unnecessary, and I loved the Army, I lived and breathed it, to the point that now, nothing I do creates the smallest consolation. I am as lost as I was as a child in that supermarket, where's my mum? Mum where should I be? What should I do? Mum, can you help me? Am I the only one who feels like this? Is there anyone out there like me? Is there another way?

Whether there is another way, we were preparing for the only way, and with todays' nuclear threat and the whole middle east having nuclear weapons we had to do CBRN training. Its fucking horrific. CBRN stands for Chemical Biological Radioactive and Nuclear weapons training. This didn't mean we were going to get trained on how to press the red button in the Prime ministers' office, that would be pretty fucking cool, no, what this meant is that we had to train in what we would do if someone used these weapons against us. Surely, we couldn't do fuck all? Well apparently, we could, and presumably, instead of using our last precious moments before our faces melted off and we grew an extra dick, to see our families, we would have to use them fighting the enemy. But first we had to learn how to use it, and not a word of a lie it's exactly like that scene in the film Jarhead. We had these rubber boots that are supposed to fit over your regular boots, no matter how you tried they would not fit over so you would be walking about with these rubber attachments flopping about like a fucking penguin. The other kit was ok, the jacket and the trousers went on quite smoothly with the hood going up fine, and the mask did its job. But you couldn't move, every one of us looked like a walking camouflaged pillow with a scary cover on, it was horrendous. It was deemed necessary that we had confidence in our kit. To give us solace in this equipment we had to use it. So, like a Jewish family in world war two occupied Poland, we were marched off to a gas chamber. How sadistic is that? Thirty teenage boys all cooped up looking like reject teddy bears at a carnival inside a gas chamber. We were all set out along the outside facing inwards with our masks off. The test was explained to us, first of all the training team were going to light a block of CS gas in the middle of the chamber. Happy days. Once this had filled the room, we would line up three at a time in the middle of the room, remove our masks and then recite our rank, name and army number, simple. So we applied our masks, the block was lit and we waited.

The first three were called forward, removed their masks and then began to recite the information, it took about three seconds before they started coughing, choking and being sick. "What's your fucking Army number?" The training team screamed at them. It continued until they were curled up in a ball on the floor, their eyes were streaming with tears, the veins in their necks were bulging with the vascular appearance of a steroid injector as their throat strained to cough up gunk from their stomachs. Once the training team was happy, the blokes were dragged outside and thrown against the fence. The wind could blow away the CS gas that remained on their face and clothes. For some of us, including myself we were able to try and hold our breath a bit longer. The thinking was that as soon as we answered the questions, we could leave. That thinking was wrong. I answered my questions and instead of being able to leave, I was asked more. "Where do you come from Greeny?" I quickly answered, "Banbury Corporal," before again holding my breath. He punched me in the stomach, not hard or aggressively, certainly enough to make me breathe inwards. "What football team do you support?" by this time I had a lung full of CS gas and I answered. "Manches...." I sputtered up and coughed, trying to spit it out of my mouth but I couldn't. I tried to wipe it off my face, it went nowhere. I felt like I was suffocating and began to panic, and the more I panicked, the more I took in. I couldn't breathe but I was trying to, my eyes swelled up and streamed with tears, my throat was closing up and trying to take on oxygen at the same time. I was poisoned with this asphyxiating substance that polluted the room. I caved, the white flag was raised, and I hit the floor. "See Greeny, this is why you wear your fucking mask." I was dragged to the door and thrown out, a mixture of laughs and help came from my peers who had already been through this torture. I profoundly sucked in the oxygen around me like a crack head who had just been handed a pipe. The lads picked me up and threw water on my face and undressed me. I stood up against the fence and let the breeze take the gas away from my body. Then after five minutes, I laughed at the state of people coming out of the chamber and in turn helped them to their feet.

The circle of life was restored, it was a nasty lesson, but I suppose in the grand scheme of things it made you open your eyes. So too did the theory lessons, seeing victims of mustard gas and other CBRN weapons is a sharp dose of reality. The real question that should be asked though is why are these monstrous devices invented? Why would you ever need such devastating consequences like these? And for the record, when I was asked what football team I supported, I was trying to finish the answer with United not city.

Learning to be a soldier - photo taken somewhere on the back area of infantry training centre Catterick.

Chapter 5
Stand To, Stand To

As we grew fitter and developed the necessary skills in weapon handling, marksmanship, and field craft, so too did the tests and situations that we would have to learn to apply them. Up to this point, we had only conducted our first three-induction exercises, these had solely consisted of the simplest of military life in the field, how to cook, clean and pack your kit. We had learnt how to apply camouflage cream and utilised our natural surroundings to make us invisible to the naked eye. We creatively used green and black lines to our faces and placed shoots of foliage through our helmet netting. This wasn't actually to make you look more like a tree, as we had all assumed, It was in fact, to distort your figure, to blend in the contours of your face and the shape of your body. It's quite amazing how much the human outline sticks out like a sore thumb in the wilderness. An arm, leg, shoulder or even the mark four helmet that was protecting our heads, were visible from miles away. By adding a bit of grass on your shoulders and in your helmet, you could quickly reduce the natural lines that could so easily give you away to the enemy. We had visual exercises of how and why things are seen. Shape, Shadow, Shine, and Silhouette, then we put into practice exercises and techniques on how to reduce these elements. We learned to blend in with all our surroundings, how to move through the land undetected, this was, for me, how I had imagined the Army since I was eight years old running through fields with a stick in my hand battling the Nazi's in occupied Europe.

In total there were three tactical exercises that we had to complete, all with different focus points on modern warfare. The final hurdle in the way at the end of the three tasks was a live firing exercise, named, Warcop. The first of the three battlefield assessments, for lack of a better title, gave me the most intense feeling I have ever felt and maybe will ever feel in my life. The focus on this exercise was conducting a reconnaissance patrol at night on an enemy position, using the intelligence we had gathered to then perform an attack in the morning. We would then rotate the responsibility of administering the reconnaissance patrol over four nights, this way each section had the opportunity of conducting the patrol.

We set off during the morning from camp, and we were tabbing out toward a wooded area in the back area of Catterick. Our platoon commander had plotted this on his map and shared this information with the section commanders before setting off. We were given a small brief of what events would follow, the information we had was limited. At this stage we were recruits and not riflemen, our principal responsibilities were to pack our kit correctly and not fuck up. From the moment we left the gate, we were tactical, this meant no talking, as we patrolled across roads and paths we manoeuvred in a staggered formation. The signal is to hold both arms at the side of the head for enough time for the person behind to see, and this is then repeated by each man as is every signal. We gave a distance of five meters to the man in front, every ten steps you took you would do a cursory spin and walk a few steps backwards just to ensure the patrol was still behind you. As we patrolled, although your focus was moving forward, your eyesight would always be on the ground ahead, to the left and right of you. Weary eyes were like steel as we searched every bush and hill point over the top of our sights, daring the enemy to pop their heads up so we could blast them down with rifles loaded with blanks. This is the shit I took seriously, fuck all the bull shit in camp, fuck polishing my boots and ironing my combats, this is what I was here for, unleash me upon the enemy. There was always a multitude of stops on any given patrol, a brief few moments where a single fist would be raised in the air that would filter all the way down like a Mexican wave moving through the crowd in a football stand. We would take a knee and face out right toward the vast surroundings. The section commanders would move forward to the platoon commander. They would discuss what way would be best to proceed, course correction may be due to an obstacle, or a vulnerable point that may be best to avoid, I didn't care. All I cared about was taking on board some water and resting my legs for a minute or two. The patrol of thirty men could be seen trying to shift their large Bergans' onto their back foot as they knelt, to try and ease the weight that so heavily burdened their shoulders. We would move off once again when the person in front of you moved off, a whisper in the ear "prepare to move" followed by "moving" would be given to let you know that it was your turn. On receipt of "prepare to move" you would check your weapon and ammunition pouches to ensure you had left nothing open or on the floor, then you would whisper "prepare to move" in the next persons' ear and so on and so forth. For a more tactical approach, one tap on the shoulder would be given followed by a second to indicate the same instructions.

As we patrol down the road, we are told to 'go firm' this is just another little army expression that basically in this context means to stop. So we take a knee just at the entrance of a large wood block, the command for a 'snap ambush' is signalled throughout the line of troops, right down to the last man who is covering the rear of our patrol. The signal for a snap ambush is as followed, snap, hold both fists clenched out right and mimic the movement of snapping let's say, a pencil or a straw. Ambush, hold one of your hands in front of your face, open palmed, palm towards the face, and move it downwards in a controlled sweeping motion until the tip of your fingers reach your nose. Those two signals given together are the hand signals for a snap ambush, and if you didn't get that, don't worry because most squads will say it out loud as they complete the action anyway, making the whole concept of hand signals redundant. It's kind of like when people try and shout and whisper to be quiet at the same time, what's the point? Or you know when your mates across the bar, shouting, "do you want a drink?" but at the same time he's swigging down an imaginary pint, It's the same thing. We had conducted a snap ambush before as part of our induction exercises, it's a simple manoeuvre that you carry out if you suspect you are being followed. You merely break track, (move off your current path) one by one and peel around each other forming one line of defence facing the path you were just on. One section would be at the rear of this defensive line with the platoon sergeant, once again covering the back of the platoon. If you were being followed, they would walk right into your line of fire, and twenty to thirty blokes would fire five thousand rounds into their bodies. This snap ambush wasn't for this purpose though. We were using this exercise as a precaution as we had reached our destination where we were setting up, 'camp' for the night. We moved off section by section as the boundaries for our harbour area were set out. Each section of eight men would occupy a side, (so to speak) of the harbour area to give an all-around defence. You would sleep with your battle buddies, so each section would have roughly four battle spaces, fox holes, bashers, camps, whatever you want to call them. One of you would lay facing outwards, giving protection and the other would build up the battle space around them, finished off with your poncho tied to the nearest trees with a bungee cord. The most common form is a triangular harbour, the section commanders, platoon sergeant and platoon commander in the middle, then either a roaming sentry or, static sentry points outside of the camp.

This was just the basic, it was one of the first things we learnt, and although the thought of living in the battle zone was exciting with all the hoorah, to be honest half the time we just fucking moaned it was too cold. There's a term in the Army, informally known as ticking, which means whining, and because we're English, when it's cold we tick because it's too cold and when it's hot we tick because it's too hot. It's something we never grow out off, the only difference is in the Army there's nothing you can do about it, they do train you to be robust and fit, but in the grand scheme of things and as in life itself, you do things because you were told. I remember a story of one bloke who, 'refused to soldier' he didn't want to continue in the field, so they stripped him. Those trousers belong to the Army, that jacket, t-shirt, and socks belong to the Army. All the bloke had left was his pants, he was sent back and put in jail, after that no one, 'refused to soldier'. I didn't mainly because I was wearing issued black boxers and it was cold out there.

Once again, I've diverted from the course I was following, "wasn't I talking about unicorns and clowns dancing through a flowered meadow?" My mind the washing machine that it is, was telling me to go and buy some drugs. 'Fuck the writing Gary, that's for idiots, go and get some lovely drugs, who needs a mortgage, that's what the banks want you to do.' I occasionally listen to myself, not for the drugs. I kicked that habit, that's up there in chapter 12 or thirteen. I do often listen to my mind, the conspiracy theories and whatnot, and it does make me wonder if I should work. "What's that brain, the banks, and government want me to work? Well fuck that, let's go and buy some drugs, those lovely drugs they make me forget everything". But then I snap back to reality, "What about your writing Gary, remember what you have done to your family, drugs won't make you forget that when you sober up." Then I'm all ashamed again, let me keep writing, and we will all end up with the same conclusion, I hope.

So somewhere between wanting to sign that crafty Oath Of Allegiance and between wanting to buy some drugs. (It makes it sound like purchasing some biscuits.) There was a moment, that moment I talked about earlier, that I don't think I will ever feel again. This moment wasn't anything elaborate or spectacular, and it wasn't a grand gesture, like I wasn't knighted or anything. What this moment did possess was a magical ambience that struck me personally and has forever stuck with me. I don't want to talk it up too much, because afterwards, you may be like, "was that it?" To be honest, I wouldn't blame you. I've skydived, scuba dived in Egypt, travelled Route 66 on a Harley Davidson, fought in Afghanistan and run the London Marathon, however this majestic moment, so embedded in my soul took place on THIS tactical exercise on the back of Catterick training area.

During our reconnaissance phase of the first of these tactical exercises, we were to patrol out in the dead of night, so dead in fact that as we moved away from our harbour area, we had to hold the daysack of the man in front. The dense forest combined with a black sky posed a maze-like effect, lose the group, and every horror movie you've ever watched will shoot to the forefront of your mind. I can imagine myself, all camouflaged up looking like an extra from a Rambo movie, yet curled up in a ball crying because I'm scared of the dark and sure I just saw the girl from that movie the ring. Luckily no one got lost, would've been a bit embarrassing really, the headlines would have read, 'British Army on tactical exercise rescued by the Scooby gang and the mystery machine'.

We moved through the dark forest of disarray and the wilderness, silently crossing tank tracks, wading through tree lines and water features. Patrolling for around one hour. We moved in between two wood blocks that gave a slight rise, as we emerged we had reached the peak of this raised land that had opened up with a group of fields. The fields rolled up and down each giving a different shade of grey to the tapestry that lay in front, at the foot of this land in the far distance was a set of lights, the origin of the illuminations could not be made out. There were enough of them to give the impression that they belonged to a small village. A few streetlights, a bedroom, maybe even the flicker of a TV shining through a dark room and a curtainless window. This was that feeling, as I moved through the field with the cool breeze gently stroking my face, my eyes fixated on those lights, the possibilities flustered my mind, what are those people doing? Do they know I'm here? It was that realisation that I was doing something incredible, I was learning techniques that would aid me when facing the enemy, this rifle in my hand would kill people and a thousand miles away people will be lying in their beds. I was a hero, but, to the unseeing world I did not exist, I was a ghost with my rifle, a soldier of the night. This was the feeling that I will never feel again, this was the feeling of embracing the cold and the dark, this feeling was being in the wilderness and feeling more at home than the people in those lights.

Now I've said it. It doesn't seem the majestic moment that I reeled you all into, I did warn you though to be fair. Something about feeling cold and seeing the warmth made me feel special. I realised I was part of a secret club, and now I know I will never belong to that club again. That moment where you stop and see something that makes everything thing else in the world seem irrelevant, that moment of calm and oneness. I wonder if everyone has one of these moments, I wonder if the Taliban had these moments, that before they go out to blow someone up that they are reminded of the beauty that the world has to offer. I wonder if they ever sit and think about the people they are about to kill, or if they wonder about the moments we have witnessed. We're all human, we were once all children, and in another life, we may have shared these moments together.

Apart from the period where for a moment I was stolen away into enlightenment, there was still a job to do. Would have been nice to stay in that moment, forever, that's why monks are so happy, they don't have day jobs that get in the way. This day job was a little bit different though to be fair, it was exciting, as soon as you patrol out and become 'tactical' everything becomes intense and deliberate. Every step you take is thought through, say for instance you're at home and you need a wee, you would get up and run to the toilet, you wouldn't think about where you're looking, where you placed your feet, you just want to unzip and dilute the water. As soon as you're in the field, everything has to be over deliberate, each step you take you're taking for a reason, the easiest route, the quietest ground to walk on, avoiding trip hazards. Your eyes are not just concentrating on those lights in the distance that send you to enlightenment, but are instead searching, every bush, tree line, raised ground and everywhere else for anything that doesn't fit in with the atmospherics. We go firm, our section commander told us to close in, it's a bit like a huddle in American Football but with Rifles and all-round observation. He explained to us in a whisper, that was hard to hear with the wind invading our eardrums, that we were approaching the enemy position and that we would be observing them from a distance. I was shaking with excitement. This is what I had been waiting for, what I heard was the prime minister speaking to me.

'Gary Green, you are MI5's most secret and lethal weapon, what I need you to do is go down to that enemy outpost and kill everyone without getting detected. Leave no witnesses behind and find the nuclear launch codes, the world is depending on you.'

My name is Green, Gary Green and I like my Stella in a glass, not a can. Not quite James Bond in reflection. I wasn't MI5's most deadly weapon, in fact, the enemy was placed there by our training team. But as a small consolation to my imagination, the objective was still to be undetected. We used a night vision scope to observe the enemy, we watched their routine and counted the number of targets there was and what weapons they were carrying. I was over enthusiastic, 'c'mon we can take them.' Regardless whether we could take them or not, the motto is to train hard and fight easy, not the other way around. Probably a bit early on in the book for this, but, when your mates start dying and getting blown up, you can appreciate the substance in a message like that. Why take risks? There's nothing glorious in holding your mates' intestines inside his stomach or placing his detached legs in a yellow toxic waste bag.

So instead of trying to take on the enemy with my one-man Army, I followed suit and observed them. It felt a bit naughty, all it took was one of them to be naked, and I would officially be a peeping Tom. Bit of a shame they were all blokes really, not my sort of thing and it wasn't an environment of arousal to be honest. So apart from trying to look at their willy's, (a play on the above statement), we observed their movements.

Did they patrol regularly? How often would they change their routine? Were any of them smokers? What weapons were they carrying? Did they have any vehicles? How many of them were there?

All these little things may seem quite tedious or irrelevant, put into the right context though, really could make a difference or provide strategic advantage. In the worst-case scenario, disadvantage. For instance, if the enemy had a tank, you wouldn't want to try charging from the front. We were told to sketch what we could see. There are features that you cannot see on a map and when it comes to planning an attack, any information you can use to gather a picture adds to your tactical prowess. It was all in all a rather exciting affair with the sneaky peaky business, but with the anti-climax of just leaving, just a bit of, "oh that's what they're up to let's go back to camp." If anything it was a bit of a cold midnight walk. It was only a brief introduction to tactical exercises though, but I have always wanted to run before I could walk.

Back in the harbour area we were rather quickly set back about our routine, which luckily for me wasn't sentry duty. Too many times I've been sat there at two o'clock in the morning, absolutely shivering from the bitter cold and rain beating against my face. Fewer things can make a man recoil than the feeling of climbing out of a warm sleeping bag in the middle of the night and placing a cold helmet fitted with a wet chin strap on his head. I had dodged the bullet this time though and was straight in my sleeping bag, not that I can remember, but I'm sure after a minute or two I was curled up snoring. If anything would give our position away to the enemy, I'm sure it would be the deep grunts I make as I drift around inside my harmonious slumber.

At some point in the middle of the night, we were attacked, the ear-piercing sound of grenades going off and the cries of, 'stand to, stand to,' shot from the stern lips of our section commanders. On the command of, 'stand to,' no matter what position you are in, you grab your weapon, make ready to fire and face the outside of the harbour area. All goes quiet, eerily quiet and we face out toward a hidden enemy. Not far from us a loud explosion goes off. 'BUG OUT, BUG OUT,' is passed on throughout the ranks of men, half of us are still inside our sleeping bags. Five minutes ago, I was dreaming about being in a warm bed with Lucy Pinder. I don't know what I would have done with her at this tender age, probably just cuddled. Now in the middle of a cold night, I'm forced out of my sleeping bag half asleep, to pack all of my kit away and run out of this godforsaken dense wood to go and play soldiers. I wasn't pleased about this if you couldn't tell. The fact was that we knew this was training, we weren't under attack, our section commanders were the ones throwing the grenades. They grabbed us and screamed in our faces, telling us to pack our kit away, "faster Greeny, you fucking cunt." In my head I replied, 'but Corporal, I'm tired I just want to go back to sleep.' Perhaps flutter my long eyelashes at him and see if he took pity, he would have probably punched me in the face every day for the next two weeks, and in reality, I packed my kit faster. With no light what so ever, eyes still drowsy with sleepy dust built up in the corners acting like glue and the bitterness forcing your body into a shiver, packing your kit away is not an easy task.

For even the slightest idea, set your alarm for two in the morning with the tone of a battlefield. Have your partner scream, 'cunt' in your face, run downstairs into your back garden in the middle of January, get dressed in the cold and then run for five miles with two weeks' worth of kit on your back.

That is about as close as you can get to the experience, of course, you would then have to stay in the field afterwards planning attacks to carry out. There's no home time in the field, no popping home for a cuppa when it gets a bit too cold. The fact is you're in the area until the end of the exercise, you cook and clean, then drink with the same water. If your feet get cold and by cold, I mean they've been wet from a river crossing and the temperature is minus ten, you put your feet in your battle buddies' armpits until they warm up, you don't get a blanket out or turn up the thermostat.

The comical side to this was as we all finally headed out to the track ready to move out, our platoon commander was at the front, his kit was perfectly packed. Apparently, with the pre-warning of what was coming, he had packed sooner, and I'm sure he would have needed those extra few minutes to plan the route on his map. Then the section commanders were ready to go, running around grabbing people up and making sure they were prepared. Last to come running out of the wood line came us, the riflemen. The bergens that were on our backs were weird and wonderful. Sleeping bags were hanging out, ponchos draping out of pouches, one bloke had even stuffed his poncho down his shirt where he was in such a rush. The two best examples I saw that were hilarious in this context was one bloke who ran out without his weapon, and another who ran out with nothing at all. This doesn't seem that funny I suppose, but to us it was hilarious, the consequences, not so much. The thought of someone thinking 'fuck we're being attacked' and to just leg it, was hysterical, especially the poor bastards face when he got on the track and realised how bad he had fucked up. I'm sure the training team had seen worse, but even when you make the smallest mistake, you feel like it's the end of the world.

The next tactical exercise started off the best, a lot of what we did was more of the same so to speak. Attacking enemy positions, fire and manoeuvre, living in the field and becoming self-sufficient. It wasn't about making mistakes and being told.

It was about learning to think for yourself, and eventually, it started to happen. The beastings began to happen less often because the training team didn't have to grip you up every five minutes. We began to mould into a team and play our parts within the section, we evolved and grew as a team. What we were learning at this phase is outdated now, we learned FIBUA (Fighting In Built Up Areas.) However the MOD deemed this as too aggressive, and the name was changed to OBUA (Operating in Built Up Areas.) Either way, we were still breaking down doors and throwing a grenade through at the occupants. A little exaggerated to be honest, you would have colour codes that would determine your level of aggression as you entered, for instance, green, would mean you would go in as a firing pair (one in front with your partner over your shoulder) and manoeuvre through the room looking just over your sights. You would break the room down between left and right and take a half each, raising your weapon up and down moving either left or right sticking as close to the wall as you could. This was called cutting the cake. If you were going in red, then you would break through the door, throw in a grenade, withdraw, and wait for the explosion. Go through as before in your firing pair and fire into the bottom corner of the room and likely enemy positions, for example, behind a sofa. Of course, the strategically practised measures of this sore far beyond red or green. It was a long drawn out process, moving from room to room, floor to floor, building to building. Once you had taken a whole building and left one person in each room, you would have quickly run your resources down and had to start recycling them. It was exhausting work but breaching a window on a ladder with a grenade in your hand is a fucking awesome feeling.

Whoever came up with the next couple of tests was trying to weed out the strong from the weak, well I suppose they were just designed to measure your character in extreme situations. What a tragedy would it be, if, you found yourself in these cases and then realised you couldn't cope with them. Like any training in the world, it is designed to make sure you can prevail in the most extreme, and unlikely scenarios so that the reality doesn't seem so daunting. It just so happens that our extreme situations were worse than most, and so was the reality.

Tactical exercise three, I can't remember the date, but the ground was cold, very fucking cold, in fact, it was so severe that you could hardly put a shovel into it. I know this because that was our objective, to dig a trench, well actually not just dig a trench, but, dig a trench the whole platoon could fit into, and it had to be level with the tallest mans' shoulder. This started with using a shovel to clear away the snow just so we could start digging, the platoon split into two groups, one group would rest for half hour while the other started and then vice versa until the trench was complete. The first few times the pick axes hit the ground, they merely bounced away from the hard mud like a bouncy ball thrown at a bulletproof window. Some tried with the shovels first, even beating at it with the metal edge in frustration. Eventually, the pickaxes began to penetrate the frosty structure, each blow gouging a piece of skin from the ground which would forever leave a scar in the soil. We were told to try and remove the turf first so that we could piece together the grass once we refilled the trench. The plan was to leave no sign of us being there, completing a landscaper's puzzle. However, we did not have green fingers, they were red and blue from the cold. Each strike into the ground sent a spasm up the tendons as the body tried to absorb the collision, our fingers were not green.

As we got further through the frozen soil the ratio of diggers and resters, for lack of a better term, had diluted, and not the way in which you would expect. More people were trying to get involved with the digging and removal of the earth, the only cause of this was the temperature. It was far too cold for even the most work-shy to just sit down and seise up, in fact, the ground was too wet to sit on from the snow anyway. The further down we got, the more mud had converted to soft clay, pick axes became wedged in the sticky substance. We began to lose our tempers as our hard work showed no promise of ending, it was taking a considerable amount of effort to remove the smallest piece of clay. We had been beating away and dug for around six hours, we were only up to our waistline. The contrast in our body temperature and the outside was apparent, sweaty bodies in issued green t-shirts would breathe out and be able to see their breath. We were digging until exhaustion, and when you were too exhausted to continue, a comrade would take your place while you drank icy water from your black issued water bottle. As the hours passed us by, so did the earth, slowly but surely, we saw progress. Eight hours in and we were nearly there, by ten hours I'm sure we were finished. After slight amendments and eleven hours, we were complete. What had started out as a morning exercise had continued into the dark frosty night, as we looked upon our achievement we realised how still the night became. No noise, just a bright full moon spilling light onto the large open field we had been digging in. Everything was still, save a small rustling of the trees talking to each other as their leaves and branches swayed in the mild wind. This was pure tranquillity, nature is so still, these trees had seen thousands of us digging these trenches. During the hours of graft, it had seemed like a lifetime for us, until we had finished. Our work here was done, but the trees remained still and in their position. Next month more recruits would be digging here, and the same trees will be providing the same oxygen for them to breathe, as I write those same trees may be watching someone digging right now. Maybe they will for another thousand years when my bones are earth, it gave me a sense of insignificance.

After this feeling of insignificance came another one, we weren't spending a night in this trench, our eleven hours of work was mainly nothing more than a lesson in how to dig a trench. This channel that we had built was to be filled back, and it took us an hour to undo our hard work, every piece of the ground we had pulled out was filled again. Right until the layer of turf we had first stripped away. The trench was only a symbol of our teamwork. We had created something. Together we had made our Mona Lisa with shovels for brushes and emptiness for paint. Within sixty minutes we had rid it from the earth forever, all that remained was the landscapers' puzzle we had left on top, we did not have green fingers, and now we did not have our trench.

Day one of the exercise was complete, and we still had to stay in a trench. As ours was now nothing more than an odd mound in the grass like a spot on a teenage face, it was not going to be that one. An entirely pleasant surprise was that we were picked up by a four-tonne lorry, they are the primary transport to and from anywhere that requires travel through rough terrain. They are the transport relics of world war two and as comfortable as being dragged across a bed of nails, still, better than walking. We arrived at our destination, we disembarked from the vehicle with our kit and split down into our sections. Each fire team manned a trench, they were slightly better than ours, perhaps my feeling of insignificance now fell more in the realms of gratefulness. Fuck staying in that mud heap, this trench had the luxury of a wooden floor, more like pallets and less like laminate flooring mind. There was even a bridge in the middle in case it rained, and the sides fitted with corrugated tin. It has to be said that sleeping in a trench was superior to sleeping in a basher, especially when that breeze sweeps across the open plane and you can lower your head to get away from it. The downside of being sub-surface is that no heat gathers or remains, it is damp, eerily quiet and secluded. We were attacked at night. Once the attack was over, we walked back to our trenches and spent the night either on sentry or trying to sleep in our metal coffins.

The next day we packed away our kit and moved out, one mistake you have to learn the hard way, is no matter how cold it is in the morning you still need to remove all your warm kit.

It's better to be shivering in the cold and wet while you're waiting to move off than it is to pass out on the way to your next objective. It's amazing how quickly your body temperature changes, from being laid in wet grass shivering from the cold to patrolling along with sweat running down your face, all in the space of fifteen minutes. Getting your balance between being comfortable and being sensible is a hard but vital discipline.

We came to a farmhouse, the objective was to take the house and bunker up for the night, as we moved close the enemy started to fire at us from the building. We returned fire and hit the deck and then returned fire. The firing order came from the section commander.

"Two-section, reference farmhouse, two hundred meters, enemy, rapid-fire."

Seems quite calm, however, in reality, this has to be loud enough to be heard over gunshots. Also, a point to note, when you cry rapid, you hold onto the, 'd,' for instance, rapiddddddddddd, and then fire is screamed slightly louder and in a higher pitch. I don't know why, it just is. Without going through the details of a section attack, again and again, I'll skip to the meaner details. We took fire from the enemy. We took the building one room at a time after a successful breach, the result concluded in all enemy dead and the acquisition of the enemy stronghold, no casualties were sustained, probably because at the end of the day, it was all practice.

Once we had acquired our shelter for the night, we split the rooms of the top floor between the sections, this is where we would complete our administration and sleep. I loved this part because it had the feel of world war two, we had captured a Nazi position on D Day with the troops of Easy Company lead by Captain Winters and were celebrating our victory with a rest. For the uneducated on the latter people, that's a Band Of Brothers reference.

"Watch it if you haven't."

We were attacked a couple of times through the evening, as to be expected, and fought them off from our house. It's a fucking awesome feeling firing from windows and doors, it feels gangsta, awful way of describing it, but it does. We put on a sentry position per section and manned these throughout the night, although all was still. In the morning, however, we heard the screams 'stand to, stand to' so we all got in position, kit packed away and weapons at the ready. Then the familiar click and bang of smoke grenades being set off, but no sign of smoke from the enemy. "Gas, Gas, Gas" was screamed and then repeated throughout the building. 'Oh you're fucking joking,' I thought to myself. The smoke grenades had been set off inside the building to replicate a chemical attack. Thirty blokes were clambering around their kit trying to find their CBRN fatigues. The boots were hanging off my feet, those fucking useless rubber boots! The helmets were lopsided where they were ill-fitted due to the respirators, but fairly quickly we were all in our kit looking like we had been covered in glue and ran through a nineteen fifties Army surplus store. "Bug out, bug out" was the order given.

We scrambled to our feet and with fifty kilograms, (at least,) of kit on our backs and our breathing significantly reduced we made our way out of the building. A sewer pipe lead under the fence and back on to the area, this was our escape route. We got on our knees and then belt buckle and scrambled through the pipe, once we were all out the platoon commander began to run off, and we had to follow. Through thick grass, mounds and humps in the lumpy landscape we doubled, sweat filled the inside of our body armour and respirators. Our lenses filled with condensation as our warm and desperate breath couldn't filter quick enough, blokes fell to the ground and struggled to rise again with the mountain of kit strapped to their bodies. This was a struggle, our minds were telling us to swing our legs and arms in full motion, but our bodies could not replicate the action. We were sick inside our respirators, our breath had nowhere to go, and our bodies could not get the much-needed oxygen. After three miles of running, we were deemed out of the danger zone, and we were given a chance to walk, even walking felt like an inevitable death. We were told to use the straw system on our respirators to take on water, they didn't work, but we sucked with all our might to try and get some fluids in our bodies.

After a few more miles of walking we were called to a halt, we were able to take off our kit and rest, with each layer that came off, came a sense of freedom. First the bergens, the release gave movement back in our bodies. Removing the helmet, and respirator allowed our red-hot faces and sweat soaked hair to feel the refreshing breeze. Once the rubber boots and CBRN kit came off, our body temperatures returned to almost normal now that the wind could flow freely against us without the charcoal barrier. Finally, off came our combat jackets and body armour, our lungs expanded as we sucked in oxygen without a restricted torso. Most of us just laid there sipping water, bathing in the freedom given to us. This was earned rest, this was free, we had not paid for this air and feeling of coolness. It was a sense of relief that could not be found anywhere else except where we were at this very moment.

A lot of us talked after this and said if this had been the price of surviving a nuclear attack, we would rather die, but we had just done it as an exercise where we knew we were safe. The human mind is so powerful, and so is the instinct of survival, if that's what we can manage just because we were told, then imagine what we can accomplish if we genuinely had to.

Chapter 6

It's time for the small fish to enter the big pond

Once we had finished the tactical exercise phases of training, it was time to complete the final exercise. This consisted of a culmination of different tasks that we had achieved previously. Completion of this would almost qualify you as a soldier that could operate in the field and would also give you admittance to Warcop, a live firing camp where we did everything we had already done but with real ammunition. The 'final ex' was much like any other, conducting observation posts on enemy locations, section attacks as we patrolled through vast ranges of field and bramble. There was no lesson learning as such, just operating as a section, blokes stepping up as second in command and taking ammo states after each firefight. We pushed through water features and fought from the water, we scaled hills and rocks and fought the enemy upwards. Each time using the skills we had learned to outflank and suppress the enemy, we took farm houses over for a night and moved off again in the morning. We lived out of our bergens for two weeks and fought the enemy every day and won, one day we entered a street and was attacked. We took the street one room and one building at a time, we were operating as a combat effective team, and we were winning.

The final test on the exercise was an attack on an enemy factory, we were awoken at five o'clock sharp, this gives you fifteen minutes to sort out your admin, wash, powder your feet etc. Also get your scoff cooking, the further fifteen minutes will be eating your scoff and then getting your kit on your back. Apply some more cam cream to your face and check your pouches to assure your magazines are in the right place. You can't leave off on patrol without making sure your grenades are in the correct areas. To leave off at five forty-five, you need to make sure that at five thirty everything is packed away and you are moving to your section rendezvous point giving an all-around defence. This will all have to be done covertly with minimal noise as possible, and the last thing we would have all done is removed our warm kit. Packing away your softie jacket at the time in the morning when you're freezing is the worst feeling, it turns a camping trip into an exercise. We moved off into the cold morning. Sunrise was not even upon us as we silently made our way across a darkened landscape. It took us under an hour to reach our final laying up point, this lull in the patrol is where you can gather your final thoughts and assess your information. It's also the point you can drop excess kit that won't be needed for the attack, swapping out overloaded bergens for a daysack and the ammunition you will need as the battle wears on.

We moved along a tree row, utterly unbeknown to me at this point was that on the other side laid the enemy, they knew not of our immanent ascent onto their position. A break in the trees came and on the other side was a steep drop opposite the structure, the morning was still dark, and we were completely invisible. We dropped a ladder down to the bottom of the fall that appeared to lead to a sewer system. One by one we clambered down the ladder and dropped into the system, we stacked up along the closest wall, weapons facing upwards and outwards, hearts racing at the thought of what was to come. We were at the bottom of the large building, it looked like a disused factory, something out of a Bond film or Ultimate Force. We passed through a large waste pipe and came to a broad open stairway that lead into the main floor of the factory. Another section had moved around the side of the building to assault from another direction. The platoon commander had come with us as we were taking the lead, we entered the building, and with the single throw of a grenade it all kicked off. The building was dark, the loud bangs and cracks of the rounds being fired filled the air as they ricocheted off every wall. The smell of pyrotechnics filled the nostrils from grenades being set off and smoke grenades being let off as the second assault began on the outside of the building. As we took the floor, moving from pillar to pillar, we fired at every shadow jumping in front of us. My heart was pounding out of my chest as I turned every corner expecting to bump into the enemy and shoot him with my pretend bullets. The rounds may have been fake, but the feeling and intent were not. Muzzle flashes blinded us every time we pulled the trigger. We battle our way through the floor and upstairs, through rooms, over balconies, under sewage pipes, outside the building and on the roof. By the time the battle was over the sun had come up and we were still in our positions making sure every nook and cranny had been searched. Once the section commanders confirmed this, we heard the call for 'Endex' (End Of Exercise, this also became military slang to say stop in any given context). Which means we're no longer playing soldiers, all tactical movement can be stopped. You're no longer allowed to shoot anyone, and your body armour and helmet can come off. It also means in a short time will we be allowed a hot shower and sleep in our beds, happy fucking days!

Now we had conducted our final exercise, we were theoretically able to perform a live firing exercise. Of course, it was very controlled, there were instructors with us standing behind checking our every shot and making sure we stuck to our arcs of fire. Your arc of fire is the direction you can shoot in, or if not firing then the points of reference that you are to observe. For example, if you were looking at a football goal, your left of ark would be the left football post and your right of arc would be the right football post and you would be able to fire at anything between.

They weren't like, "right boys good job on the final ex, here's five hundred bullets, stick em' in your shooter and go and brass up anything ya like." Also just for reference right now, we were moving through firing ranges essentially, with figure eleven targets placed in set positions that we would then be told had contacted us. We would then conduct a section attack on those areas with live rounds. Another quick reference, the positions we were attacking were never fifty meters away, the positions were usually two to three hundred meters away and were quite often obstructed by large hills and water features, meaning by the time you had finished the attack you would be blowing out your ass and wet.

For Warcop we travelled to Scotland by coach, when we got there we were put up in a local barracks for the night, we had our safety brief and a rough going through of what we were doing. We spent the morning on the range zeroing our weapons, to zero your weapon means to adjust the sight of the rifle you are firing. By firing five rounds at the centre of a target at one hundred meters will give you a reasonable estimation of how the sight needs to be adjusted. If your shots fall to the right change the scope to the left until your five rounds land in the centre of the target, this is to ensure that where you're aiming you are firing. No weapon fires straight by itself. The beginning of the exercise was an indication of what was to come, the four-tonne lorry dropped us on a main road, a steep main road that verged off to the left and disappeared. We marched off up the hill in single file with a Bergen full of kit and our helmets and body armour. We kept going and going and going and no matter how far we went the end of that road did not seem to come and showed no sign of the gradient lowering. It was one of those times where no matter how you arch your back, shrug your shoulders or bend over to subdue the weight from the straps, the pain and struggle do not ease. For five miles we climbed that hill and by this time we were in May and for probably the only day in Scotland the sun was fucking blazing. By the time we had reached the top, we were ready to throw in the towel and all the kit off our backs. However, the exercise had only just begun.

The exercise was much the same as all the others, sentry positions were set up, and battle buddies were chosen. The only difference was that when it came to the section attacks, we were slowed down. Our movement was monitored, the positions were set for us rather than played by other troops. When it came to the attack, our arcs were covered and observed. Instructors were right behind ready to jump on us should anything had gone wrong. One of the attacks that stick vividly in my imagination was up a hill, to the naked eye it seemed relatively close, however, upon advancement, it was anything but. The ordeal was less desirable than running the London Marathon barefoot three times over. The novelty of using live rounds wore off due to the fact you had little freedom of movement, and your function was dictated by safety guidelines. It was mainly long and tiresome insertion tabs, if you were the lead section, there would be short bursts of fire and manoeuvre followed by lulls in the battle to regroup and to give the rear lads a chance to catch up. Swap around once the regroup was conducted, then it would start all over again.

I know this seems like I have skipped through quite a bit of training, this wasn't my intention, but I don't want to go on and on about the same things. I could spend hours repeating the section attacks and talking about the scenery that surrounded me, as I patrolled through wood blocks and fields at all temperatures. This was normal and happened every day, so it wouldn't be a good read or support the agenda of my story or why I'm telling it. Plus, as you go on through this book, you will understand that this is just an explanation of how I was developed and transformed. From that innocent virgin that went in and signed the dotted line, to the chaotic whirlwind that now sits in his baggy pants on the sofa writing this book. Having just been signed off from work for two weeks because of my mental state, spoiler alert, in the future I have a job. The main point to take away from the past few chapters is that it was fucking hard, hours and even days spent in wet ground observing the enemy. Countless lessons spent learning how to take apart weapons and put them back together. Full days spent freezing on the ranges of Catterick practising the marksmanship principles, over and over and over again until we got them right.

Physical training ranging from tabbing with forty-five kilograms up to eight miles in less than two hours, running until the point of throwing up, punishment, mental mind games, limits pushed and reached. This is all even before the obstacle course races or the steeplechases. Once in the freezing winter, we did the steeplechase. We came to the sheep dip, a pool of water followed by an obstacle to climb over and the water was frozen solid on top. For no reason, no punishment, we had to break through the ice and just sit in the water and then dunk our heads under. I didn't want to, so I tried to cheat and just put my face in. The PTI held my head under the water, I thought I was going to drown, I came back up and laughed about it. This happened every day, the full screws would walk up and down the line whilst we would stand there and then smack us between the legs with their regimental canes. A battle camp was another of the obstacles we faced around week twelve that I haven't mentioned yet, everywhere you go in battle camp you have to run, whether it's the toilet or the cook house, you run. We also learned unarmed combat, not your usual run of the mill punch them in the face either, it was learning all about the pressure points and how you can hurt someone with little amount of force. The sum of the six months concluded with the passing out parade, we spent hours and hours banging that parade ground with our boots, it's easy to do nothing, but to be standing in the same position for hours on end with a rifle held tight against your side, is not.

May 30th, 2008, the day that had taken six long months to arrive, six months which had me broken down until all that remained was the desire to succeed. Six months in which the chubby eighteen-year-old boy that had stepped off the platform at Darlington train station was transformed into an infantryman, my insecurities, my dignity and my weight had all but disappeared. What was left was a man who stood proudly, a man who was ready to fight and die beside his friends for his country. A man who now had a number two short back and sides haircut for life, and a man who stood in his number two dress uniform alongside thirty other infantrymen who were ready to pass off the drill square in front of their families. Before the parade had started, we were all in the corridor of our block, this was nearly the end, all the bonding, laughs and tears were over. Our platoon sergeant stood talking to us, giving us a speech of how proud he was and that our careers were only just beginning, he gave us all a glass of port. We drank the shot as is the tradition in the rifles, a drink that represented the beginning of our journeys to war.

We waited just away from the parade ground, we stood side by side, every inch of our uniform was in perfect condition for the parade, the smallest hair, cotton or dust particle had been brushed from our bodies. The legs of green trousers fell perfectly above our boots, the boots that had repeatedly been polished for weeks so that even the faintest of images would mirror perfectly. Every insignia of the regiment that lay upon us had been cleaned, re-cleaned. The facial hair that would usually sprout from the pours on our bodies had been removed from our skin, the hairs on the backs of our necks had been shaven to the point of our number two haircut and checked with a ruler. Hairlines were as straight and precise as a plasterers trowel. Any imperfection had been corrected and ironed out days and weeks before this day. We were rifleman now and every action was intentional, there were no mistakes, we looked like this because it was our honour to. We looked like this because every second of this parade had been drilled into us from our first day here, we looked like this because we could do this in our sleep.

Our families stood with pride in the audience as the band marched onto the parade, the sound of military music filled the air and set the atmosphere. A class and unique performance, seldom seen by the typical eye, they too matched in perfect uniform and followed each other step by step as they moved across the parade in formation. Nothing out of place, deliberate and precise movement as they played their instruments for the crowd, arms swinging, trumpets playing and drums banging. Once they stopped, lined up at the back of the parade square, a moment of silence fell, our hearts were pounding as we knew this was our moment, DUM dum dum dum DUM dum dum dum. The first drum beat in the sequence was louder than the rest and it was on this drum beat that our left foot was to hit the ground. This was to keep the step as we marched onto that parade square at one hundred and forty steps per minute. The initiation of this movement was the sound of the bugle and the third set of drumbeats, we moved off on the left foot all in sync. As we stepped off, the left foot triggered a movement, three separate manoeuvres taking our rifle from our shoulder to the trailing of it in our right hand at our waist side. As rifleman our traditions are slightly different to the rest of the British Army, we set off on our own, our movements faster and shorter than the rest, cheers from the crowd came as we moved like a complete body of men in front of our families. They saw the young faces they had been away six months ago, boys who were normal teenagers, listened to loud music and got drunk, got in trouble with the police, and now the same faces were showing the most dramatic form of discipline in front of their eyes. As they cheered and as the music played and we swung our arms with the most amount of purpose and swagger, the hairs on the back of my neck stood up.

The parade continued, we heard lectures from Colonels we had never even seen before, giving us inspirational talks and reassuring our families. All I was thinking was, 'shut the fuck up I wanna go home'. We saluted to the Generals and Colonels with our rifles, they came around and inspected us. "30037006 RFN Green ready for your inspection SIR." He looked me up and down and asked me which battalion I was going to and wished me luck. My spotty little face and broken front tooth passed the inspection. My arm ached, I was bored, I wanted a few beers and to get home. The parades are fantastic to watch and show the discipline that we had earned. It wasn't my cup of tea, I was happier covered in mud and sweat, shitting in a field. There were a few drills we had to carry out throughout the parade where we split into an open formation and back again, the officers carried out some exercise with their regimental swords. The moment came that I was waiting for, shitting myself but waiting for intently, I was here to pass out like everyone else, but because of my achievements, I had been awarded best recruit. This didn't mean I was the best recruit ever, or better than anyone else, it just represented that my training team had seen something in me, a desire and an ambition to succeed. I had excelled and taken on every challenge that was set for me and also gone slightly beyond. To be awarded this and to accept this reward in front of my family was the most satisfying feeling in the world. That last final push before you ejaculate, that was the feeling. At the time the pre-mentioned analogy meant nothing to me, I would have probably referred to it as a hard wank or a long-awaited constipated poo, either way it was mega.

We set ourselves into an open formation. All the prize-winners were set out at the front, and the command. "PRIZE-WINNERS," was given and we all came to attention. "GROUND WEAPONS," came next, without moving our heads or necks, we lowered our bodies and placed our weapons forward facing on the ground. "UP," we shot back to attention with our heads stern in the air, and our arms tight to our sides with our thumbs trailing the seam of our trousers. As the order was given, we marched out to the front where a table stood with our prizes on. The Lieutenant Colonel of the training garrison stood ready to hand these out. I have a video of our passing out parade, at this point you can see me, ears sticking out of my head like I was trying to pick up a radio signal and my legs shaking with fear. The prize-winners names were called out and the prize awarded, the drill was to salute and then march over to another table to hand them back and join your platoon in the ranks. Mine was last to be called, I was handed the Baker Rifle, which is the rifle used by the founding fathers of our regiment, this was the come shot.

After the prize giving I was slightly relaxed, no more pressure, the two other platoons were marched off the square, they saluted as they passed the crowd and thinned out back to their block. We conducted our march past, but, we did not leave the parade ground. We halted at the end of the square, we turned and faced out towards the opposite end, once again the square fell silent, the bugle played, and so did the drum beat. Dum dum dum dum, Dum dum dum dum, on the third hit we began to double on the spot. Rifle trailing, arm tucked up swinging nipple to the collarbone. On the fourth set, we moved off in a perfect symphony, our knees rising all in line and all side by side. The sound of the bugle called for an eye right, a salute without the hand, head tilted over but our bodies still facing and moving forward. The sound of the bugle again gave the signal to carry on, and our heads snapped forward. As we passed the crowd, we had to begin marching at a normal pace, not comfortable, and not only that, whilst moving perform a turn so that we were back in our ranks facing the right way. We completed the manoeuvre in perfect sync and marched off the square. As we disappeared from view we could still hear the cheers from the crowd from our double, we felt like rock stars and were cheering and celebrating as we got back to our block. Our families met us shortly after, for photos and cuddles of congratulations, they met our friends that we had spoken so much about. We all had a drink in the naffi, which is just a shop within a barracks where you can buy stuff, but there was also a bar and pool table etc. Also, there was a bloke selling DVDs of our training and parade, photos of our training and rifles memorabilia. I didn't stay long. Before I knew it, I was in the minibus with half my family and driving back to Banbury.

I was gutted, I had waited for this day since the first day I had got here, but it was shit. I wanted to stay, 'I don't want to go home, please let me stay here forever with all my friends.' I was proud of what I had achieved, but now, I was leaving what

I knew, it was change all over again. My friends that I had bonded with were leaving, and I didn't know when I would see them again. Not only that, I was going to a battalion where I would know nobody, what if I didn't like anyone? What if they didn't like me? I was shitting it. I went home and just decompressed really, I didn't do anything interesting, by nature although meeting me you wouldn't believe I'm quite a shy and anti-social person. Some blokes went on holiday, but all I done was sit at home and watch tv, I think I might have had a couple of nights out, but I wasn't indoctrinated into that lifestyle, yet.

Training was over, no longer were the rains strapped around my back, I was now a Trained Soldier in the British Infantry. I was to report to 4th Battalion The Rifles, Bulford Barracks, Salisbury. The former Second Battalion The Royal Green Jackets, the Regiment I originally wanted to join, I was assured that even though the amalgamation had taken place that the history and virtues of the Royal Green Jackets still ran deep within the Battalion. I was back to that crossover point, from being a big fish in a little pond to being a small fish in an ocean, a daunting realisation. Toward the end of training, I knew I was best recruit, I had faced all the challenges and excelled, I was at the top of my game. Now, where I was heading, I was the new fish amongst a sea of sharks who had been in this territory years. They had all been to war and bled together. They were part of the furniture and me, well I had nowhere to sit. Another anxious train journey stood between my new home and me.

My first memory of battalion life is one of anxiety, fear of the unknown. The picture of a child leaving his primary school education and taking the leap into secondary school. At training I was on top, seeing the recruits turn up with their oversized luggage and grinning at them smugly as you know two things. One is that they don't know anything about what is to come and secondly that you have already completed what they are about to face. At the end of training, we were cocky. We knew everyone, and our surroundings were familiar to us. There was no fear of the unknown, corridors that once seemed dark passageways in a labyrinth of hell were now just short cuts to different parts of the camp. But now, at battalion I was the small fish, I was the recruit fearing the unknown, every corridor and road was unfamiliar, every step I took was on the original ground on which my feet did not yet feel comfortable. It was as if I was carrying a sign on my back that read. 'Do not speak to this boy!' Everyone I looked at stared back at me as if I was out of place, I had not yet earned the right to speak to anyone. I was a nobody.

Once I was given my bed space and sorted my room out I felt slightly at home, not much, but at least I had a base at which I had stamped as my own. I had only my bed and a book to read but this was mine, this little space in the middle of this arena was the only place that felt familiar to me. This safe place was where my learning curve began, much like driving a car, passing your driving test is only the beginning, then you need to learn how to drive. I had moved out of training, I was a fully qualified soldier, (so to speak) now I needed to learn how to be a soldier. There is a long process, not one put down on paper and taught as a lesson in a class of civilised students. It's learned through unwritten rules, a process that has no end point but starts with the first person you meet and is practised through your entire career. It has been enforced and handed down through Rifleman to Rifleman since time began. There is an invisible boundary in which it is acceptable to act, as a NIG (New In Green, which means new to the battalion) your limits are minimal and moving out of those boundaries will find you in boiling water. The longer you are in and the more you progress socially with the platoon, your borders grow. However, there is always someone waiting with a fist to knock you back into your box should you get too comfortable.

My first night in Battalion as a naive young Rifleman consisted of laying in my bed trying to read, this at first was fine as no one spoke to me. I had no introduction and had no disturbances. I was a ghost and my position in the platoon at the moment was unnoticed by anyone. I was nothing but an intruder inside of a band of brothers, these men had been to war together in Iraq and had shared sweat and blood and laughter and here I was in the middle, nothing but an outsider with his bed and his book. The cocky young Rifleman had laid his head to rest anxious of what the next day would bring, whom would I meet? Would I fit in? A lot of questions for a head that wanted to sleep.

Once I had gotten over my anxiety, I managed to fall asleep, but the slumber was cut short by a bang. The origin of the noise came from the sound of our first door being flung open and crashing into the wall of the hallway. I lay petrified in the same spot I had woken up in, too scared to move, I prayed that the noise would not head in my direction. I faced the wall, 'crash' the noise of the second door flying open into our room."Greeny, oi, oi, Greeny," came the distinguishing shouts from our senior Rifleman. I still lay facing the wall with my back to him hoping he'll think I'm asleep and leave me alone. I was dragged from my bed and onto the floor to the command of, "don't ignore me Greeny you little cunt." As I hit the floor and got a glimpse of him I could almost not believe my eyes, he stood over me completely naked with nothing but a curtain tied around his neck like a cape. "Greeny, I'm a superhero." He was steaming, the curtain around his neck dragged across the floor and his penis dangled between his legs as he giggled and shouted. What could I do, I was a NIG, I would probably have to suck his dick if he told me to.

I got up and sat in my bed, I was like a hostage negotiator trying not to let the situation get out of hand, like I was pleading for him not to hurt me and let me sleep. "Fucking move over Greeny," I faced the wall, and he got in bed with me. His arm wrapped around me spooning me, I have never been so scared in all my life, my first night in the battalion and I'm going to get bummed. Of course, I never, he was just drunk and wanted to sleep. I woke in the morning, and I was on my own, I looked up, and he was sat on his sofa with his feet up on his table with a fag in his mouth. He was so cool, he didn't speak to me he just sat there, I didn't know it then, but he was going to be one of the best friends I've ever had. For now, he was like a god within B company, and I was barely noticeable, his only words to me were, "go and do the block jobs." So I did, I cleaned the toilets, mopped the floors and took the rubbish out. You didn't say no, that word didn't exist. You do as your told.

The morning parade was with the Platoon Sergeant, Pratty, he seemed pretty sound. He introduced me and called me a turd, his insults were funny, the most common he used was, moon head or to change it up you would get, goats teeth, sheep head or dogs breath thrown at you, after six months of being called a useless cunt, I could handle moon head. Once we had the morning parade, I had met everyone in the platoon, most of the blokes were pretty new, we stuck together like sheep. After the platoon parade at 07:00 you go and get breakfast at the cookhouse or finish getting your stuff ready, then you parade at the company headquarters, (COY HQ) prepared to begin your day. There is a detail on the COY HQ, which tells you what you are doing, you are to read this each night, so you know what to wear to the parade. Too many times I'd been seen legging it back to the block because it's PT and I've started to walk down in combats. As I got down to company parade, I was pushed to the front, Kev was behind me, I didn't know him at the time or even know that was his name. All I know is that he pushed me to the front so I stood in front of him. This was the first time I was with the whole of the company, not one person spoke to me, except Kev and when I say spoke to me, take that with a pinch of salt. As I stood within the parade, I felt a hand go in my trousers, and a finger pushed right into my ass and squeezed tight, I shot round, and there was Kev, sniffing his finger and said, "fresh meat." Either of two things was happening, I had accidentally turned up at an aggressively homosexual battalion, and they found me irresistible, or the most likely of the two, they were fucking with me because I was the new kid, the outsider. I decided from that point that the best way to get along was to go along, plus you have to serve your time, I fucking loved it, do more, punch me, induct me into your brotherhood and I implore you to do so at full capacity.

The first few months were like this to be honest, the butt of every joke and pushing of the social limits. As a mechanised unit, we had the Bulldogs to take care of, each section had a dedicated driver that had to complete weekly checks, and this included general maintenance and cleaning. At these periods we would have to go clean, sweep the yard, mop the floors, put away oil and clean tools etc. Of course, the senior rifleman wouldn't do this. This was a job for the new blokes, this was a job for me, what the top blokes would do was smoke and talk and find ways to entertain themselves. Once this consisted of attaching bungee cords together and strapping them to bollards to create a giant catapult, they then made us take our trousers down and released the sling on us, it left a bruise or two and I'm sure someone will still have videos on their phone. Another is when Mac and Ron tied me up with tape and placed me in a metal bin full of brake pads. About five blokes then persisted to throw break pads at my head, I laughed along, but each blow fucking hurt and I wanted to cry. This is the Army and this is what happens. This incident subsided when they deemed I had had enough so to speak, this is how you fit in, the more you resist the more frequent it happens and you're seen as a shit bloke or a rat.

Within a month I had been locked in a locker room naked, shot with air guns repeatedly and forced to punch (now one of my best mates) in the face. Each time I hit him I was told, "fucking harder Greeny or I'll fucking hit you?" Talk about stuck between a rock and a hard place, but fuck it, I hit him. I'm not saying all this to moan or to say it was bullying because it wasn't, it was initiation. I was going to be going to war with these people and I loved it, it was character building and if you can't take a bit of horseplay then how can you face the enemy on the front line? This was where the bonds were made, friendships were forged for a lifetime, and a trust that could never be broken was cemented in the hearts of each man. Fucking look left, and right of you, this man that's just pissed in your mouth because you fell asleep will carry your broken body off the battlefield. The man that just punched you in the face because you fell asleep on stag will take a bullet for you. The man that just shoved a finger up his sweaty ass and rubbed it on your top lip will give you covering fire as you cross open ground in Helmand Province. But Gary, the most important thing, is that the man that just punched you in the side of the head for getting a bit too big for your boots, will die in less than a year. It will be the hardest thing you've had to deal with, and in years to come, you will still be writing on his Facebook wall. Never take this bonding for granted, once it's gone it's gone and you will never get it back, nothing in life will ever compare to the life you knew then.

Chapter 7
Never talk about the BC

What a contradict I am, the title of this chapter informs you that I should not talk about what I am going to talk about. I won't release names of members or anything but more the importance of my indoctrination and what this friendship meant to me. If possible, it was even stronger than the regular bond I had with my brothers. If anyone asks about the BC, the only answer you can give is "shut the fuck up." So any questions after this paragraph or two will result in that answer, "shut the fuck up." The BC meant more than just the tattooed insignia on the right wrist. It was a circle of trust, those within the BC were the closest of friends. To be involved in the BC meant a member had to nominate you and then at least four members had to accept your nomination, then you were initiated. But we will get to that. To be chosen, you had to either, just be an excellent bloke or help a member of the BC in conflict, that's where my nomination came.

Once you start mixing with the blokes and showing that you want to be one of them, sounds stupid but I just mean that you want to fit in. It takes the right kind of personality I think, being able to laugh things off and be one of the blokes. If you do that you're okay, like prison or school or anything densely populated by males, it's just a way of life, have a drink, have a scrap and laugh it off. Once you do that, you start your socialising and socialising requires drinking, drinking involves violence. This is where it all started to go wrong for me, I took the BC so seriously and loved the buzz of being part of it. I developed this alter ego almost when I drank, I could never and have never been able to let it go. When I drink I'm that person that has to fight, live up to the title, fight for that acceptance. Every time we went into town we had to fight, for whatever reason, someone was from a different regiment or blokes were looking at us the wrong way, we would have to fight them. As a new bloke, it would be my job to initiate it, "Greeny go over there and kick off with them." So I would, I would have my double vodka red bull in my hand, dance over to a group of blokes and bump into one of them. I would turn around, push any of them and accuse them of barging into me. The rest is history, throw my drink at them, punch one of them and then the boys would come and jump in. That became my aim, to have a scrap, to hurt someone, to get the cheers and the praise from my brothers. We were on a night out, we had gotten into a scuffle, my mate Mac was about to get bottled, as the bloke came forward I smashed him in the face. This along with my friendship with everyone in the BC got me nominated, and one night in the local at Bulford, that is what happened. Four unsuspected hits from the members that wanted me in, the last one from Ron was when I bent over and he kicked me in the face. I was in, the next day we went down to Salisbury, and I got my tattoo. From then on I was in the BC, a bond that could never be broke. Ron said to me one night that no matter how many years passed or how long we did not speak for that we could show up on any doorstep of the BC and be taken in. It meant no matter how outnumbered, we stood by each other to the death, we were more than brothers and this was for life. For the first time in my life I felt tangible affiliation and connection, I felt at home and from then on the violence continued. I never stopped loving it, from a boy at home that didn't go out drinking, to a monster in the BC that couldn't stop drinking and fucking enjoyed a good scrap.

One night Cas and I were out, I can't remember whom with, but we ended up kicking off with some lads, one in the middle for some reason we thought was called Specs. I grabbed the geezer, he head-butted me, by the time I looked back up Cas had caught him. He launched a head-butt at him and missed (still one of the funniest things I've ever seen,) and this Specs lad punched him in the side of the face. The look that Cas threw back as his head snapped straight back could have burned the devil to the ground, the face of a fucking psychopath. Neither of us were hurt, the bouncer had split it up before we could reach him. Our egos were bruised, and for the following week, we were taunted about how we had got beat up by a skater boy. So the next weekend we went hunting, myself, Ron, Cas and Ads. Low and behold we saw him, and we conducted a fucking section attack on the cunt. We skirmished through the outside of the dance floor and on to the raised platform where the first incident had happened. Ron was giving me the. "You aren't gonna do anything Greeny." taunting, testing my metal. So off the back of that I dived off the platform and punched this lad straight in the face, he went sliding across the dance floor and then all hell broke loose. When we got outside we were all laughing and sharing the tale, it was a glorious masculine celebration and forever added to our battle honours, 'the specs assault.'

To an outsider, I can see how this was thuggish, but to us, it was a way of life, this is how we bonded in blood sweat and tears. This was our life, our legacy, the brotherhood, the men you fight with are more important than anything else in the world. The BC was my religion, the nightclub was my church, I was christened in the blood of people we fought, and fighting was my way of prayer. We weren't looking for women, all we were looking for was a fucking good time. What better way to spend your money than on a Lyle and Scott T-shirt, a pair of G-Star Raw trousers and some K-Swiss trainers? A thirty-pound taxi to Salisbury and get them fucking covered in blood, sick and piss. This was real battalion life, fucking brutal. You had to know how to drink and fight. You had to take a joke. You had to do things you didn't want to do, the only thing is, In the end, I wanted to do it. The problem was that I never really liked fighting, I just loved afterwards, the stories, the comradeship. It was satisfying, it was family, and I was good at it. I had friends at school but I was timid, I wasn't popular, here I had started over. I was accepted, I wasn't frightened, and I was addicted to it, a bit like a gangster, cutting around camp with my BC tattoo, I felt invincible.

Behind this feeling of invincibility, this mask of bravado, was confidence, a confidence that I hadn't felt before. I believe this manifested from a social awareness. Growing within the platoon and finding yourself in this family puzzle created a bond, an invisible bond that struck through the hearts of all of us. There was no feeling of emptiness or segregation. There was just a family of people connecting and socialising every day. Wherever you were in camp, you felt secure, I never felt lonely or misunderstood, I felt accepted for being exactly who I was. As I walked through the lines of our accommodation, I knew I could pop my head into any room and find a friend sitting there. I could sit with them and talk for hours and know that even if we were from the most different of backgrounds, that we would have that bond and something in common. In our hometowns we may have hated each other, we may support rival football teams, we may have a different religion. He may be rich, and I may be poor, but, in this environment we were equal, we were all brothers, and we were all human. I miss that, I sit in my office alone writing at the minute, and I could cry, I could cry at the fact that I will never feel that content again. An effortless and unconditional friendship that had me so secure. My time before deployment in battalion life was short, twelve months and nine days to be exact, but within that time I had made a complete network of people who would die for me and in turn, that I would die for. Never will you meet people like them, people who will give you absolutely everything they have and ask for nothing at all in return.

Around February 2009 things around camp started to ramp up, we were gearing up for deployment and the training schedule had taken a very steep turn. There was less time for drinking because we were always away training. Implementation was about six months away but had not been entirely confirmed as we were deploying as the election support force for the Afghanistan elections. We had briefs from the CO every Friday. They were as useful as a fucking fart in an elevator. He would have us all parade on the field next to the H block and give a similar speech. "When are we going? I don't know, how long will we be going for? I do not know, what will we be doing there? I do not know, but I can tell you, we will be going."

'Yeah, cheers for that mate, massive help.'

Every week he would make us go through the same bull shit, he would gather us all there while we were waiting to go home and tell us that he knew nothing.

The training began to get attractive, hard but exciting, during PT sessions we started to wear our body armour and helmets during tabs. Each time we would have a casualty so we would have to carry them back to camp. During my first year there, training had taken a gradual slope down, we were quite lax, but when you get ready to deploy everything supercharges, range days with every weapon you can think off, casualty evacuations and battle PT every Friday.

The fitness was excellent, and so were the range days but we needed to put our skills into practice, so as training ramped up so did the exercises. We were off to all parts of the country taking part in various tasks, weeklong training in pre-deployment specific locations, a bit like a harsh Butlins, each training facility had different terrain and reasons for its existence. Like Dartmoor, the only reason I can think that the place exists is to piss squaddies off. The area is horrific. The site is tableau for sure, what you see is beautiful, the natural water features and landscape is very much untouched by urban reprobates, but, moving along and upwards is hard work! We conducted an exercise there in November 2008, R Company deployed the week before us, it was so cold that thirteen of them got evacuated off the ground by helicopter due to hypothermia, it was in the papers come to think of it. The whole thing was a fuck up from the beginning, one of the first things we encountered was a river crossing, by boat luckily, but to get to it was a vertical drop down a muddy, slippery bank with full kit weighing us down. Once down, and still holding onto the wet rope that was saving us from icy death, you had to scramble into the dingy, worst fucking idea ever, and once across it was the same up against the other side. Before we had even started the exercise, the night sky was black, the temperature was minus twenty and my feet were soaking and turning black with frostbite. That training was indeed one of my worst experiences, out the other side of the river, Nosh and I were so cold we were doing press ups to keep the blood circulating our bodies. The first assault we conducted, consisted of a night march to battle, we made our way to the bottom of a mountain, literally a mountain. The 'Yes Tor,' we were at the bottom, we had to march up the side of the thing, at this point, it was probably about three in the morning. Everything I was wearing was either soaked with sweat or rainwater. The bitter cold was clinging to every inch of my body, my forearms felt locked in position and stiff, my fingers burnt from the cold as the gloves I was wearing had become wet and were as now insulated as a fishs' tail. The Yes Tor was a vertical climb, with my weapon in my hand and sixty kilograms of kit strapped to my body. It was a stop and start exercise with the stopping a small chance to catch your breath, necessary but not all that effective as the air became colder and denser.

We were contacted about fifty meters from the ridge, possibly further as my memory isn't all that clear on the fact and I wasn't the first man so the distance would obviously vary. All I remember is that it just made the climb fucking harder, fighting up a bastard hill, first thing in the morning without a wink of sleep, barely able to carry myself from exhaustion and now trying to fire at the fucking enemy. Whoever put this together was an undeniable massive prick. The assault was horrendous, the mountain was like a treadmill, no matter how far you went it just kept going and going. By the time the attack was over, we were breaching the ridge, we could then see that the side of the mountain we had climbed had completely blocked out the light, even the sky. We had been in complete darkness throughout our ascent, the summit unveiled the sun, it provided not a single ounce of warmth though, just a bright cold day, the eye of the storm. The ascent up the Yes Tor had been cold, also the wet and damp ground flooded the air with a dense texture that stuck to your lungs. The top of the Yes Tor was still freezing, but a dry cold if that makes sense, silent and frozen. We moved under a rock and tried to brew up but our water bottles were completely frozen, the stone had icicles hanging from the ceiling where the water had given up its liquid structure, morphed into an icy knife. Starting the gas cookers was hard because of how cold they had become, once began we filled our containers with ice and used it to make a hot drink, a well-earned and well-needed brew, what a fucking start to the morning. Such a lasting feeling and ever so familiar, seldom on these exercises are you kept in comfort or a content feeling of warmth and serenity.

The rest of the exercise contained fewer mountains, just miles upon miles of travelling on your mark one boots. Attack after attack, casualty after casualty, and mile after mile. It just didn't seem to end, and the terrain was, as you would expect, horrendous, it would have been a nice break to walk on a bed of nails.

Dartmoor was the most laborious exercise I had faced in a mental aspect. There was some severe digging in that had to be done to get through it, the attacks were attacks and no matter where you are they take your breath away because of the sheer velocity of them and the movements incorporated. But with Dartmoor the terrain had wholly battered us, every three steps you would trip over a knot in the ground or struggle to climb a hill, there were no paths so everywhere we went we were carving a new walkway out of the field. Every step was a challenge and climbing up with your kit on your back was exhausting, I remember once I fell, and as I got up I fell again. I wanted to cry there on that spot, just give in and cry, but I couldn't, the emotions of exhaustion and frustration had grabbed me by the balls, and I felt entirely at its mercy. I know it was a testimonial of resiliance, but fuck ever doing that again!

Another one of the shit places we went to, was Lydd Ranges, what a fucker that was, I'm not sure if it's a commonly known thing but they are famous for their shingle beaches. Did you know that? I do, only because I had to go there, but now you know, see you learned something through this book, well actually two things. One, Dartmoor is shit and cold. Two, Lydd has shingled beaches and is shit, don't go there. I'm not a travel guide or anything, in fact, Dartmoor would probably be a beautiful place to go with the misses, get a log cabin and have a romantic walk, if you're into that thing, you can go to Spain for eighty notes now, so maybe you would instead go there.

Anyway less of my 'where's shit' holidaying advice and back to the famous beaches of Lydd. It was another one of those places to piss us off, the Army goes, "right where's shit?" I imagine someone who knows where everything shit is, goes, "Lydd is shit." That will conclude the conversation and the Army decide to send everyone there. Or the other way they decide is by going "those section attacks are quite hard, how we can make them harder?" Someone who knows how to make things harder goes, "well they're quite hard and tiring on normal ground, how about we make them do it on shingle?" That concludes the conversation and the Army will send everyone to do it on shingle.

Or perhaps the land is just cheap because it's always shit there? Who knows? The central fact is that when you're preparing for war, you need to be as robust and as fit as you can. If you can perform a casualty evacuation on shingle with full kit on, or you can perform an attack up the side of a mountain in minus twenty degrees temperature, then you can probably conduct it them in Afghanistan. That's what we were training for, train hard and fight easy. Well, so the saying goes anyway.

We were all trained soldiers, the whole unit was, although I moan about the conditions of where we were because it was shit, as we went on and on, our fitness did progress, we became stronger and more effective as a unit. We grew adaptive to the environment and the ground, we were less cold because we could handle colder climates and knew how to prepare for them. It was like they said in training, passing out was just your driving test, here we learnt how to be soldiers, packing your kit right transferred into buying the better kit and stowing only the necessary inventory. I no longer wore big and bulky webbing that obstructed my movement. I wore slimmer belt kit that just had a few pouches that strapped to my body. I had molly grip pouches that attached to my body armour and held magazines of 5.56 ammunition. My day sack became tailored with bags that carried my essential kit, and I learnt to be able to take a lot less yet be able to use it all to my advantage. I had become a deadly and tactical killing machine, I was faster, slicker and more dangerous than I had ever been before. I was able to conduct a compound clearance with my section, carry an injured comrade to an extraction point, run three miles in my full kit, stand up and hit the enemy from three hundred meters away, all before I needed a rest or a drink of water.

To learn to be a soldier, you have to be trained in conventional warfare, which is all well and good for Northern Ireland or The Falklands, but Afghanistan was an entirely different beast. The extended fields we had trained to fight in would prove useless when faced with miles of sandy tracks and compounds, there's a tremendous leap in tactics in a section attack across the familiar ground to that of a dynamic three sixty enemy in unfamiliar territory. Our training had to change, we departed on a weeklong battle camp, and we were not staying in the field for this exercise but instead would complete one battle scenario per day. This was to test us at section level in our drills, observation, and durability. These were set in model towns, fighting from vehicles and interacting with crowds of civilians. A normal. Actually... Normal? I'm not sure if that word can be used in any of these contexts, so instead, we will use standard, even that's a bit abnormal, but, we will use it nether the less. Thus, a standard firefight that we had trained for from day one was an enemy attacking and us diving on the floor and attacking that position. Real life had to be a lot slower, for a start we were about to face the threat of I.E.D's (improvised explosive devices.) This meant everywhere we tread, first had to be scanned with metal detectors. This also limited our movement for just jumping on the floor to get out of the way of incoming fire, we now had to conduct five and twenties before taking a knee on the ground. This meant first of all when you went firm. You had to visually and physically check the surrounding five meters of your position for anything out of the ordinary. From the first chapter of my book, you can see I apparently wasn't very good at that part. And then once firm you would need to visually scan the surrounding twenty meters, anything that looked even slightly aberrant. Of course, this is dependant on the environment, a coke can in the street is regular in England (unfortunately – pesky litterers) but in the middle of Afghanistan would become novel. A whole patrol could quite quickly be stopped because of a single coke can. Its very existence would be questioned, was it placed there? Is it a bomb? To be complacent is to be dead. Add to this the bulky chest and back plates we had to protect us from fiery metal projectiles and fifty-degree heat, and you start to build up a picture of what we were training for.

When we had kicked down more doors, thrown more grenades and tactically conquered more miles of the ground than ten men could shake a stick at, we were then also after said door kicking and grenade throwing, supposed to be able to give life-saving medical treatment. Two people from each section were to be trained as team medics. I was one of them in my section, that was not a pleasant course to be a part of. We learned how to save a dismembered limb, at twenty years old, learning how to stem a severed arm or leg is daunting. Believe me when I say it doesn't prepare you for the real thing, but at that time in my life, it was still enough to make me shit myself. It's the little things that come with it as well, like, if your mate gets blown up, yes check his legs and body for bleeding, but, also check their mouth. You see in a blast injury it's common that a victim can bite his or her tongue off and choke on it. Also, there may be debris from the blast or blood in there anyway, so be prepared to fish hook it out. All this was helpful, even the tests were pretty realistic, having someone screaming that they've got no leg and fake blood spraying like a champagne party, but it was still just someone I knew and fake blood. When your mate is there with a missing leg, scorched trousers, the smell of singed skin and leg hair filling your nostrils as you hold onto a flap of skin, trying to tuck it into a first field dressing as he screams in agony. It's quite the different story. And also they forgot to mention what you do with the other leg that isn't quite detached yet, just a shattered mix of blood and bone, what do I do about that? A shot of morphine in the arm and a kiss on the cheek as you wait for him to be carried away.

So by April time 2009 the unit as a whole was deemed deployable, all we awaited on now was our orders, which at some point in time I remember getting, I can't remember when to tell you the truth, but I can promise you we did receive them. The advance party was to go about two weeks before us, and we were to depart on the 9th June 2009, four days after my 21st birthday.

"Ooh, lovely late birthday present, thank you ever so much it's what I always wanted."

In fact, it might have been. I'm still too emotionally corrupt to know whether I was sarcastic or not. Around some point here I should mention my first relationship, her name is not essential. Like Voldemort (she who should not be named.) She needn't be either was it not for the fact that she will play a critical factor in my first of many downfalls. Not to pin the blame on her, just sort of the straw that broke the camels back really. I met her in early May 2009. I was gimpy looking back then, I have matured like a fine wine now, I guess that makes me a bit of a grape back then. Either way, this was my first encounter in many respects with the opposite sex. We fell in love quite quickly and unfortunately for her, neither of us realised that we were entering a chaotic time, at first it was rather lovely and very 1944, the young soldier boy finds love with a nurse and fucks off to fight for his country. It just didn't turn out like that, although at that time in my life I was really in love with her. We promised to write to each other, and we cried when we said goodbye. I even had two photos of her, one I kept in the side of my helmet and the other I carried in my pocket, she was my first love, and I had only known her four weeks before I flew out to Afghanistan.

I was ready to deploy, my kit was packed, I had said my goodbyes and I was as mentally concrete as I have ever been, I was physically as fit as I had ever been and I was as robust as a land rover tire.

Ron, Cas and I were in Salisbury. I remember this point in my life clearer than any other moment, we were in Boots looking at the men's shower gel and just generally messing about when my phone rang. I instantly recognised the number. It was the number that came up when you're receiving a call from a satellite phone from Afghanistan. I knew it would be one of the lads from the advance party, the advance party was made up of lads from the Battalion who had the relevant qualifications to be trained to drive the Mastiff vehicles. It was Kev, a mate of mine from five platoon, I had spoken to him while he was out there during the previous weeks but this phone call was much different. Instead of the usual upbeat, hyper voice which we usually conversed with, he spoke in a low tone. There was a sense of hesitance in his voice that suggested he didn't quite know how to say what was about to come out of his mouth. The exact words were stuttered, unclear and lacked information, but from what I could manage to interpret into sense, was chilling and probably the soberest news I had ever received. That moment of realisation yet utter disbelief. My heart sank, disappeared, swallowed somewhere inside of my stomach where you store those painful feelings you are unable to digest. My friend Cheesy was dead. We were told that he had collapsed and had been taken to hospital where he had died. The news came that he unknowingly had cancer before he had deployed, he had just felt ill and never woke up. It is something that has lived with me since. That phone call made me feel sick, it wasn't supposed to happen at all, but especially not like this. As we got back into camp, we went to Battalion HQ to clarify the news passed on to us. As we arrived the flag was sailing in the wind at half-mast, this told us everything we needed to know. On the 7th June 2009 Cheesy was pronounced dead, two days after celebrating my birthday I was mourning the death of my friend.

We had not even flown out yet, and we had our first death, it was in the cruellest of ways. Upon the hour of battle, God took away one of his most exceptional riflemen, for what reason I shall never know. We shall just move forward forever with the sun a little less bright but with an extra star in the sky. I would never lie or pull any punches or for the sake of being mindful sugar coat the truth, in this instance though there is no need. The loss of Cheesy was indeed a devastating blow, and I don't believe that there would be anyone that can say they were not gutted when word touched their ear. Part of being a rifleman though is being able to move forward, those feelings are to be bottled up and the hardest pill to swallow is that there was still a job to be done and we had to be motivated for it. In other lines of work you could go home, you would not be expected to carry on your employment. Here it was the opposite, death was expected. You were sent to your function. The memory of Cheesy has never and would never be forgotten, but for now, it had to be cast to the back of the mind and we were to be thrown into the battlefield.

Between us and Afghanistan stood a lot of bullshit and administration, clean kit, check kit, recheck kit. Section commanders check, platoon sergeant check, check, check and fucking check. Our four-man room, once communal, full of sofas and TV's where we had spent nights sharing food and movies, laughing and giggling as banter shot back and forth, was now an empty space. Everything had been packed away awaiting our death or return. If we died, our kit would filter through the system and be given to the next person who turned up at battalion. Our possessions sent back to our families.

The Sausage Factory

The sausage factory, now contrary to the euphemism this is not a reflection on how at times I shared a room with twenty other penis's, this is, in fact, the analogy I use to transfer my thoughts on the process of the British Army. So it all starts with the consumer, in this case, the consumer is a politician, a fat politician brandishing a Savile Row suit, I'm not sure why I just like the thought of portraying them as a Bond villain, much sneakier and slyer than a Bond villain though. This consumer needs sausages, so he hires a farm, this farm is run by sausages, and although the sausages have been through the same process, the consumer has convinced them to run the farm and to persuade innocent pigs that they want to be sausages. These naive pigs sign up, they watch movies on how good it is to be sausage, and they leave the farm and head off to the butchers to become sausages. They are slaughtered, they are ground up in a meat grinder, filtered out and forced into a camouflage skin and cooked until all that's remembered is how to be a sausage. They are fed to the consumer who munches on them to fill his need, and when they are done with they are tossed into a bin, no one can go back to the farm as pigs, they are always sausages and this is the sausage factory. We're just created, chewed up and spat out. They profit from our death and the next recruit lines up and wears our kit. I give you, the sausage factory, yum yum.

Sat in that room with our bags of kit, one black grip bag full of comforts, if you like, should you be wounded you would have this stored with the rear party in Bastion and brought to you. Bergans packed with our essential kit that we would be living out of for the next, well, however long really. The minimal amount of equipment to last you six months in the field, to be honest, though it was less than most people would take on holiday for a week. I remember my mum was packing us two suitcases each to go to Great Yarmouth. I had less than that now to spend six months in the desert, no disco kit needed! For some reason the night before Cas and I decided to shave each other's hair, we both went for the Marine look. I don't know what possessed us because we both looked like a pair of tits, just one of those things we did. Our relationship was like that, how could we both be proper bell ends? We would brainstorm it, and then the ridiculous idea would come, and we would do it.

We loaded up our kit and got a coach to Brize Norton, not far from my hometown, I contemplated asking the driver if he would drop me off to say another goodbye to my Mum but thought better of it. To be honest, I wanted to feel sad, I thought that was the right thing to do, but I wasn't. Anxious perhaps but I was with my family already, I got homesick sometimes and hadn't become detached from my family at all, it's just I was back when I was with the boys. Plus this is what I felt my whole life had been building up to, for me, it was as if I was a football player and we were about to play in the world cup final. Everything we had ever been taught was about to get put into practice, every run, every tab we had been on was all for this. My skills were so sharp that if you touched me, you could cut yourself. I was ready as if I had lubed this bitch up, my cock was hard, and I was ready to fuck shit up. That was the feeling amongst everyone. We were excited. No one seemed sad or scared, even the youngest of the faces were laughing. I had turned twenty just four days previous, lost my virginity about a month before, this was the first time I had ever been on a plane, and I was off to war without a hair on my face.

Chapter 8
Bullshit of Bastion

I can't remember why, but we didn't fly straight to Bastion like everyone else, there were about six of us I think, we flew to Kandahar first, may have been because of space on the flight, either way, I can't remember. What I do remember is getting off the plane, we had to run past the jets as we got off and it was boiling, the further we got away the heat stayed with us, it was evening, and the air had not cooled. Partially because it's a ridiculously hot country but also because we had not acclimatised to the weather, like when you first go on holiday, the first few nights you're sweating in your bed sheets begging for air conditioning. This was not going to be a holiday. We were escorted from our flight, I can't remember who by, possibly an American, it was dark, I was anxious and played follow the leader. We were lead to a hanger with all our kit, and that's where we were to sleep for the night, but fuck going to sleep. I'm on holiday mother fuckers, straight away I went out for a walk, I know that sounds crazy, but I was so excited, excited to see Americans, aeroplanes, sand, buildings, anything. All was the culmination of a lifelong waiting for everything I had ever wanted. That's how it felt at first, naïve Gary Green sightseeing in Kandahar, "ooh look at that Humvee quick take a photo." I was a bit like an idiot abroad, utterly clueless to anything outside of that wire, we were safe here, and this was the first time I had left the country. Exception actually, I had been to Belgium on a battlefield tour while in training, and I went on holiday in Wales, if that counts? But this was the first time I had been on a plane and left the country, I felt like I had a pass to a film set, I was an autograph book away from looking like a complete an utter tourist, like a five-year-old in Disney land asking Micky Mouse for a signature. It was tremendous, even just seeing sand and feeling the heat, it's all rather exciting, and the atmosphere just draws you in. Americans are so cool man, and they're like they are in the movies, US Marines were staying in the hanger next to us, that Humvee I mentioned earlier was their's. I did get a photo sat on top of it, posing like a proper chopper, but it's ok I was new to Afghanistan at the time so that can be excused. A pair of Wyley X sunglasses I had bought from the Naffi, while I was in training, was in my pocket, I swapped them with one of the US Marines for a pair of Oakley's, which was one of my most gangster memories, you can't be in Afghan without Oakley Flackjackets!! I still have them in my daysack, which, said daysack has been with me since pre-deployment training, Afghanistan and everywhere I have been since. I used an old ammo pouch to use as a sunglasses pouch, because one, I'm a gangster like that and two, I don't need ammo pouches anymore.

We awoke in the morning, tied our desert boots to our feet, buttoned our untucked desert shirts, fitted our moulded desert pattern jungle hats, fitted our Oakley's to our faces and slung our weapons. All this and we were only going for breakfast, we had to walk through a small part of the base to get there, I don't think I could ever truly convey that feeling I had. Apache helicopters fixed to the ground ready to shoot off into the war zone at a moments notice, armoured personnel carriers riding through the camp in their tanned coating, smudged with bullet holes and damage from I.E.D's where they had been caught up in blasts. Kandahar base was gigantic, a scale that my eyes could not take in at once, the sun shone down so bright, and although this may seem strange, everything looked pretty. As we got into the cookhouse, I don't think a man between us could believe our eyes, and when I say they had everything, you can take my word that I am not exaggerating. They had fridges full of every can of drink you could imagine, stacks upon stacks of m&m's and other chocolates, muffins and pancakes. This was a far cry away from what we were used to when people make the constant comparison between the USA and the UK's equipment and resources etc. they should start by looking in the cookhouse. I wonder if they would like to swap? The US's luxury beef burgers and burritos for our lasagne and chips? I need to mention that any pasta dish or any dish for that fact is made with the same ingredients and tastes the same, like tomato and plastic. Perhaps they would like to trade some of the cold cans of mountain dew for some diluted orange squash? Maybe not, on their behalf.

After scoff we went for a wander around the dusty camp, there was a square in the middle, full of shops, even a café that sold cold milkshakes made with ice cream. I think it was a Swedish place, if all camps out here are like this, this is gonna be a dream. Soon before long though we had our orders to catch a Hercules flight to Camp Bastion, a Hercules isn't quite to the same standard as the Airbus that takes you to the US or Dubai. It's a giant baked bean tin with a set of wings, not the most comfortable of flights. Due to the lack of soundproofing, it sounds like you're sat inside of a formula one car. Pretty soon after the trip, we were united with the rest of the company, the room we were all kept in, was a brick room full of sandbags around the outside, it looked like the kind of bunker you would set up to repel an impending zombie invasion. The guys had slept here for the night, because of security and it being located next to the airfield, nobody was allowed to leave the room. Although it was a big room, with a company full of blokes it soon became enclosed with a humid temperature, the blokes were not happy with the fact that we had been swanning around Kandahar drinking strawberry milkshakes and eating with the Americans. Win some you lose some though, we were happy. It took about two hours of being stuck inside that room before we were allowed to clear out. A bus took us to a hanger, it was pretty much a replica of the one we had stayed in the night before only this time there was more than six of us, we had air conditioning and a block of toilets and showers outside, luxury! We had the next day to square our kit away, explore the sites and we could even use the internet booths if we so wished, nothing like updating your Facebook status to let people know you're in Afghanistan, oh and of course to let loved ones know you're ok. Bastion was a mile's length away from

Kandahar in regards to comforts, there was a pizza hut, run by Afghanis and it was horrendous. It did make a change from the cookhouse where they served tomato pasta with a side of tomato paste. It wasn't the pizza hut you get at your local though. It was more like a microwaved dough covered in tomato puree and cheese made from cats milk. I would have preferred to travel into the desert and found a local who was serving up deep-fried dogs asshole. Still, every cloud has a silver lining, and this one was that we would probably all get out of training because of diarrhoea and vomiting.

The next day we were back on the leash, we were about to start our RSOI package, which is your, Reception, Staging and Onward Integration training into Afghanistan, this lasts roughly two weeks and is to educate on the latest threats and intelligence. Also, it aids you in acclimatising to the environment. From the wet and cold green climates, the fake streets, townhouses and mountains we had been training, to this fifty-degree heat, dry, vast landscape we had found ourselves in was entirely different. This RSOI package was the time to decide what kit was most important, where were your ammo pouches better placed, how did you want to sling your weapon, what was the best way to break your kit down and what equipment would better suit this. The day started with a run, five miles I think we did around Bastion, boring and not much different to a run on a sunny day in England, Cas and I spent most of our time making up raps as we made our way around. Then a few health and safety briefs about the facilities, basically all I got from it was not to wank in the internet booths and that horse flies will get in your eye and blind you. Also actually that camel spiders were not to be approached, not like I fancied tangling with a fucking camel spider anyway, what planet were they on? Have you seen what they do to people? Their bite numbs the flesh of their victims and then they start eating around the bite, thanks for the advice, however, I had concluded that I was staying away from those motherfuckers all by myself.

After the basics, by basics I mean that anything out here can kill you, we started to learn about the other things that can kill you, the Taliban. We had learned about I.E.D's because that was a method used by the Taliban for years upon years, we had not learned about the statistics though. By the summer of 2009, when we had arrived, the stats for British troop casualties in Afghanistan was a limb a day and a life a week. The Taliban were adapting their methods. They had learned that we were using metal detectors, so they started combating that by using pressure plates that contained no metal. They would fill likely pathways used with pressure plate I.E.D's and then place them around that, so if you found one you could bet that they had them around you as well. They knew our tactics. When shot at we would look for cover, so they started placing bombs in likely places we would look for protection, they would ambush troops and wait for them to move. All they had to do then was wait for someone to land on an I.E.D. The Taliban was indeed a cruel and a cunning enemy, they watched and learned our every move. Moving through the irrigation ditches became a frequent route that troops used, so they started placing bombs in the bottom of the water. You could be trying to make your way through the waist-deep water, then end up losing your legs and potentially drowning to death. If you made it through the irrigation ditch, you would most likely find a bomb as you climbed out, imagine climbing up a slippery bank out of the water with sixty kilograms of kit on your back and then having a blast go off in your face. Losing arms, fingers, legs, eyes, covered head to toe in blood, sinking to the bottom of an irrigation ditch, gargling muddy water for air as blood pours from every orifice of your body from internal bleeding. Imagine trying to hold onto the bank but finding you have no arms to do so, not being able to stand out of the water because your legs have been ripped from your body. Limbs replaced by bone and torn flesh, arteries singed shut from the heat of the blast and your skin bubbled up hanging from your ripped muscles. You know your only chance of survival is your men pulling your drowning limbless torso from the water, this was not just the reality, it was common. Afghanistan 2009 was littered with I.E.D's, if you escaped one you were hit by another. Travel by vehicle and they are buried deep in the ground with tonnes of explosive ready to turn your Mastiff into a scrap heap. Travel by foot and every bridge, pathway and piece of land is available to uplift and snatch you limbs or life away. Even trees and walls had become likely targets, they were called TV bombs, and they were head height ready to separate your head from your body. It was a terrifying thought that this was happening daily, a limb a day was being lost by British troops on the ground, they were now initiated by pressure plates, command wires and even remote controls.

Hearing this was not easy, it still didn't bring the situation to life entirely, and it was all again talk and no action. We were still training. Lanes had been made for us to use metal detectors (valums) to go up and down trying to find I.E.D's and the drills that followed. If something was found, you were to check the ground around you, lay behind the finding and tuck one arm under your body armour and use your other to brush the dirt gently to try and uncover whatever had set the valum off. Many times it went off, to reveal a coke can or even a crisp wrapper, we quickly learned not to take that for granted as they would place these on top of a pressure plate so when you thought it was clear the explosion would go off afterwards. Hours we would spend up and down those lanes uncovering devices that had been planted, it was one of the most important jobs, if you didn't discover the device someone in your platoon was going to get hit, it was a lot of responsibility and took a lot of patience and attention. It was one critical piece to the puzzle, and it's when you realise that war is not all shooting, ducking and diving, there's no fun at war when you understand the actual reality. Our fight was not going to be against the Taliban, it was going to be a hide and seek game with bombs and spending hours searching these lanes made me feel like we were going to lose. We had specialists from the bomb disposal squad taking us through the different types of pressure plates, and I.E.D's that we would be facing, we never had a clue what they were talking about, our philosophy was simple, try not to stand on one.

After all the talking and checking for bombs, we got to do something that was more our kind of style, after all, we were rifleman, we don't deal with explosions we deal with bullets and grenades. We headed out to the ranges, over the days we spent there we got to do all sorts of things, first of all, we had to zero our weapons, the marksmanship principles and all that. The sites need to be zeroed, the last thing you wanna do is get a clear shot on the Taliban and miss because your weapon wasn't adjusted correctly, that's basics, it would be like tripping over a football in the world cup or missing a penalty. So we sorted our weapons and conducted our five-round check groups, we did some range practice and fired while on the move, emptying magazine after magazine into the targets. We shot from all positions possible, we learned to shoot over each others' shoulders covering each other as we changed magazines, the gunners had their chances to get rounds down range, the air clattered as the sounds of light machine guns and general purpose machine guns ripped away. Their 5.56 and 7.62 rounds can fire up to eight hundred and fifty rounds per minute until their barrels start to glow bright orange, there are stories of the barrels even melting due to the sheer heat that the volume can produce, they certainly make light work of anything they fire into. Every rifleman in the company was fully competent on these weapons, pass any of us a rifle, pistol or machine gun and we could run through the drills with our eyes closed, we could pick up the weapon system and take out an enemy. We then got to play with some more of the specialised weapons, plays not the correct word there, you didn't play with weapons at all, so instead, I will say we got to take part in training for the more specialised weapons. The first of these was on a range created for the UGL (underslung grenade launcher) for some reason these were only given out to the section commanders, not sure why? There must have been some purpose for it though. These were quality to fire, they weren't the most effective of weapons as they are not very accurate and have a danger radius of about five meters, but they were fun to fire. They were an attachment on the end of the SA-80 rifle (the British Army's primary assault rifle in 2009.) When fitted, you would elevate the weapon and find the required angle through the vertically attached sight and pull the secondary trigger. It would give a little thump as it left, then sail gracefully through the air detonating as it landed, the small yellow face would silently fall on the enemies head and have them looking like someone had cracked a melon open with a sledgehammer. I remember some numpty on the ranges fired the thing completely vertical by accident it flew directly into the air before coming down towards us. Everyone had to leg it before it landed, fuck being killed on Bastion ranges by some silly twat. Gave us all something to laugh about though I suppose, lots of funny things like that happened, it must just be human nature to fuck up with dangerous objects.

Then we got to play with the big guns, oh yes, the grenade machine gun was first, that even sounds like something that was purely designed to fuck shit up. Oh by the way if you haven't realised I tend to swear, excuse me for my poor manners it's just my way of expressing myself, a rather bland excuse, but it's almost slang and culture in the Army to swear. For instance, calling someone a good cunt is a compliment, don't call your mum a good cunt though she won't take it the same way.

"Mum is dinner ready?" you may ask.

"Yes." She replies, mums always have the dinner ready.

"Oh thank you, Mum, you delightfully good cunt." Would not be the response to use, just say thank you and eat your fish fingers.

The drills were quite similar to all weapons, well sort of, you had a top cover like all guns, yet rifles and pistols are mostly magazine fed, so for guns, I guess I'm correct in saying it's similar.

Cock the weapon, pull the top cover up, check it's empty both visually and physically, close the top lid, take the safety off, point it away from anyone and fire off the action. Pull the top cover up, load in the belt of ammunition, aim it at what you want to kill and pull the trigger, simple.

It was like the UGL just on a bigger scale, instead of one grenade flying at the enemy inaccurately then having to reload, you could fire five hundred of them consecutively. As the gun fired away, it made the small thud and clicking noise as the grenades flew towards their targets, and the link that binds them together breaks away. The landing party is slightly different as they explode with small interventions in the desired direction. Due to the recoil of the weapon as your firing, the grenades tend to not land in the same place. The burst of explosions are usually a few meters apart, it seems as if the ground is dancing as the explosion kicks up the Afghan sand with a delayed clap of thunder belted out from the bombings. That was a fun day at the ranges, pounding grenades into the desert around us, aiming at a disused car off in the distance. Next of the big guns was the heavy machine gun or HMG as it's known. This was a significant old gun, I should mention that both the GMG and HMG are vehicle-mounted weapons, you wouldn't run around the desert firing them from the hip or anything. The HMG is a fifty-calibre machine gun. It's a beast. The recoil shudders through your whole body as you fire it, it makes a tremendous sound similar to that of a formula one car as it roars past you. It's said that the round would not even have to hit you, that if it narrowly missed you, the sheer force and velocity it generates would rip your limb away. I still preferred being up close with the enemy, give me a pistol, show me the door to kick down any day, nine milometer SIG Sauer P226 in the face, I want to be the British Army sponsored photographer for the Taliban, smile and wait for the flash. Our weapons were zeroed, we were slowly becoming acclimatised to the heat, we were trained on the more specialised weapons. We took a long walk in full kit, arrived at a staging area, it was a makeshift compound with no roof, quite small and an area above for people to observe as we moved through, practising the drills. In pairs we drove through the compound, we entered doorways with our rifles central to our chests, we looked just over the sights keeping our backs to the wall, moving from wall to wall, doorway-to-doorway we cleared the compound.

After all this hard work we were rewarded with shit pizza and wanking in fifty-degree heat toilets, the reason we had these luxuries was that we had taken our chequebooks, we could write these to the clerks, and in return, they would give us dollars to spend. The one real treat we did enjoy was in this little café next to the Naffi, they sold mountain due slushy's, they were incredible, apart from that all we had was piss tasting pizza and recycled Nuts magazines to knock one out to. Apart from the lack of anything fun to do, we had to contend with the BOB, (bullshit of bastion) as a lot of officers liked to cut around camp bastion, it was imperative that we looked the part. This meant that even though we were only a stone's throw away from a war zone, we had to shave every day, our shirts and trousers had to be clean and even the bottom where our combats met our boots had to be turned over with ties. Every time we had to do something ridiculous, we would call it BOB, there were loads of silly little rules that we had to follow, some were in our interest, others I think was just because the head shed was bored, perhaps the fact we were not trusted came into it as well. In the middle of the desert, they checked our hairline, made sure there was no hair on our face and made sure our kit was clean. You would see blokes coming in off the ground covered in blood and dust. Facial hair was overgrown where they had been living out of their daysacks for weeks on end fighting the Taliban. As they got into camp they were shouted at for being unclean, forced to shower and shave, replace the combats they had been fighting in for fresh ones before they were allowed in the cookhouse. Even your issued sun hats had to be replaced with your beret while walking around the camp, I sometimes wondered if the people who run that camp had been on the ground. Had they even seen the conditions we had to live in? Perhaps if they had spent more time out of the wire, they would not be so strict inside it.

Cas and I thought we had come across a bargain, one of the Afghan locals had a shop inside Camp Bastion, he was selling DVD's, fake sunglasses, cigarettes etc. One of the box sets he had was the complete Dragonball Z box set, it had cost something like thirty dollars. When we got it back to our bed space, we eagerly opened the box set, I had a portable DVD player, I ended up leaving that in Camp Bastion due to the fact where we were going had no electricity. We still had it for the meantime though, so, back to the story, we put the first DVD inside and pressed play, it started, we were faced with Chinese subtitles and what we interpreted as the Chinese language as well. It was awful, that was our childhood dream flushed down the drain, and thirty dollars. So again that was something less to fulfil our spare time, there's only so much time you can spend on Facebook, primarily as it wasn't the domineering popular social network that is today. So boys will be boys, and we started getting naughty and bored, we started playing pranks on each other, the Company was rife with unsuspected blokes being smacked in the balls, especially the newer blokes of the company. I don't know where it came from, but someone had a mini rugby ball, which started to become fun, not to play rugby with of course, but instead to be launched at anyone who had dropped his or her guard. Walking quite pleasantly along minding your own business, perhaps pondering what you're going to write in a letter home to your mum, then out of nowhere, 'SMACK' a ball twats you in the side of the face. This happened to me once or twice, it's incredible the amount of anger you can build up in a split second. Regardless of your social status within your platoon, there's always the likes of senior NCO's in snipers, recce etc. who will fill you in for the fun of it, so best just to keep quiet sometimes. You see I had only been in battalion just over a year, although I was in the

BC I still wasn't a senior rifleman at all. It's only because of the likes of Iraq and Afghanistan that has caused a high turnover of people that it became less significant. So Gary Green who had been in battalion a year would mean fuck all to the likes of Doris the ten-year full screw from snipers who coaches the battalion boxing team, if he launches a ball at your head, you know your place and say thank you.

Things carried on this way in-between briefs and last minute training because we had nothing else to occupy our time. Not like we could just pop down the local pub, we didn't even have a TV, which sounds stupid but we're so used to numbing our senses with these devices that once taken away from them you don't know what to do. The last night before we were flying out to our patrol base things got a bit too far out of hand, Wils and I were play fighting. Penny was sat writing a letter and had put his pen in his mouth, building up the picture here, aren't I? It's sod's law, so you all know what was about to happen. As we were fighting, I jumped on Wils back and swung round to choke him out, as my foot turned round I kicked penny in the face, we found this hilarious, until Penny's head resurfaced from his bed space coughing up blood. Unbeknown to us I had just kicked that pen straight down Penny's neck and ripped the back of his throat open. I had never seen a man panicking so much, he couldn't get his breath and was spluttering blood all over the floor. I know it seems wrong but all that was running through my head was, 'oh I'm going to be in the shit now,' I felt bad, I just knew that the potential repercussions for this could be a whole lot worse. Through gargled blood, he kept trying to shout "I swallowed my pen," I knew it was terrible but I couldn't help laughing. I don't know why? Perhaps it was the way he was saying it, or just nerves because the sight of my mate holding his throat and coughing up blood wasn't funny although, that being said, we laughed about this for a long time and imitated Penny coughing up blood. No comeback came to me for this, I don't know how really, maybe the full story never came out, the worst part was that because Penny was held in the med centre whilst we deployed to the PB, his tour was changed, and he was posted with the Dragoon Guards as a driver. We were proper good mates, and I felt awful that he would be spending his tour of Afghanistan with people he didn't even know, but, I also felt relieved I didn't get punished for what I did.

One of the things I hated, really fucking hated. I packed my kit perfectly as we were about to board the chopper, my equipment was perfect, my pouches, my rifle, all squared away, so I was more or less comfortable. Then we had to take the platoon weapons and other section kit, so although my kit was squared when it came to boarding the chopper, my rifle was hanging from my body, I had a GPMG in each hand and grab bag wrapped around my neck stuffed with radio batteries. I looked like a life-sized game of buckaroo as I reached the back of the Chinook. It was always that way, and you could never just be comfortable with the kit you had because there was still more shit to carry and you was only expected to take it. I could fit my fighting kit in my small personalised daysack, each pouch was perfectly able to hold precise equipment, then it all get's fucked up because you have to carry ECM. You can't even take your daysack on the ground with you, so all your kit gets fucked underneath a massive piece of Electronic Counter Measures, and you end up running around Afghanistan with a suitcase on your back. It's not efficient, you can't manoeuvre correctly, how can you be expected to fight an enemy that is running around in flip-flops with an AK-47 while you're chasing them looking like a passenger running through Heathrow trying to check in to a late flight for Costa Del Fuck Yourself. So the band of happy go lucky holidaymakers, and I piled inside of the Chinook, it was my first feel of actual war, I wasn't in contact, there were no bullets being fired at us, it was just the view, the sight and the feel. As the Chinook took off, a feeling comes over your body, a sense of weightlessness, we effortlessly soared altitudinous, the camp became a painting, the tremendously formidable Bastion became a picture that I felt if I reached out

I could touch. There was a gunner, crouched on the loading ramp, he manned a Gatling gun, behind him we could see the sand, desert and mountain ranges appearing and then disappearing. Random compounds, patchy green zones came in and out of view, it was the scene that had been plastered all over the news since the invasion of Iraq. This was the beautiful vision of war I was used to seeing yet the first time I had experienced. I looked around at the faces of seven platoon. These were my comrades; shaved baby faces overlaid with the desert pattern helmets that weighed down their heads. We were at the final point, no turning back now, the safe refuge of Camp Bastion was behind us, what lay ahead was a minefield manned by radical extremists. This was the final flight path, once we landed and our feet hit that ground, we were in bandit country, their country, when our feet touched the ground we would be at war.

Chapter 9

It's all shit's and giggles until a bomb goes off

We landed, I was still carrying the excess kit like Buckaroo, I was about to be let off though, as pretty sharpish we were on patrol. We landed in FOB Silab, which was to be manned by 'five' platoon. It had electricity, an ISO container which was converted into a freezer. It had been used for storing bottles of water. There was an internet room with two computers, a welfare tent with a big screen TV and a PlayStation and a selection of games. If Michelle Keegan was walking around topless, then it would have been a lads dream. We weren't staying here though, no, we were waiting for the sun to set so we could patrol off to a PB about the size of a football pitch. We couldn't land there because it was a red zone which meant you could only land inside if there was an emergency, casualties, etc. Which gives you a slight indication of what it was going to be like. As the night drew in, we readied ourselves for our first patrol. It was only a patrol down to our patrol base, which was just under a mile away as the crow flies. The ground was pitch black though, we had never even stepped foot on earth or ground like it before, and we were working on a map, well the boss was. We aimed to perform this patrol as low key as possible, we had all our kit with us, so the last thing we wanted was a firefight. We had been outside the wire, (a term meaning outside of Camp Bastion) for almost two hours and we were about to conduct a real patrol in enemy territory. I had butterflies in my stomach, partly excitement and partly nerves as I was under no illusion that any one of these steps could be my last. You put these thoughts to the back of your head otherwise you would never get anywhere.

We were the lead section as we stepped off, I swear to god that every step I took on that patrol was so deliberate, a bit like a driving test, every movement was so exaggerated. It was as if I expected the enemy to be around every corner, I was so profoundly strung. It was a waiting game, I was just waiting to be shot at, waiting to see the enemy stood there, life or death, who would shoot first. I came face to face with no such enemy, we moved through dark Afghan roads, although by roads I mean sandy tracks, some big enough to fit two cars and some narrow where we had to move into a single line. We were in the green zone of Helmand Province in the summertime, so the desert we expected to face was replaced by greenery, not quite the Oxfordshire countryside I am used to, but more mud, sporadic trees and farmers land. These were all made possible by the Americans who had introduced Afghanistan to irrigation ditches which spread far and wide through the green zone allowing water flow and vegetation to grow.

During the patrol between compounds a dog had started to bark, I could see it's silhouette at the end of the track in front of me, we halted the patrol, and the dog continued to shout in its native tongue. I was lead man of the patrol at this point. I didn't know what to do. 'Shall I shoot it? No that would completely give our position away, shall we wait? Would that be too long with this dog barking? Will the Taliban come? We would be sitting ducks.'

The thoughts spun my head. Luckily the boss had decided for me, I was to fix my sword to my rifle, move forward at speed and kill the dog. My section commander, Jonesy, was right behind me, I felt like I was in that scene in 300 where Leonidas confronts the wolf as a young boy. It was my time to become a man and strike down this foul beast, for he who wishes to alert the Taliban shall feel the wrath of Greendog and his steel blade. As I drew closer, I stared at the shadow, and I telepathically told him I was sorry and that it was either him or me.

Plus these were feral dogs, not like my Freddie at home, my little French bulldog is clean and house trained, these beasts were full of rabies. They were wild animals, still, with all this in mind I had compassion for the creature, he was just in the wrong place at the wrong time.

My hands were shaking, I was terrified, I haven't killed before, 'what if I fuck it up and it bites me?'. I swallowed my 'man up pill' and decided this was it, I'm going to stab this dog in the face and be done with it. My hands shook more with each step, my stomach was bubbling inside as I approached the dog. Five meters away and I was certain I would lunge at this dog, then it just ran away. All that anxiety about to be released in one swipe of my sword, gone. The dog was probably just scared, just minding its own business and fucked off to have a shit in someone's garden I assume. My manly trial was over, I passed the test through intent, not through deliverance. I needed to change my pants though, if the dog hadn't given us away, then the smell of me shitting myself just might seal the deal.

All that business with the hound of Afghanistan, it was a rather anti-climax to be honest, exciting at the time though. The silhouettes of compounds contrasting against the bright full moon in a cloudless sky, the giant clay walls that divided tracks, tall trees that gave shallow whispers as a breeze caught their broad leaves, it was all new, and it was all exciting. A wide-eyed Greendog embraced it all.

PB Parang, our home for the foreseeable future. It was dark, so we could hardly see what was on offer as we arrived. The previous occupants were already packed, they too wished to use the darkness to cloak their escape. There was a handover for the section commanders and the platoon commander. We went through a similar but less detailed affair in the sangers, which of course was next to useless because it was pitch fucking black. But the basics that we were given were as followed, the Taliban religiously attack the compound three times a day like clockwork, at first light, midday and last light. Anything south of the PB was bandit country, and you will get attacked as soon as you moved in that direction. The village a couple of hundred meters to the north is full of Taliban spies. The Taliban will always attack from the south, from three primary compounds but of course, it was too dark to see them, and last but not least, anywhere you go, the next day will have an IED waiting for you. Each rang true, we would find this out straight away, and also some of those lessons took a while to learn, and a hell of a lot more we discovered for ourselves.

I finished my sentry duty, I started on Sanger one, so I had a shitter and had to do two, three and four as well, forty-five minutes on each. I can't remember whom I was with, but at night we always doubled up the sentry positions. I clambered into the first cot bed I found and got my head down, my sleepy drift didn't last too long as loud cracks ripped through the air, 'stand to' echoed through the patrol base. I threw on my body armour, ran into the centre of the PB wearing flip flops, dirty blue Nike shorts with my helmet hanging off my head. My body armour wasn't done up properly, so it was flapping about as I cocked my weapon. The guys in the sanger were shouting out the direction of enemy fire, and they were engaging heavily with the GPMG's. The two sangers facing south (one and two) were in contact. The rest of the platoon began to climb the south wall of the PB, two layers of hesco protected us from the enemy outside. We climbed it and fired into likely enemy locations, almost a whole platoon of men firing out towards the enemy. Every time the sound of the battle quietened, the enemy would fire at us, and all hell would break loose as we retaliated. This must have carried on for thirty minutes until the Plt SGT started calling us down, we had all got a bit excited in the heat of the moment. There was no need for us returning so much fire and we were accomplishing nothing except wasting ammunition.

It was time to do quick lessons learned, we needed to fight smart, one thing I can say about my Battalion, something that echoed true throughout, that was that we were thinking fighters. These videos you see where troops are firing thousands of rounds may look good, but unless you're hitting a target, there is no point. That amount of firing would only be useful for suppressing an enemy. Apparently, the fact that they kept firing back meant it wasn't working, and also we didn't need to subdue the enemy as we weren't advancing towards them. So this excited burst of aggression was nothing more than a rise in tempo from a situation meeting expectation, it's sort of like pulling down a girls' knickers and then whipping your dick out and coming, you need to put your dick in first. The first few times we got a bit excited, but after a while it just became normal. Pretty quickly we went from troops climbing the hesco in their pants and flip-flops to lads that just sat there. You learn to gauge the enemies intention. If it got a bit too hairy we reacted, these little firefights though were only the enemy pushing our buttons.

In the blazing sunlight, PB Parang came to life, it was maybe one hundred meters by one hundred meters, give or take a little perhaps. The hesco walls that surrounded us stood roughly fifteen feet high, hesco blocks were laid two thick at the bottom with a single file wall across the top, there were four sangers, one in each corner, each raised from the ground with either a ladder or steps to climb. There were two ways into the PB, the front entrance, the wall had a corner built at the front of the PB big enough to fit a mastiff through yet designed so no one could see in or out and for good measure a meter high rail of barbed wire. The second entrance was a secret one, covert, hidden and camouflaged at the side of the PB. It lead out into large foliage before a long track, invisible to the eye. Next to the secret entrance, you had the 'bathrooms' one side and a washing station on the other. The toilets were made from hesco railings, the rim of the seat was even covered by a sandbag. There was a metal grid to piss on, we also had showers, after a fashion, plastic pallets to stand on with solar showers hanging above. The receptacle that produced the water was the solar showers, a large bag that you would fill with water, the sun heated the pool and then you just release a catch, and the water drains onto your head. This was a short-lived luxury because we had to ration our water bottles. Next to the showers laid remains of what used to be a smaller compound, this consisted of two large rooms, one was used as a medical centre and the other as a store for water bottles to keep them out of the sun.

Along the south-facing wall, we had a large tented area that divided into two parts. The furthest away was for three section, then another area where two section (including myself) were staying. Next to us toward sanger one, was the land rover, this was fitted with a canopy and was manned at all times as it was our only source of communication back to HQ at Silab. Between the land rover and sanger one was a smaller tented area, this is where one section stayed. Our layouts were all pretty similar. However ours was slightly more extensive so in the middle we created a communal area, it was just a massive wooden crate with some chairs around it. Our bed spaces were a cot bed with a single bed sized tent shape on top, this was our mossie net, it did its job as more than once we awoke to camel spiders waving us good morning. Apart from this, we had various ways to store our kit, ammo tins to keep letters in, sticks in the ground to keep your boots to stop creepy crawlies making their way inside, your body armour and weapon was always right by your side though. Outside of the two-section bed spacing, we had an even more substantial communal area, pretty much the same setup. There was also a small gym next to sanger four. It incorporated a punching bag and some ammo tins filled with sand, all pretty makeshift. The support vehicles were parked up with us, two mastiffs, one fitted with a GMG and one with a HMG, the support guys made a home outside one sections' living area. I should mention as well our one treat, a welfare tent, it was a canopy and a small flat screen TV. We could only use it once a week as it had to be run from the generator and we needed that for communication. That was home basically, the only other addition was the burns pit, a big old roofless square that was also a relic of the previous compound, it was full of human shit, covered in petrol and set on fire.

One good thing about the toilets, while it lasted, is that when the Americans had been there at some point previously, they had left behind a crate of 'porta-johns.' A foil bag, which opened up with a plastic bag that would fit the size of a toilet seat, the bottom was filled with a lemon smelling powder and the packaging contained an anti-bacterial wipe. You could open up the bag, do your business, fold the bag up inside itself with a lemon scent, wipe your hands and dispose of the container in the pit where it awaited incineration. Once these ran out, we were left to take turns shitting in a black bag until it was full, once full you would struggle to carry the sloshy remnants across the PB and sling it in the pit. I had to take it a few times, the bag never split on me although once throwing the pack in the hole, the bag exploded when it landed, shit and piss splashed out the sides, a wet mixture of smelly waste.

The communal areas were used for playing cards. We played two main games out there, the first that we used to play inside the living area was Shithead. Last player standing becomes the shithead, of course. If you were the unlucky one, then you had to wear the shithead sign, this was just a piece of cardboard with some para-cord attached. The sign read, 'I am the shithead of PB Parang.' It was only something to add morale.

The second game that we didn't start playing until a bit later into the tour was poker. I won't bore you with the rules of poker, there are too many variations and to be honest I can't quite remember, I had never played poker previous, and I have not played since. We had a ten pound buy in rule, we kept a log as well because no one had money out there, not much use for a ten-pound note in the desert unless your going to start a fire with it. Some blokes came back two hundred pounds in the green, some came back two hundred pounds in the red though, bit harsh but the same rules apply I guess. I used to love it though, at that point, with all the lads sat around the table, all laughing, it didn't even seem like we were at war. We could have been in a Vegas casino, all chips in, one million dollars for the winner, but we weren't, we were in Afghanistan. In the same clothes, we had been in for months, unshaved and unwashed. This is the real sense of brotherhood, freedom. Equals. Serenity. There was just friends, humans passing the time and enjoying each others company, bonded through one course. It's when you have nothing that you can find something, we had no fridge, so we found ways to keep our water fresh. If you dug a hole, placed your water bottle in a wet sock, left that water bottle in the hole, your water would remain cool. I don't know why it worked, but it did, that was the best water I'd ever tasted in my life. We had no phones or laptops, so we read, we played cards and talked for hours on end, we honestly learned to love each other. Enjoy the richness of conversation, it's funny, but no one will tell you that they never felt more at home than when they were at war. It's kind of like being a child I guess, all you have is time to find something fun to do, a football provides hours of entertainment. You find joy, I grew up without money, and before the age of the Xbox and PlayStation or whatever, so I was out after school knocking for my mates and climbing conker trees. That was what it was like here, rounding up your mates to play cricket with a plastic set that looks like it came straight from the pound shop, but we loved it.

There was nothing like a dose of reality though to snatch you away from a juvenile state of happiness. You always had to make sure you planned a game of poker right, the worse thing that could happen is being halfway through a match and realising you're on stag. Nightmare. I've spoken before about stag being a right shitter, and that's for a perfect reason, it's entirely one hundred percent certified tonk, especially at night. None of us were robots. It's tough to stand for three hours looking into the desert, you can't help but become complacent, you start to learn the surroundings and the atmospherics. At first, even a car or a bike coming towards you becomes exciting. Then after the hundredth vehicle, it's just another fucking car. Another farmer tending to his crops, staring at the same compounds, farmers, and tracks every day becomes tedious. Very quickly you start to come up with ways to entertain yourself, the first and the easiest is masturbating, I unloaded more sperm into those sangers than I did anything else, everyone did. There even became a competition between the blokes, who could wank in every sanger, I don't think anyone ever managed it, sanger one was a bit dodgy because you were close to everyone. Sanger two, three and four were comfortable, well out the way and you could sit down in sanger two, staring out into the rural surroundings, all the time you're sat there knocking one out. There's a story about one of the lads in five platoon who got caught wanking on stag by the colour sergeant, one of their lads would be able to tell you the name. Apparently, he got a right beating, must have been mortifying. Great banter and morale for the rest of the platoon though, I can imagine his poor face as he realised he had been caught.

By the way, we didn't spend all our time wanking and playing cards, I will get to the gory stuff, I'm just not into glorifying the whole thing, war isn't what you read in the papers or see on Ross Kemp. We were on patrol every single day, and there's nothing more exciting than kicking down a compound door with a nine-millimetre pistol in your hand, not knowing what's on the other side. That is just a small fragment of the puzzle though, compared to everything else that went on out there I would hate for you to think that it is simple. I didn't come home and want to kill myself because I had a whale of a fucking time running around the desert with a rifle, the reality is far more complicated. Look into the eyes of an amputee and dare try to condescend to him that he spent his time wanking and playing cards, don't dare try and tell him that it wasn't the best time of his life either.

Anyway back to being on stag, another way, a harsher way as well to enjoy yourself is to play with the Afghan locals, not with their dicks. The wanking part is over. This practice works better if the locals are on bikes, scooters or whatever to be honest, what you do is crouch behind the hesco and wait for them to get close. Then jump up screaming stop, cock your GPMG and aim it straight at them. Shouting things like, "stop, or I'll fucking shoot." They can't understand you anyway so just make it sound aggressive. You could probably shout, 'I love you' aggressively, and they would still shit themselves. I don't agree with this behaviour or condone it, but at that time that's just how it was, they would shit themselves and fall off their bikes, start lifting up their hands and pleading in their local language. Fucking awful when you think about it, but at the time we would be cracking up. It's against everything I stand for now, but, we were trained killers, we were in an abnormal situation, our morals were shot to shit. The thresh hold for compassion had been numbed, above all else, we were fucking bored shitless. Plus sometimes they had watermelons on the back of their bikes so you would stop them, guys would wait at the gate and call them forward to be searched. While two guys were covering, someone would relieve them of a watermelon or two and send them back on their way. Again heartless stealing from a third world person with nothing, but we were starving.

It wasn't all like that on stag though, the first time I was shot at I was on stag. It was on our second or third day in the PB, it was midday, and the sun was blazing down. I was leaned on the GPMG in sanger one observing the south, as you can't watch an actual enemy, you look into possible enemy firing points, which for us were the compounds to the south. I can spend time trying to remember every building and the number of it by its grid reference but, to be honest, I really can't remember.

(I do have a sketch that I did, I sent it to my auntie while I was out there and pointed out a few of the major incidents and the location).

As I was facing out toward the possible firing points, I heard the bang of a round fired, then the whizz of the bullet passing me and the thud of it hitting the sandbags behind me. I'm not ashamed to say my first instinct was to dig into the ground and hide behind the safety of the hesco wall. After that initial round, all hell broke loose. You can judge how close the bullets are by the sound they make. If you hear a whizz then they are close, if you hear a crack, then they're above your head and not very accurate. The sound of the GPMG from sanger two filled the air as it let rip, I had no idea where the shot had come from or if the bloke in sanger two had any idea. I swallowed a load of fear and jumped up. I had no idea what I was firing at, I just aimed at likely enemy positions where I thought it could have come from. This happened daily, as I said before we were attacked in our PB three times a day like clockwork, sometimes it was a few pop shots and sometimes it was a hell of a lot more. I don't know what governed their decisions on how much they would fire at us. Maybe they got bored. I know we did. Sometimes we would initiate our contacts and fire into local positions to try and get them to fire back. It was a bizarre feeling after a firefight. It could last anything from fifteen minutes to three hours. Shooting back and forth with the enemy, then just nothing, the area falls dead quiet, from what was a battlefield only becomes an area of nothingness. Then the farmers just come back out and start tending to their crops, literally one minute you're engaged in a full-scale firefight then the next you're back to sitting in the sanger bored, trying to decide what the first meal you're going to have when you get back home. I often wondered what the Taliban were thinking, why they stopped.

Why didn't they just try and kill all of us inside the PB?

Why didn't they work to overrun us?

Maybe they had things to do, perhaps Terry the Taliban turned around to Thomas the Taliban and said.

"Yo Thomas, I've gotta go in ten minutes so we better not make this a long one. The wife's put a nice curry on, and we're gonna catch up on Desperate Housewives."

Or perhaps we killed them, and it was someone different every time.

We had a goat once, we called him Billy because all goats are called Billy ain't they? We brought him from the locals, and the Fijians had to slit his throat and skin him. It's on video actually, a rather grim affair but we were starving, fresh meat was going to make a nice change from rations. They had made this underground oven, with the goat butchered, put in foil, they shoved him in. As night drew in I was on stag, the communal areas had been brought outside, and everyone was sat around them, except the four people on stag. To make it fair we rotated the sentry so everyone could join in, I was swapping with Walps. Everyone was laughing, joking, having a good time, eating their goat. It was supposed to be a fifteen-minute change around so that they could eat and then come back, he didn't come back. I was absolutely fuming, I could hear them all laughing, about an hour I was there before he came back, by the time I got down to everyone they were clearing up. I went back into that sanger and gave him such a debriefing about what a jack cunt he was, I struck him so hard that he fell backwards and his helmet fell over his face. I was right in what I had done. He had been jack, so he got a slap for it, the reason though that this gets' put into perspective is that the next day he got blown up and lost both of his legs. A weird feeling that was, it wasn't that I felt guilty or that in some way it was my fault, it just put things in a different light, in the grand scheme of things was it worth me punching him in the face for an hour of my time. Inflicting, not only pain but also upsetting someone and mentally damaging them, I know before he got blown up he wasn't thinking about that, but, I had converted this happy memory into one of shame and sadness.

I don't know what happened because I wasn't on that patrol, our section was on sentry duty, the patrol moved north back towards FOB Silab, it may have been a patrol to get the mail or something I can't remember. We heard the explosion, we rushed to the Platoon HQ to try and find out what happened, we knew there were two casualties, and we got their zap numbers. As soon as you hear double amputee, your heart just sinks. The nine liner was sent, a chopper picked up the casualty, Walps was the casualty, no one saw him again until we got back to the UK. Mac was the second casualty, he had been knocked unconscious but he was okay, he was brought back around and continued the patrol. The patrol returned to camp, it was the same people minus one that had left, but when they returned they just seemed a little different, it takes a long time to wash the blood away from your hands. The next day things only continued, as usual, another patrol around Kalshaw Kallay, more times getting shot at, more card playing, more drinking warm water and eating shitty rations. This was the routine, and this is why we were here, cannon fodder. Our job was to live in these conditions every day, we are infantrymen, we do the dirty work. Our job was to fight, to kill the enemy on the ground, we were expendable, and we were trained to be so. Lose the men beside you then keep pushing forward, then when you get back to camp you've got to carry a black bag full of shit to the burns pit and set it on fire.

There's a couple of things that I have left out, there just isn't enough time or space for me to go through every single thing. These are a couple of highlights that I have not mentioned.

- I was once sent back from a patrol to change my top as I had cut the sleeves off my shirt.
- A Fijian corporal threw a rock at a Riflemans' head and split it open because he wouldn't pass him a ball.
- We smoked weed that we got from local fields.
- I held my pistol to an Afghan locals head and told him I would shoot him in front of his family if he didn't give me information. (He had two sim cards, one we found hidden under his car seat with a book of contacts, the interpreter told us they were from Iraq and Pakistan).
- We were once sent on a patrol to buy cans of fizzy drinks for a meeting with local Afghan elders.
- One of the lads was 'Injured' because he smothered

himself in baby oil and got sun stroke from sunbathing.

- Every week we had 'shave day' where we were forced to shave as we were not allowed facial hair.
- Once 'someone' shot a dog, we set it on fire with a phosphorus grenade.
- 'Someone' disarmed an I.E.D by themselves and carried it back to the patrol base in their daysack.

Looking back, you had the two sides of tour right here in this chapter, the monotonous day-to-day life of living in a patrol base and the devastating reality of life outside of it. I must say that on the whole I much preferred the latter. Compared to living in England, I would much prefer either. Strange concept that and possibly hard for those that abstain the experience to understand. For some reason everyone I have spoken to concur, although it was the worst experience of our lives it was also the most endearing. The loss of a limb a day and life a week in Afghanistan was no joke, as devastating as Walp's injury was, he was not our last. Statistics say that 2009 was the bloodiest year of the conflict in Afghanistan and we were there for its hottest months.

Chapter 10
Casualty, Casualty

Once again, I awoke with a sweaty ball sack, tired from sentry of which I spent three hours of the early morning observing the quiet Green Zone as mosquitos used my skin like a takeaway meal. I tried to stay alert as my mind drifted in and out of life at home, the lads' who took over from me must have done an excellent job as I was not killed in the night. Less could be said for the makeshift tent which protected us from the boiling hot sun, if anything it acted as a sauna which explains the fact that my balls are clinging to the inside of my leg as if I had applied super glue before I fell into the land of nod. It's Sunday, July 26th, 2009, life in the Patrol Base begins, as usual, a short trip to the corrugated tin which directs away my yellow dehydrated piss. With no cover from the rays beaming down from the sun, my urine evaporates before it has flowed to the soak away in the sand, the smell of misty piss reaches my nostrils as I try to rehydrate myself with a warm bottle of water. As I head back to my bed space I pour the remainder of water over my head, the clear water is lost for a second in the overgrown hair before it reappears trickling down my face brown and distorted, carrying away a build up of dirt, sand and stone. The water dries as it runs down my skinny body, at first glance I look like I have a healthy tan but as the water channels down me and dries, it leaves a slightly paler trail behind it, the filthy tan I am sporting is just dried dirt and blood that was acting as a sunblock.

The Platoon, in full apart from those that are on sentry, is sat around the Platoon HQ, a land rover with a high-frequency radio in it. I always remember in these times feeling somewhat detached from my body, not like an outer body experience, perhaps nothing at all and it's just strange to look back? Whatever the feeling was or wasn't I can picture it in my head like a movie, perhaps wishing myself to go back and do things differently. Look at the men different, I see their faces, unwashed, unshaven as it's been six days since, 'shave day.' A mixture of rugged looking men and young boys, at that time I was just a young boy, sat with my warm bottle of water, my rifle in my hand awaiting the Boss to give us a brief. First Pratty does the Platoon Sergeant part of the brief, something along the lines of.

"Right you scruffy little cunts, remember it's only five bottles of water a day so make sure you ration it, don't forget to fucking shave tomorrow."

Then an ammo count, a quick rundown on anything we had been doing wrong, then we'd be allowed our rations for the day because we weren't trusted to have more than a 24 hour supply.

Then Boss comes from behind the Land Rover, tatty combats that were perhaps once fitted now hang slightly from his body, I'm sure at home he would be a gentleman all prim and proper, yet here he stands as dirty as the rest of us with his overgrown hair standing up slightly. "Morning chaps" came the greeting and start to the brief, it was that accent that had come straight from Sandhurst, 'the rain in Spain falls mainly on the plane' a far cry from the manner of how Pratty gives his briefs out to the blokes. I would have to be rain man to remember precisely how the talk went but the points to note were as followed.

During the past month, we had conducted a patrol to bring an MFC (Mortar Fire Controller) an expert in calling in Air Support and Fire Support (nothing to do with fried Chicken as the letters suggest.) He was attached to Six Platoon in PB Haji Alem, and his tour was due to finish. Now we had him with us it was our job to secure a HLS so that he could be transported back to Camp Bastion. The reason that the Chinook wouldn't land inside the PB was that they were scared the tents would get caught in the propellers and would take down the helicopter. One section was to set up the HLS, and Three section were to conduct a short-range roaming patrol to set a presence just broad of the HLS. My section (2 section) was to support on overwatch from the PB. So, in short, a reasonably standard operation, which should be conducted in less than two hours, back in time for some scoff and a game of, shit head.

We kitted up, manned the Sangers and provided overwatch for the patrol. I was in Sanger four directly facing the HLS with the HMG. The two sections left the PB, the patrol began, I observed ahead as one section lead the patrol dominating the ground with their presence as they broke track and moved into the area, which was to become the HLS. They were sweeping the area with metal detectors as their second men covered them from any enemy threat, you are left vulnerable as a valum man, your concentration and focus are on the ground directly in front of you as you scout for I.E.D's. You are moving slowly, you only have one hand on your weapon as your other is engaged with the metal detector that sweeps in front of your feet, for this reason, a cover man stands behind you with his rifle, he becomes your eyes, his weapon becomes yours. As one section move forward with the HLS clearance, three section pushed out. They make their way up the track that leads West, this trail leads to compound 24, a compound that we had been attacked from daily.

Three moves up, the patrol is in single file with a man at the front sweeping for I.E.D's, using a valum reduces the speed of the patrol dramatically, it's a necessary slow, an intimate relationship with the ground is needed. A nasty surprise is rewarded should it hide any secrets. As the patrol passes the compound a sigh of relief is exhaled, this was the danger point, this is where we anticipated an attack, an attack that did not come. One section had cleared their HLS, they had now begun to set up all around defence and mark out the signals for the pilot to follow as he approached. Three section pushed west of the compound and slowly moved out of our sight, they crossed a small bridge through a tree line that obscured the full view of compound 24. Shaw, the last man of the section, moved across with his LMG held at his waist side, as he crossed that bridge he triggered a pressure plate I.E.D. First, the noise shattered the eardrums of us all. It's a noise that shakes the bones of even the strongest of men. I watched as the cloud of dust formed in the air, a mushroom of sand and dirt kicked from its resting place, rose like a nasty fog, a ghost of the bomb haunting all those that were brave enough to see it. Before the dust from the blast had even settled back on the ground, rounds were getting fired at us, this tactic is a cowardly example of how the Taliban fought. As the men of three section were giving first aid to eighteen-year-old Shaw, the Taliban were shooting at them, trying to kill the men that were now fighting to save his life. All this chaos was happening within one hundred meters of the PB, yet we were helpless, due to the position of three section it would have done more harm than good to try and provide fire support for them. The rest of my section kitted up to push to the incident position and give a casualty evacuation. One section had gone firm in the HLS, there was not much they could do as the enemy was almost impossible to spot anywhere this side of compound 24 and the tree line that followed the western track. The two mastiffs with our fire support element left the PB and headed fifty meters down the southern route to try to give fire support from a flanking position while the rest of my section moved to secure the casualty.

Whether it's just my memory playing tricks on me, or just those haunted nightmares reoccurring over and over in my head, but I'm sure I remember seeing his leg fly from his body. I probably never, it's just one of those things where something is so surreal that your memory can't even recall it accurately. I don't know if that makes sense or not. It's just how I remember it, those feelings are as real writing this, as they were when it happened. That fright, guilt, anger, all come rushing back as I sit with my palms becoming sweaty and my heart beating a little faster. It's as if my hands are filling my keyboard with sand, and my throat is clogged. The stifling heat and the chest plate of my body armour still restrict my lungs. The ghost of Afghanistan has never left me, and maybe it never will. The tablets, the therapy, the love, nothing will never take it away from me. Perhaps I don't want it to, it might be the only shred of self-identity I recognise now. Who is Gary Green without PTSD?

The battle rages on, the screams of Shaw can be heard from where I am, above the bullets that fly around, the shouts of commands and even the voice inside my head. The screams are the only thing I listened to. The mastiffs attack the enemies flank with the GMG and HMG, it did not deter the enemy though, they continue to fire and move from compound to compound. Like a snake in the grass, they are almost undetectable until they shoot from their murder holes. My section moved to the casualty. They get him on the stretcher under cover of three section who fight disorientated against the invisible devil. Sometimes I felt as if I could hear them laughing at us, we skulked about like rats chasing cheese in their viscous sand traps. From the noise and chaos, I saw my four men moving back down the track with the stretcher in their hands, covered by two men who ran at their side, rifles in the shoulder as they retreated. This is why we had practised a thousand times, a thousand times more even, we had to practice on a beach in Lydd or the mountain of Dartmoor because here, it was a thousand times harder. I remember those screams as they got nearer the PB, tears streamed down my face in anger, frustration that I was helpless, I could do nothing except listen to those screams and see the pain in his face. Doing fucking nothing but observing that situation is the hardest thing I've ever had to do, like a nightmare where you're stuck. A sick dream where every fibre of your body wants to do something, yet you can't. The closer he got the more visual it became, one leg hanging on like a chicken drumstick that you haven't quite bitten into it properly, twisted, covered in blood and facing the wrong way. As if you had rubbed it a thousand times with a cheese grater and then bent it the wrong way. The leg that was the primary cause of injury was gone, severed below the knee, not like you imagine, not clean cut, but instead blackened from heat, sand and dirt, it looked as if it had been hacked off with a blunt knife and then set on fire. I watched him enter the PB and get taken to the med centre, I didn't see him again until back in Selly Oak hospital, in the UK. I heard his screams right up until the point he was taken away though, I still hear them now, screams like that you will never forget.

As three section withdrew down the track, we were able to engage, I began to open up with the HMG, and it was exciting for about ten seconds until I got a stoppage. The HMG was a good bit of kit, however in the sandy sanger it just kept getting stoppages, we had it taken apart and oiled up weekly, it just didn't make much difference, a few shots in it would just jam up, an anti-climax to any good gun fight. Three section moved back into the PB, one section followed suit under cover of sporadic bursts from my HMG. Shortly after this, in the distance we could hear the sound of propellers, this was the sound of approaching help, it all seemed so sudden, though I imagine for Shaw, this had felt like three lifetimes, and death all rolled into one. Glow sticks were snapped and thrown into the centre of the PB along with a blue phosphorus grenade. This was just to adequately distinguish the landing zone for the pilot although I'm sure they would not have found it too difficult to see the big square patrol base. However, this is the British Army, and stranger things have happened. We could see the Chinook helicopter fly low, a majestic sight, that's one of the moments that makes it feel like war. I know that sounds stupid, but those views are seldom seen through the eyes of men. This was stuff that I had only ever seen on a TV screen. We kept our eye out for the enemy, scouring every tree line and compound for the slightest movement or indication of foul play. This was explicitly a dangerous time. They would love to shoot down a helicopter, especially during a casualty evacuation. Although my focus was outside of the PB, I couldn't help but look back as they carried Shaw out of the med centre. They had him on a stretcher, his legs were bandaged up and covered over with a toxic waste bag. This is just what they use to limit the amount of sand and dirt that gets trapped inside the open wounds. He was followed on by the MFC, once loaded they did not hang about, the Chinook lifted from the ground, in almost no time at all the flying ambulance had disappeared from view. It left behind a slight buzz of the propellers. Eventually, that drained away yet the screams of eighteen-year-old Shaw and his limbless lower body ringed in my ears.

It was only later when people started talking that we became aware of the fucking irony that the patrol had just been sent out to secure an HLS because the RAF didn't want to land inside the PB. Once Shaw was injured and he had to be brought back into the PB for the med centre, they landed inside anyway. If they decided to evacuate the MFC from the PB in the first place, perhaps Shaw would never have been injured, it's challenging playing with these questions as I'm sure they lurk around the heads of all of us. They are something you can get lost in and become tormented by. However, those screams will always stay with me and so to the irony of that day, this was not the only stupid decision ever made, but it was one with devastating consequences. I heard stories of a game called barma-roulette. It involved turning off your valum while minesweeping, it was not something I recall our lads doing. I never heard of it being done on patrol, it would be one thing risking your own life, but we would never do that to our brothers, that sort of guilt would kill a man. The only time I did something like that was in a doorway, we would usually check for I.E.D's first, we were not going to cross the threshold of the doorway until it had been swept. However, I laughed and stepped through it. Although this was a stupid mistake, it, fortunately, had no repercussions, I don't even know what I would have done if I would have lost my legs in that way. We heard that Shaw had stood only a footstep over the bridge where it had not been checked for I.E.D's, one step, if he had stayed in that safe lane for that second he would still have his legs today. A sobering thought, look down at your feet, move your left foot slightly to the left, that was the step that lost an eighteen-year-old boy his legs. The sort of games you do seem so stupid and pointless when you look back, I remember being on a roof of a compound on patrol. I was with the sniper of our platoon, Doris, to try and draw fire from the enemy, I kept standing up. I was skylined on top of this compound trying to get the enemy to shoot at me, imagine if I had been shot? What a pointless tragedy that would have been, but this was war, and these were the things that happened.

I would almost be ashamed to admit to a couple of things, but we are human, I know anything we did, a thousand other squaddies have done. One thing I got caught doing, falling asleep on stag. Everyone does it, no matter how much of a trained soldier you are, as soon as you get a bit complacent, the boredom sets in, the eyes start getting heavy, and you try and fail to snap out of it. I tried rubbing water in my eyes, jumping up and down on the spot, everything, it doesn't work, then your head starts dropping and snaps you out of a sleepy fall. Next thing someone shouts, 'cunt' at you and you wake up. Once I could hear something rustling about in the sanger, I was shitting myself, I was falling asleep as well, it was sanger four about three in the morning. I was terrified at the thought of sharing the night with a camel spider, so I went outside, laid my body armour on the floor and went to sleep. Awful thing to admit to, but I know I wasn't the first or last to have done it. I remember on sanger three once I was dying for a shit, my stomach was hurting. I was looking around for someone to cover me for five minutes, no one was around. It was only about half eleven at night, people were still up, but sanger three was out of the way. I thought, 'fuck it,' to myself, ran down the sanger leaving it completely unattended, done my business in the toilet and then went flying back up. Again such a bad thing to do, but I guarantee I'm not the only one, though someone was more committed, we found a chocolate pudding wrapper in sanger three, and it had a shit in it. Someone apparently got caught short and went in their ration bag, I was crying with laughter. I can't remember what poor bastard found it, still makes me laugh to this day though. I got caught sleeping on stag once, I didn't get punched for it though, maybe I was liked too much, not sure. Jonesy made me dig a well as punishment, better than a punch in the face I suppose. Digging through sand and clay in fifty-degree heat, I could have thought of better things to do with my time. Seems like a fruitless enterprise, a well in Afghanistan? We were in the Green Zone, surrounded by man-made canals. One thing that strikes me as bizarre to this day is seeing crabs just walking around in the irrigation ditches. I saw crabs in Gt Yarmouth when I was growing up as a child, never thought I would see them in the middle of Afghanistan. Frogs as well, for some reason every morning we woke up, there would be hundreds of tiny frogs hopping their way across the PB.

One of the less friendly encounters I had was one that I never even knew about, I went down with a fever, I felt cold but my temperature was through the roof. They thought it was heat stroke at first until I started getting a pain in my left bum cheek, at first it was like a tender spot with a black hole in the middle, a small chasm of rotting flesh. Then it grew, becoming a tomato hanging from my backside, erupting with puss like one of those model volcanoes at an American science fair. It turned out a camel spider had bitten me. I had never even felt the little fucker as it munched on my skin like a pizza. I honestly can't tell you when it happened. Maybe when I was having a poo and let my guard down, perhaps the Taliban had sent the camel spider in a drastic bid to knock me off. Either way, all I know is that as I squeezed it, the puss ran down my leg like a small creamy Niagara Falls, it came back about three more times. The last time it happened was when I was in the UK, the same day I passed my driving test, I had to have an operation to cut it from my skin, literally gave me another asshole, six centimetres long and three centimetres deep.

It's safe to say that Afghanistan was a peculiar place, it was bizarre, things were just so different out there, hard to explain. One day you're fighting on the front line, the next you're bored on stag, then it's movie night, and you're huddled around a TV like children watching a DVD from 1999. I tell you what's a strange feeling, I have an abscess at the moment, I have a cup of tea, I'm writing on a £1500 laptop sat inside a warm house, yet because of this abscess, I feel like my life is so unfair. Says everything about how our society has changed really, I'm writing of a time where I had nothing and yet wanted for nothing, though here I am with everything and wanting everything else. My happiness has been completely depleted because of an infection in my mouth. Perhaps if I had an abscess back in 2009, I would have still wanted for a cold drink and warm bed to sleep in more than I would have wanted for the abscess to go? I certainly know I wanted those things more than I wanted a Rolex or a BMW. Needs at war are not based on class as they are out here. The status of a man wasn't measured by the car he drove or the clothes that he wore. It was governed by the way he was to his men. It's so false as well as most people in a nice car are paying it off on finance, the clothes they wear don't fit the nature of their work, they just prioritise the image over anything else. In Afghanistan, nothing was false, it was life or death on a daily basis, you wore the same clothes, drank the same water, shed the same blood. As I write this, I realise that I felt secure in my body, more confident in my skin at war than I have ever felt since I returned to the UK. A lot of terrible, unimaginable things happened in that green zone, but I would trade back the house I sleep in, the clothes I stand in and maybe even the sense of purpose I have from this writing. One trade with the devil just to feel that sense of content in nothingness. Only men looking after each other, no worries in the world except the task in hand, our stature came from how we comforted each other, and our value came from the inner peace we shared in the chaos of war.

The thing about Afghanistan is that nothing is guaranteed, every step you take can literally be your last, the desert holds no punches, the sand gives away no signs of what may lurk beneath. The real fear is looking into the eyes of your friends and seeing fear in their eyes, each time on the ground knowing this may be the last time you see them again. Recognising this anxiety makes it hard to take things quite as seriously out here, at work when targets are not met, or we're short of the annual budget, I kind of think to myself, 'who cares?' Are you going to die? Life's so short, there is so much more to it than money. When you've lived in life and death situations, civilian life can seem trivial. The only thing this world gives us is less and less reason to recognise the things we're thankful for. Imagine if a bomb went off in this room right now, would the snobby business man reach for his presentation full of facts and figures? Would he grab his car keys? Would he even reach for an injured woman? That's what I want to know, what would his priorities be. How much would he value his work, or would he be struck with an epiphany and grow a sudden empathy for human nature, that which matters. Nothing gives you this rationalisation like war, once you've been in battle and fought to save a mans life, not much becomes more important or significant, for dying is the only thing you can't change, everything else can be. For this reason, a life outside of war is hard to take as serious or motivating. I appreciate priorities, but I don't appreciate how important money has become, how controlling and strangling it is, I never saw a £20 note suffocate a man in war, so why do I see it outside of war? Putting things in perspective is quite easy from my position, I've lived at the farthest edge of the spectrum, and not much can question your sanity as seeing the same grief come from money as it does from war.

We patrolled up to secure Green Four, (Kalshaw Kallays grid reference and nickname for the town.) The rear section manning the sangers in the PB covered the stretch of road between us, and Green One (a junction south of our PB, the grid reference was Green One, so this is how it was known to us.) Green One was manned by six platoon. The reason our platoons had moved off to cover these points was for a resupply. By controlling these points, we had a secure route for Five Platoon to pass through, this stretch of road was a significant bridge between FOB Silab five platoons' residence and PB Haji Alem, six platoons firm hold. Somewhere in the middle was PB Parang. I'm sure this was for resupplying battery packs as six platoons were damaged, don't quote me on that. I'm sure also the patrol would have carried mail down in the vehicles due to the rotation of airmail dropped into Silab, and the considerable lack of it supplied to ourselves and six platoon. The patrol was ok to start off, it sounds bizarre I suppose to say it was the usual, to me the concept of being at war at that point in my life, was normal. It wasn't out of the ordinary to have a weapon, to be weighed down in kit surpassing my body weight. If I said it was abnormal, that would be to say that we never went on patrol, "no one was shot at today, that was abnormal." Or, "I wasn't dehydrated today and at no point was I struggling to find a break from the blistering sun, that was abnormal." Pronouncing a statement such as, "I fucking hate Afghanistan, it's too hot, and I'm sick of having to drink warm water after a patrol. I'm tired of seeing my mates get injured and not being able to have a fair fight with the Taliban." Was usual, it was far too normal to be used to these conditions.

Back to this routine patrol, the atmospherics were average, we conducted a small staggered march from the PB and secured the first checkpoint at the south of Green Four, it was a significant crossroad at the start of the village and the route leading to Lashkagar. Quite often you would see tractors and other vehicles covered with the lively possessions of Afghan residents wishing to move from the area to Lashkagar. I suppose they felt it would be safer, these vehicles would be stacked fifteen to twenty feet high and tied up, topped off with children perched on a mountain of objects resembling the angel on top of a Christmas tree. We would search them, head to toe before letting them pass on their way down the dusty tracks, a home removal conducted by a tractor. Entirely unsettled by our appearance, to be honest, they probably thought we were foolish, watching us struggle to move off the spot while they hopped back on their mobile home and set off on their business. That was our primary services on patrols like this, just avoidance technique, stand there and look menacing until they either shot at you or chose not to. Everyone else just went about their daily routine, barely even acknowledging your existence unless you purposefully engaged them. As we manned the checkpoint locals would wander in and out, each time we would stop them, rifles pointed at them by the cover man, one false move and they would be shot down. The command given was for them to lift up their dish dash, dish dash is the word given for an Afghan garment, generally speaking, it is a long shirt worn with matching bottoms. Over the years British forces had spent inside the country, the locals were familiar with the practice and often perform the raising of their clothing without being told, they would then turn around to do the same again. This was a cursory check to make sure no weapons or explosive devices were hidden on their person, a more thorough inspection would be given once they were cleared to move closer. For us it was a break from the mundane task of sitting on green four, what you don't see behind the scenes in videos of firefights is the four hours of patrolling it took to get there, it was never all bombs and bullets.

We acted as a buffer zone, as good as any explanation I suppose, if you drew an imaginary circle and drew points on that ring, you could imagine at each of those points were two of us. This gave us all-around defence, the critical organism in a three-sixty degree war zone. After a few hours we had successfully claimed the ground, it was firmly under our control, for lack of a better word we had almost blended in, became a part of the natural order of things. This was communicated through to the company HQ, giving five platoon the capacity to move farther south to our position to then pass through on to green one. At this point, although we were technically in control, it never felt like it, stationary in this central beacon of activity we were completely exposed. The locals looked at us as if we were flies that had wandered into a spiders web, outcasts distinguished by our superiority, superiority in context but not in reality. This was not our land, the spiders' web was not our comfort zone. Although we had the weapon systems, the tactical movement to control this ground, the eyes of the local elders would have suggested differently. It was a stare of pure stillness, not a flicker of emotion gave way as they stared through every one of us. A group of elder men stayed in the exact position from the moment we got there, drinking green tea, made with boiled water taken from the nearby irrigation ditches, they seemed neither bothered nor worried about our presence. It pissed me off a bit, not that I wanted them to be scared of me, I wanted my presence acknowledged, my status confirmed, all the guns we had, the helmets and body armoured that preserved our appearance as warriors were still not enough to make me feel safe. The equipment could not outweigh the glowing savageness of their stares, and whether they meant to or not, I could not help but feel intimidated, watched, threatened. Nothing had happened, the atmospherics were normal, nine out of ten times you could tell if something was about to kick off because all the locals would suddenly disappear, the only ones that would be left in sight would be yourselves, that's when it was time to worry. The Taliban relied on the locals for information, so they didn't want to kill any of the local people, although they controlled them with fear, they had a balance. It was working. The locals wouldn't want to talk to us or be seen with us through fear of what the Taliban would do to them.

We remained on sentry, controlling the ground with our presence, coming from the north, we could see five platoon, they had men in front of the vehicles sweeping the area for I.E.D's at vulnerable points. Once checked they would get back inside the vehicles and drive to the next marker, It was a strenuous technique, but it was a way of minimising the risk of the trucks initiating a pressure plate bomb in the ground. It was refreshing once they reached our position, we were reunited with friends that we had not seen in a long time, sharing quick laughs and stories before they had set off again. Wils and I were chatting with Dan, we quickly shook hands with a smile before he re-joined the patrol, this was the last time we saw him with his head intact. After they left us, I would say half an hour went by, give or take ten minutes or so, the sun had started to drift away, and the blazing rays that came with it became less irritable to our skin. The worst noise shut down everything else around us, a shock wave ripped through the entire area, once again everything drained from our faces. Talk of home, what we spend our money on once we got back there became redundant and secondary to what had just happened. We were powerless to help, all we could do is listen in to the radio communications to try and find out if anyone was hurt. What had happened? Who had been hit? The commotion followed like a whirlwind of chaos, I don't honestly know what had happened in the following minutes as they fought through the carnage, but we received the following information through the headset. One casualty dead, one critically wounded, or T4 – dead, T1 – critically wounded. We only heard the zap numbers come through, I can't remember the last four of their numerical license plates but once you get the first two letters you instantly tried to work out who it was. HU and BO, were the two initials of the surnames, in order not to upset anyone, I will not give their names.

Due to the significance of the incident, the casualties had been moved to PB Parang. A radio call came out for extra medics to be sent down to help. We answered the call and were about to realise the real devastation of what had happened. As the patrol had left PB Parang, they had got some distance south down the track and had got out scanning the ground. As they returned, a pressure plate I.E.D had been initiated at the front or rear of the vehicle. Bar armour and a wheel guard of the mastiff had been ripped from the vehicle and had struck a member of the patrol in the head, splitting it in half and killing him instantly. It was never one hundred percent confirmed what had hit him, also I never received clarity of which end of the vehicle he had been walking toward, it's not the kind of questions you ask. In the explosion was five platoons' sergeant who had been sent backwards into an irrigation ditch by the blast, he had received injuries all over his body. These had left him with his stomach ripped open and his intestines hanging from his body. This was one of the worst incidences of the tour, it had left a sour taste in everyone's mouth.

This is what I mean when I say it makes you question everything in life, how can you see your mates head split like a watermelon, then expect to go to work the next day? How can you take the world seriously after seeing some of the most unusual things that can be bestowed upon humanity? You have blood on your hands, that blood will not leave you when you come home, that blood always remains there. Every time I'm asked to do something at work I find it hard, it's a bitter pill to swallow to have someone tell you what to do. Have someone moan at me for doing something wrong. It makes me angry. I earned my status at war, I have blood on my hands, for that reason I will forever carry the mark of war on my chest. Because of this streak, I don't feel I will genuinely fit back into a stable life. My senses are too aware of my surroundings, my temper is carved to that of a killer, and my attitude will forever be that of a rifleman. My swag will always be to swing my arms lower than the rest, hold my head higher. This will be the thing that stops me integrating, I am intelligent enough to see the needs of the world, I just don't take it serious enough. I know I need money I just don't value it as much. I have been on a higher wavelength where money did not matter, I have seen the real cost of living and its real purpose. I have lived on the edge of my seat, at the edge of that seat I needed no five-pound note, money could not have saved His life. Looking back at times like those I feel grateful that I was able to do my bit. No matter where I go or what I do now, I was allowed at least for those moments in time, to reach my full potential. Fuck this class based falseness that everyone else lives in, with their pretentious problems, fuck reality TV and all those who are a part of it, moaning about daddies money and their cheating boyfriends. How can I take that seriously? How can I be a part of a world where that draws attention and gives fame? How can we as a civilisation condone that when people die every day? It sure as hell isn't why I went out there but it's a big part of the reason that given half the chance I would go back again. Just to be part of a world with no TV, no money and no civilians that will see no further than the clothes I wear, if you judge the calibre of a person by what they have then you're a fucking moron.

Me on the right hand side helping 'V' give combat first aid to Abdul John

Chapter 11
Abdul John

I was doing what I usually done with my downtime, playing poker with a few of the lads and listening to music on the iPod dock. We had it charged all the time via a solar power charger. We lacked in electricity, not many plugs in the Afghanistan desert, yet the supply of Sun power was insurmountable. Sat there chilling, just another day in paradise. There were no patrols out, so the blokes on stag were just observing in their arcs, not much going on, almost too quiet. That's when it happened. An explosion came from about one hundred and fifty to maybe two hundred meters east of sangar three. First instinct when hearing a blast in our environment is to get your head down, an explosion doesn't just mean a single static I.E.D, although as I have pointed out I.E.D's were our primary threat. It could have been an I.E.D with a follow-up attack, it could be an RPG miss fired, so another one may be about to get fired, or it could be mortar fire in which case this attack could last a long time. So, first instinct is to get low and see what happens next, to be fair though we were all reasonably confident we were safe behind the thick layers of hesco walls, we barely flinched as we looked up to see the thick cloud of sand being kicked up in the air.

Whoever was on radio stag would be listening out for a contact report, just in case one of the other call signs were out on patrol, and for some reason, we never knew about it. Nothing came over the net. We started to cheer because the only explanation that we assumed was that a terrorist had tried laying an I.E.D and blew himself up. A few chants of 'own goal' were shouted by the blokes, 'serves you right you cunts' was another favourite shouted out by bloodthirsty poker players. It could have been a stray dog or a civilian, either way, we were happy that as far as we knew it wasn't one of our boys. It was a small pocket of relief, a few of us would regret this for the rest of our lives. It does pay to never take anything for granted, especially out there where anything can happen, and all seems to go wrong. A few moments later the bloke on sangar three was calling for the interpreter as one of the locals was shouting up to him, the language barrier being what it was meant that he didn't have a clue what the local was trying to say. We got the interpreter over so he could speak to the local from the sangar in safety helmet. We all busied about, getting our kit on, speculating what had happened, we were all a bit excited about the drama. Anything to distract from the mundane existence. The information received then relayed by the interpreter was devastating, there were two civilians in the explosion, one was in critical condition, the other was killed instantly, both were children. No one could properly take it in, you hear that information, and it doesn't register. It's a game. It's a film. It's anything that you don't have to process straight away, anything that stops you having to feel, if you feel something, it makes the job a lot more difficult.

The word had got to Boss, he agreed to have the casualty brought in to get treated within the PB, V, the platoons medic started setting up the med centre. As a qualified team medic and quite a competent one, I was going to help with the casualty. Jonesy and I were kitting up to go out and secure the victim. We had the cover from the sangars, as soon as the child came we were able to move to the back gate while the search team, Stants and Wils, provided cover form our sides. It could have quite easily been an ambush so although there was a child casualty to consider, there was also the safety of the men.

"There are two blokes, and the casualty is being carried in a wheelbarrow." Called the sentry. As they passed sangar three the four of us left the back gate, Stants and Wils went first and called the Civilians over to one side to begin searching, Jonesy, and I gave a quick search of the wheelbarrow. What we saw was a young boy no older than eight years old slumped lifelessly, heaped inside like you would pack your shopping in a bag. He had a dish dash wrapped around his legs which were covered in blood, arms rested on his chest with no effort or desire to move them. A lot of small lacerations peppered his arms, his head had a lot of trauma with many cuts to his face, he looked like he was laid there ready to die. We decided we needed him as quick as possible if we were going to save his life. We put a stretcher next to the wheelbarrow then prepared to lift him, Jonesy took the child softly under his armpits as I took hold of his legs.

"Three, two, one lift," as I lifted him up he seemed light, too light, yet Jonesys end hadn't moved. I looked down to see the child's legs were in my hands, they had separated from his body, the dish dash was just to keep them in place. There was a moment of horror as the situation gripped me, then it passed, I knew what I had to do. I put the legs to one side exposing the true nature of the child's injuries. Few things will burn in my mind like the horror of what I saw at that moment, the charred flesh of the child will forever stain me like blood on a white shirt.

The child's legs were both amputated like a maniac surgeon had removed them with a chainsaw and a flamethrower. Both above the knee, the left leg was detached as far as the hip bone, there was a small fraction of the child's femur protruding from the wound. A small amount of skin coming off his buttocks went to a point with a small piece of muscle attached to the end of it. It rested in the soggy wheelbarrow as if it was the discarded fat from a sirloin steak. The second leg was detached from just above the knee, it was almost entirely stripped of skin right up into the child's abdomen. The injuries were so unclean and savage that the child's testicles were missing, his penis was still attached to his body, but the scrotum was ripped apart, and his actual testicles must have been lost in the explosion. This child was almost the same age as my little brother, what a parallel, evil world this poor boy was brought into, he was just a child, he had not asked for any of this, but now was not a time for reflection. This boy had been completely smashed by the blast, his small body looked like it had already given in to the injuries, but we were not as ready to give up on him yet though. The wheelbarrow would not be his grave.

I knew what I had to do, I placed my left hand under his leg gently to not add any more trauma to his already horrific injuries, I tucked the lump of skin and muscle onto his leg, so it wasn't just hanging down. I then as softly as I could, took the weight from under his right buttock. The only way I can describe it is like handling an uncooked chicken. The skin was wet, cold to touch, I guess he had landed in an irrigation ditch after the explosion as the area of this type of injury was often hot and covered in sand. We placed him down on the stretcher, I had to leave the legs in the wheelbarrow. The casualty extraction was a quick one, as we carried him off, Stants and Wils carried on the search of the civilians. Alex had come out and placed the child's legs into a Chemical waste bag to be extracted back to Bastion hospital with the child. We got him straight in the med centre where V was waiting with the trauma kit. We laid the field stretcher we had onto the makeshift operating table, so when the chopper came, we could get him away as swiftly as possible. There was an extra dignity carried out as we handled the boy, something sobering, home-hitting fell over all of us, apart from orders I don’t think any words were spoken.

Apart from his visible injuries, the boy was peppered over his entire body with shrapnel wounds. These included gashes to the head. You thank your lucky stars when you have someone as composed as V next to you. We started with the most severe injuries, which was his legs, I had my tourniquet out and tried my best to get it round what was left of his leg. The small protruding bone was moving as I struggled to tighten the tourniquet. It was almost pointless as the blast had not lead to much bleeding, just burnt skin and muscle, I felt helpless, I didn't know what could save this boys life, I just tried to do what I could whilst he was with us. Patches of hemcom were placed on the legs, the tourniquet was tightened, I'm not sure what difference it had made as he still looked as he did before. V had placed a first field dressing around the right leg, the limb of muscle and ripped skin was wrapped tight to compress the wound. I remember having to hold the large flap of tissue in place as the dressing was wrapped, throughout this time he drifted in and out of consciousness, Will was by his side with the interpreter. He fought over and over again to talk to him, I could hear the desperation in his voice as he asked if he liked football. Only whimpers ever left the boys lips. I tried to wrap the leg with dressing but what was left was too small to get anything around. I ended up tucking it under his bum which had been blown apart and forming a nappy to cover his buttock and the exposed stump. I remember V placing the bottom halve of his body in a toxic waste bag to try and reduce sand getting in the wounds once the chopper came. The last thing I did for this eight-year-old boy, was clear the blood from his eye. He was whimpering as a hole in the side of his nose leaked blood into the eye and filled the socket. It was irritating him, I wiped the blood away and placed a plaster over his nose to stop the bleeding at its origin. Two American helicopters arrived not long after the wheelbarrow came to the PB. One circled above looking for enemy activity as the other smoothly drifted in and landed. We grabbed the stretcher and moved swiftly to the Blackhawk with our goggles pulled tight to our face to avoid the sand that blasted against our bodies. The boy was loaded, followed by a toxic waste bag that held his legs, before we had got back to the med centre to take cover from the down blast, the Blackhawk had aviated and moved away, the second completed a last circle of the PB before it followed the first. That was it, the fate of this little child rested in the hands of the doctors and surgeons of Camp Bastion. Boss came to me and said well done on how I had reacted to the incident, I nodded, washed the blood from my hands, went on stag and cried until the point that I was relieved by the next person.

At the brief the next day, we were informed that there had been communication from HQ, the eight-year-old boy was named Abdul John, he had died at Camp Bastion. I wasn't surprised by the news, his weak little body had been destroyed by the explosion, just a small part of me had hoped that we had done something to save his life. He was innocent, he had been playing with his brother, they just stepped in the wrong place at the wrong time. They both died, we had never seen the other boy, we were told the locals buried the body. My Mum told me I rang her that day, she said I told her of the boy and cried as I spoke, she also says there were times when I first got back that I would scream his name in the night, that I always said that there was nothing I could do. I don't remember this, what I do know is that the very mention of his name is like a dagger in my heart. That is the single piece of evidence I will ever need to justify my feelings toward peace, anything that can cause harm to an innocent child is not worth it. That day Abdul Johns Dad had come to the PB, he was told of the news, the reaction in his face was one of sadness, tears streamed from his eyes, the words from his mouth were not, they were words of desperation. He said, not in these exact words, in fact they were in Arabic (Pashtu) and interpreted to us through the interpreter, his words were along the lines of.

"I'm glad he died, I could not afford to look after a child that could not work, it would just be another mouth to feed."

At first, I was mortified by this statement, fucking cunt his child's just died how he can say that? The sort of aggressive reaction you can expect from almost anybody. But as I've got older and grown as a person, I can empathise with that statement. I can see the sadness in the words, the desperation in his life that he would even need to say those words. How sad is it that a man who can cry over his childs' death, is still in such a desperate situation that he can even find reason to think of finance. What a savage life he must live. He also stated, once again I must say this is along the lines of, although the statement is correct the actual words spoken to those I type, will naturally become off key, kind of like Chinese whispers.

"Please, can I have compensation for my sons' death? The Taliban have visited me and said they want money for the bomb. They say it was meant for a British soldier and my son ruined it. If I do not pay for the weapon, they will kill me."

I'm not sure if the Taliban had visited him or if he was trying it on like a whiplash claim. I don't know if Boss had given him any compensation money, what I do know is that after he left that PB, I never saw him again. This may have been coincidence, but nothing would surprise me with the Taliban. They had controlled, bullied and terrorised the local population for years. I don't believe that all Afghanistan people are terrorists at all, I think they want a peaceful life and want to be left alone. It just so happens a war going on in their back and front gardens. So many times we had burst through compound doors ready to kill, instead of finding an armed terrorist, we found a family, a scared mother or crying child. The most challenging thing is that the moment you show weakness, turn your back, that child or mother could be the one to detonate the bomb that kills you and your friends. On the other hand, it could have been Abdul John. In a war, he never asked for, that he didn't even understand but was probably one of the only things he had known his whole life. Or you could prematurely pull the trigger, kill an innocent mother, child, and live with it your whole life, all the time you were just doing your job, they were just living their lives.

Afghanistan was the most bizarre place I had ever known, ridden with disease, heroin addicts, pedophiles, murderers, rapists and animal abusers, I suppose not much different to anywhere else in the world. Perhaps it was just the post-apocalyptic appearance of the green zone that, maybe that's what made it so obviously twisted. Maybe if there were a few star-spangled shops, skyscrapers and somewhere to grab a nice latte in my high street fashion coat, then the murders and drug abuse would seem a bit more normal. It was the primitive living that distinguished Afghanistan, the sand and the compounds, no furniture, no roads, the green zone was a baron wasteland, these people had made home here, their resources were low. In the same irrigation ditch, you would see locals gathering water in a makeshift copper kettle, taking a shit and brushing their teeth, all at the same time. It's enough for anyone to brandish them all as terrorists because they live in a sandy compound with dish dashes on, they instantly gain that miss trust, I was one of them. It's only as I've learned more, perhaps even educated myself that I have become less ignorant to their troubles.

There was an Afghan National Army soldier that used to flirt with me. When he would see me walking to the sentry position, he would scramble to his feet, clumsily putting on his body armour, racing to get to the sanger before me, so it looked as if he was already heading there. His name translated to 'Holiday' apparently, it could have been Osama Bin Laden for all I know. I still have a seven of spades card with his name on it. I showed him a picture of me and who was my partner at the time, he would say in a high pitched broken English accent, "Greendog" pointing at me, "Holiday" pointing at my partner. He would repeat this suggesting that we were a couple. Once he even tried ripping her out of the picture just before I stopped him, he was obsessed with me, all the Afghan males would say that women were for babies and then men were for pleasure. I never saw this, but we always saw the men hanging around with each other and coming out of compounds together. Of course, this is only speculation, it could all be innocent, but from the stories, it did make you think. I remember once in a compound I found Polaroid photos of a man and a young boy with flowers all over them, again could have been innocent but was altogether quite disturbing. The children would come to us using two fingers as a circle, poking their other finger through shouting, 'jiggy jiggy'.

A friend who was out there told me he had heard members of the Afghan National Army taking turns to have sex with a donkey, again this isn't proven, but you just believe it. When you've been out there and soaked in that sun, see the way they live, you have a feeling deep inside of what's going on, you can feel it in the air, it's all very barbaric. Although looking back, it's easy to see how this happens. They're not dropped in from the UK, they've grown up in these mountains, these sand compounds. I'm not exaggerating when I say they have nothing, on top of having nothing they are bombed and shot every day, no wonder they shag a donkey here or there, they have nothing else. There are people in the UK shagging animals, in a place where sex sells, there are prostitutes all over the country, yet someone decides to shag a dog. So, in the middle of Afghanistan, it's almost to be expected, I was out there for three months and a one point I cut a hole in the hesco wall and tried shagging it, after thirty years that donkey would have only had to look at me and I probably would have jumped on it. If you look back through our history you will see that we weren't much different, the ancient Greeks were raping young boys in those bathhouses for years, it's only because we have moved away from it, developed a moral code within our civilisation that things changed. Look at the BBC thirty years ago, the likes of Jimmy Saville, the Osama Bin Laden of pedophiles, the government cover-ups of child sex rings within the houses of parliament, it's mental, maybe they're all terrorists in disguise? Perhaps they only caused a war in Afghanistan so they could fly over to bum some donkeys and children? I feel like I've gone off topic here but my whole point is this, I had spent a lot of my life demonising the people of Afghanistan, and its primitive ways. Something about Abdul John has changed my perspective. I realised that they were and are human beings, just like me. Not perfect, uncivilised in a lot of ways, but humans nonetheless, they didn't want this war. The Taliban and extremists are not people, they are the soulless creatures with a blackened heart of pure evil, they are the ones with no regard for human life, but, look in the mirror and ask if we are much different. We are all partly responsible for this war, we all sought blood after 9/11, we got it, but it came with such a price that at no point could we just turn around and undo what we had caused.

It's easy to reflect now on it all, a lot of my life has already been twisted and darkened by what I had experienced, seen and felt in that country. I wish I could show everyone the actual cost of war. Perhaps if we had all had such foresight, things would not have been the same. At least if everyone understands the fall out from a just or unjust war, then peace might be an option for the future. Would I have joined up if I could see what my life was going to become? Of course I would, that's one thing I find strange about myself, I hate PTSD, I hate some of my ways, my anxiety, my mood swings, my aggression, but given halve the chance I would go back and do it all again. It was the one period of my life that I knew I was alive. I could feel my heartbeat, before every shot I took I had learned how to slow it down to reduce the movement in my body. I had learned how to embrace the cold, accept that it was just my body letting me know that I was still here. It has given a unique insight on life. There is a lot we take for granted, the central heating that keeps us warm, the cars that make us unaware of our surroundings, all just numbing the essence of life. I'm not saying that I don't like cars or central heating, I'm just saying that once those things are taken away from you, you start to notice the other things in life that are more important. There was a time that I valued a cold bottle of water more than anything in the world. It's a precious and luxurious thing when you don't have it. Now that it comes from a tap, I would prefer a coffee from Costa as I write. I have lived on rations for months on end, wishing for a steak, perhaps even one of my mums home cooked Sheppard Pies, yet now in my car, I quickly opted for the more convenient drive thru McDonald. In the Army I was lean, I didn't diet, I never took protein shakes or fat burning tablets, I was just living how a human should, minus the alcohol and odd take away in my bed space. I was active, enjoyed life and ate when I was hungry. I do my best now to avoid it, but at one time though I was just numbing my senses with the comfortable takeaway life, driving everywhere, take away meals for convenience and alcohol to make me feel better. So, would I go back to my more primitive utopia to allow once again the cold to remind me of my mortality? Yes. Would I trade in my life now though if it meant that Abdul John had to die again? To know the horror of war for the rest of my life? That question might never be answered. I don't know if I have the heart to say yes or the willingness to say no.

So that was it, these chapters were the yellow brick road that had to lead me from the boy that hid behind the sofa in a council house when the rent man knocked the door, to the battlefield of Afghanistan with an I.E.D exploding in my face. All the above need only be reflected upon, need only be questioned because of what happened on the 21st August 2009. We're back to somewhere in chapter one now, just before I was evacuated from the battlefield and after I was blown up. If I had nothad been blown up, would I be who I am today? Probably not, I would still be in the Army, I know that for a fact. This is when the book gets hard for me to write I reckon, all the previous stuff was just me sort of pondering on my glory days. The events after are a lot darker, in a sense anyway, no children die but the mental effects of life afterwards and what I put many people through are comparable. Those are the actual demons that I carry as a direct result of everything you have read thus far, rather than the theme of the content or information itself. As they say all things must come to an end, the explosion was the beginning of that end, the expression out of the frying pan and into the fire springs to mind. So lets get back to the blast, my final and lasting memories that summarised my time in Afghanistan.

"I stand up ready to move off and take one step forward with my left leg, the next few moments are a muffled memory from my

senses reacting to the most significant shock my body has ever felt. Firstly I remember the feeling, the shock wave of the explosion going off, it was an immense power that seemed to rip through me and had sent my LMG flying out of my hands and somersaulted me into the middle of the track, parallel to this was the feeling of the debris smashing into me."

I was sat in the sand, ears still ringing from the penetrating noise that came with the explosion, in those moments I wondered, why me? Was I just in the wrong place at the wrong time? Am I going to lose my eye? It may not have been the longest time, but I had asked myself a million questions. I can't remember being in pain immediately afterwards, I was in shock, but I wasn't hurting. You know when you get punched in the face or just bang your head, that rattling feeling, distorted, it just felt like that. I know it seems a bi-polar comparison, knocking your head on the table compared to being hit head height by two I.E.D's, but that's the only way I can describe the pain, just dull. The feeling was peculiar, my skin was numb, my whole body felt like my gum after a trip to the dentist. I was shaky, my breath had been knocked from my body. I felt drunk in the moment. A cloud of brown sand and dust swarmed around me, it never seemed to clear, at least I can't remember it settling, my memory of those seconds are just sand and blood.

If I remember what I was told correctly, then V had heard the explosion, it was loud so of course, he had heard it, he was only a stones' throw away back in the PB. He had heard the bang and just ran straight to me. Not knowing it was I perhaps, but just running to the aid of whoever was injured, that's heroic, that man proved himself on that tour as selfless, caring and a true safeguard. I was pulled to my feet by Jonesy and V, I shouted, "Is that the best you can do? Is that the best you can do?" Towards the point of explosion. It's a quote from the film 300. We were Spartan 7 after all. I've always been a bit of a clown, I suppose if you can't laugh when you get blown up in a war zone, when can you laugh? I was scared, I was always good at hiding my insecurities with a comical mask, whether it was insecure about my weight as a young teenager, or the bullies that had called me names before that. I would always use my humorous tongue to avoid fighting, swallowing the fear and embarrassment rather than face my fears, that all changed when the Army had turned me into a weapon, but this, this was different, I felt vulnerable. I was pulled inside the mastiff. This was to take me back to the PB where I would then be extracted. In the mastiff was Doris the sniper, myself and V. At this point I had my first cigarette ever, I didn't like it, but it did feel pretty gangster, kind of Vietnam war style. Once we were in the PB I went straight to the med centre, my face was dripping with blood, I had fragmentation wounds to my cheek, jaw, neck, eye, nose, head, left arm, left bum cheek and my left leg. The piece that hit me in my neck went straight through, stopping as it hit the inside of my jaw, this had cracked the roots of two of my teeth which had to be removed. My right eyelid was torn in half, the parts that weren't hanging off were swollen up like a golf ball. Before treatment, I done the obvious thing, took photos of myself looking like a badass! Once the adrenaline had begun to wear off, the pain started to settle in. My face was agony, my eye was irritable, I had a piece of frag hanging out of my arm which was sore, but above all else, my ass felt like it was on fire. V covered up my wounds because of the PEDRO coming in, I pulled my trousers back up, delicately placed my shirt over my frail body, then set my helmet back on my broken head. The helmet was covered in blood and had a crack on the rim. I wanted to get this framed in a glass box as a memento of how narrowly I had cheated death. Pratty was to join me in the ride back to civilisation. He had a perforated eardrum from the explosion. We had never really seen eye to eye, but since that day I've shared an affinity with him.

That noise came in, the pounding, 'thud thud thud' of the black hawks propellers as it closed in our position, then the gust of wind that plastered the whole PB in a sandy embrace. This was exciting shit, I know that sounds bad, but it was. The medical crew in the back pulled me inside. There was two of them. One looked after Pratty, the other had me. I would love to meet that bloke again. He asked me if I was in pain, I laughed and shouted back to him, "yeah my ass hurts, I've got frag in my fucking asshole." He laughed then wrote, 'frag in ass copy' on my bloodied combat trousers, again another memento for this blood red hall of fame of mine. During the twenty or so minute flight I stared outside, such a beautiful looking place, the blazing sun was shining down upon the landscape. I could see no war, no bombs, just a majestic land that I was now leaving covered in my own blood. How had it all got so fucked up? That moment of pondering was interrupted by the medic sticking a needle in my arm, somehow during this rocky flight he managed to find a vein, stick a thin needle into it and release a cannula in me, first try as well, I've been in hospitals where they've had to try twenty times. As we landed, I was placed in a wheelchair by the medical greeting team of camp bastion hospital. I waved bye to the black hawk, the way a four-year-old is told to wave goodbye to relatives by its mother, what a plonker. I remember being rushed into surgery, placed on a bed and swiftly having my clothes cut away from my body. Danish, American and Swedish nurses surrounded me with my little todger hanging out, weren't the most arousing of moments though, but I was close to trying to rub myself to get a semi. All that was over quite quickly, a male nurse or doctor came up to me, he told me I was going under sedation, the next thing I know I was woke up surrounded by other casualties with my right eye completely covered up.

As I came to, Cas was at my bedside, he was returning home for an NCO, (non commissioned officer) cadre. He had been waiting for me to wake up and had cried when he found out I had been injured. Although when he saw me, he called me a puff and asked why I didn't have a proper injury. I had a parcel by my bed space as well, full of shortbread biscuits. I'm sure he had eaten half of those as well. I requested for all my other parcels that I was yet to receive, be redirected to the blokes, they would be no use to me now, plus I know how desperate you can be for some decent scoff after having nothing but rations followed by warm water to drink. I was laughing with Cas, telling him what he had missed out on, laughing about our Chinese box set of Dragonball Z, talking about what we were going to do when we got home, then he had to go. I asked the nurse where my helmet and day sack was, "lost" was her answer, I was absolutely gutted, all I was leaving Afghan with was the greasy hair that capped off my smelly body. Due to the injury in my eye, I was to be flown straight home, it was less than twenty-four hours from my injury. I needed surgery otherwise I may be blind in my eye for the rest of my life. Once again by wheelchair, I was transported to my flight, I quite liked being looked after like this, I felt like royalty, but the trip home was less than luxurious. I was strapped down to a stretcher like a person with a mental health condition in the back of a Hercules. We had to stop off in Dubai to refuel. I was allowed up for a short period, one of the guys in the back gave me a snickers bar and a packet of crisps from his lunch pack. It tasted so good, It was worth three months of rations to find such excellence in a snickers bar.

There was a small part of me that was happy, it was all over now, I was going to be able to drink cold water, eat ice cream, wear clothes, go shopping, anything, anything from my civilian life, something different from the sandy routine I had been used to. No more stag, a bed, oh my god a bed, how divine, I was excited about every little thing, it was all going to be a novelty for me. Then I was struck by the most gut-wrenching feeling of guilt I had ever felt, I was going to get all this yet my boys were still out there. I had my arms and legs, I wanted to go back, I couldn't face the shame of being in hospital with my injuries, I wanted to go to PB Parang, I wanted to be with my platoon. There is no way of being able to express the emotion of coming home injured. There is a thousand, anger at the Taliban, fear that you won't fit back into your life and fear for your friends left behind. Sad to leave your friends behind, happy to see your family, to see normality, fear of your injury, relief that you're out of the country. Each of these emotions conflicts the other. You don't know how you feel and that in itself can spark different feelings until they all snowball in your head. Has your head ever felt like a washing machine? Like every thought in your head is being spun around, that if you just tried to pick one out and open it up and understand it that you would get hurt? So instead of being able to understand your thoughts they just keep turning and twisting inside over and over. That is my head almost every day. I don't understand the feelings, but they are there, they cause me to do things I don't understand, cause me to hurt the people closest to me, cause me to punish myself by destroying my life. Almost as if my mind has started a chemical war against itself, this was the beginning of that process. The thirteen-hour flight gave me a chance to soak my feelings up in an isolated state. The journey was for a wounded serviceman, injured fighting for his country, but what they were bringing home, was a monster.

The Plane touched down in Birmingham airport, there was a medical transport service waiting to pick me up and take me to Selly Oak Hospital where they treat all soldiers wounded in combat. Coming out of that plane was a moment I will never forget, my body felt so weak it was hard to walk, inside the aircraft was so dark, so the sun made my eyes squint, but I wanted to see it. I wanted to see England, the air smelt so fresh, clean compared to that which I was used to, at that moment I felt like I could cry. I was home, and I was safe. One of the medical team got me into a wheelchair, yes another wheelchair. I was wheeled into the transport vehicle, the journey was so strange. I just stared out the window the whole time, cars, houses, people, grass, animals, trees, roads and paths. Everything was as if I was seeing it for the first time. I will just fit this peace in at the end of the chapter as it's quite relevant. My Mum said that when she first saw me it was like looking at a ghost, she said there was nothing in my eyes. I didn't look at her I just stared past her and said, "there was nothing I could do, I couldn't save him, Abdul John has died, he's dead, there's nothing I could do." Then I laughed.

Chapter 12
Home, But I Was Not Home

I had first seen my family through a small pane of glass in a door window. They were in the day room, I'm not sure how long they had been waiting for my arrival back in England. I caught the eyes of my Uncle Martin, I laughed and stuck two fingers up at him. It was such a bizarre feeling, to see them sat there. When I had deployed I didn't even know if I would ever see them again, yet there they all were, just like when they had come up for Family Day at Catterick. Just like they had come to see me in my passing out parade. I was on my way for initial surgery, my wounds needed to be cleared of any infection that may be lurking within them. I think that's how it went, to be honest, I can't remember. I know that the wounds in my arm were still open, so was my eye, I was bandaged from the work they had done to me at Camp Bastion but the wounds were not allowed to be sealed until I was in England. I was allowed to go into the room to see them. My skin was dirty, I had a shiny glaze over my face where I had not washed for days, maybe even a week. My hair was overgrown, thick and greasy. I was skinny and brown from being fed on rations with intense physical activity in the blazing sun. My family barely recognised me. I wandered into the room, I had no idea what to say, I felt like I didn't even know them, they were strangers, we had nothing in common. For the most time, I just sat there silent, staring out of the window. My Mum tried to hold my hand, talk to me, but I just wasn't interested, I didn't want to be the subject of conversation. I didn't want to be there. I wanted to be in England, but I also wanted to be back with my men. I didn't know what I wanted, but I know I didn't want to be sat here in silence, I wasn't happy, I've had spikes of happiness since that day. Sex has made me happy, watching a good film that I enjoy, holidays or having a good laugh. But since that day I can't remember a time where I have been happy without anxiety. My Mum said that she knew from the moment she saw me that her son had not returned from the war, that I was back but her son was not, I was home, but I was not home.

A few things happened in that Hospital, I was visited by the Sergeant Major of the ward, I was nil by mouth because I had to go to surgery, but he was bringing cakes to the soldiers that were donated by a local bakery. Although I couldn't eat, he hid one in my drawer for when I came back, that made me smile. I would take Shaw outside for a fag, me with my one eye bandaged up, him with no legs in a wheelchair, quite the pair we made. His family had bought him the whole collection of Winnie the Pooh teddy bears, he gave me Eeyore, that meant a lot to me, I still have that teddy and I probably will for the rest of my life. The kind of thing I will give to my first child or grandchild and tell them the story. I got to see all my brothers that were injured, I visited them all throughout my stay, their injuries made me feel like I didn't deserve to be there. Apart from Shaw, the first person I got to see was Black Chris. He was in a critical way, I spoke with him for hours, we shared something that our families didn't. I felt more attached to them than I did my own family, not because I didn't love my family, I just didn't have that connection, something was different. I then visited Captain P, he was optimistic, when I saw him he was creating a hand sculpture made from clay applied to a wire mesh, I'm sure I remember him saying his sister had got it for him. The last time I saw him was at the Battalion HQ, he had made his way up two flights of stairs carrying his wheelchair behind him. I don't remember seeing Walps there, I'm sure if he was there I would have seen him, perhaps he was in a unique unit, I don't know either way to be honest. I spent my days either in surgery, having my eye tested or trying to convince the nurses to let me go home. I was agitated, I felt like a caged rat, the ward was full of amputees, and there I was walking around with a patch on my eye. I felt as if I was teasing them and I fucking hated it. I knew none of them would feel that way, but it was a ward of such pain and devastation. The spirit of the men never changed, it was full of military banter and jokes, not many would understand it. I would call Shaw hot wheels. He would call me Cyclops. Behind the jokes though, we were all tortured, Shaw would tell me about his phantom pains, he would wake up thinking his legs were still there and tried to walk. He could feel pain in his feet that had long been incinerated. I remember one night my dreams were of being captured and tortured, I awoke with my bed full of piss, I had to call the nurse, my sheets had to be changed. I had to be washed down in the shower because I was too weak to do it myself. I felt so degraded, the mind plays horrible tricks on you, many times I was waking up with my eye patch pulled off with the blood on my face. I joked about it, I joked about the piss, I laughed about my eye, that was my way of dealing with it, but the ward was too quiet in the night for me, when there was nobody to joke with, I cried.

After my surgery, I had gone to see the ophthalmologist (eye doctor - don't worry I didn't know what it meant either). I had to see him as an outpatient many times. The surgery had sorted my eyelid out, that is still to this day pulled higher than the other where the eyelid had to be sewn back together. But the eye itself was damaged inside, I had a corneal scar on my retina. This meant that the light would not reach my retina in the centre of my eye, my vision would be blinded right down the middle. It was too early to tell if this would obscure my sight forever though. I also needed to take eye drops daily to bring the balance in my eye back to normal. I got back to the ward with my eye patch off, it felt like a relief, the stitches in my eyelid irritated me so much, my ass was covered in stitches from frag wounds and where they had to dig the shrapnel out. The shrapnel that had gone through my neck and face had been left in, because of the nerves that run past those areas, the decision had been made to leave it where it was. If they hit a nerve by accident, then my face would sag on one side like I had had a stroke. Each time I woke up from surgery, I would find myself surrounded by my family. It was nice, but each time it was a vague conversation, I didn't know what to say to them. My Mum just said I mumbled about Abdul John a lot, and she said she would cry each night because she didn't recognise me. I wouldn't laugh or smile. I didn't interact with them I just stared, I was jumpy, every noise would make me jump out of my skin.

The day before my last day, or my penultimate day, I was allowed out, the welfare team dropped me, my Cousin, my Gramp and my Aunty off at the Bull Ring. I went to the bank, I had a whole £2,500 in there, three months fighting for the country, getting blown up and that was the fortune I came home to, although it was two days before payday, I had been £1000 overdrawn before I left as well. I had never had that much money in my bank before. I just wanted to spend the lot, I don't know why I figured maybe that would make me feel better, perhaps it would be a numbing distraction from reality. It felt good spending money, something ordinary, It's terrible, but you do feel better when you have money, nothing else seems to matter, it was ok being blind in my right eye because I just bought a beautiful coat. Bizarre really but it worked. I felt good about myself because I could walk around and buy things, it was like I had nothing to worry about, my family remembers it slightly different, my Mum and Auntie say I wouldn't let them out of my sight. I wouldn't let them leave me. We went to Argos where I wanted to buy a G-shock watch as mine was lost in the explosion. My Mum wanted to go next door to get cigarettes. Apparently, I grabbed her arm; I don't remember this, to be honest, the more painful things my Mum has told me I don't know. She said I kept looking around at her.

"You still there?"

"Keep up."

"What are you doing?"

My Mums recalls me as shaky, scared, like that lost boy in the supermarket. I only remember the coat, although I recognise that behaviour within myself, I tend to suppress it, ignore its existence.

The first thing I did when I got home was go drinking, I had two weeks at home, I wanted to have fun, it didn't end up like that though. I was steaming drunk on the dance floor with one of the twins I joined up with, my sister and my cousin. It was all fine until a group of lads behind us started getting a bit loud, dancing a bit too close. I lost control, but I enjoyed it, I loved that feeling, it was like the relief when you pop a spot that's been pressing against your skin, once the poison is gone, the tension is gone. I started swinging wildly, wanting each blow that landed to kill the person I struck. Once it was all over I was happy, I had got my fix, inflicting pain on others released that tension that I felt in my body. Fighting was a way of draining the valve inside myself. By the time I got home the valve had needed bleeding again, the only person around was my Mum, in my drunken stagger through the house I would swear at her.

"You don't know what I've fucking been through. You're a shit fucking Mum."

The same was for my partner at the time, she became my verbal punching bag once I had a drink. I would fight in town then need a fight when I got home, something had changed in me, I was always aggressive as if I hadn't got whatever it was in Afghanistan off my chest, so I was doing it then. Either that or it was just the only thing that was normal to me. My men were still in Afghanistan, the only thing I knew how to do without them was drinking, then fight. That had been my reinforcement of position in the battalion, and now I was on my own, I had no one to prove it to except myself. I remember causing trouble a lot in town, so I could unhook the leash that I felt so tight around my throat. My Mum said in those two weeks that I was at hers before I went back to camp that I would just scream in my sleep. She remembers me shouting Abdul John at the top of my voice. She barricaded herself in her room holding my little brothers' ears, trying to help him sleep as I fought invisible demons in my nightmares.

This was the beginning stages of what I now know as PTSD or Post Traumatic Stress Disorder. I suppose it's not uncommon or surprising that my first emotion was anger, anger at the situation, anger at myself, anger towards my family. To be honest, I clung to rage because of my lack of comprehension of my position, I wasn't supposed to be in England yet. I didn't know what to do, the only thing I could do was mimic the behaviour of my pre-deployment self. Attacking a situation with violence was my instinct then, I didn't have a clear mindset to analyse what I was doing because I was too busy trying to keep occupied. A more mature version of myself would potentially do things differently, at that point in my life though, my way of dealing with things was through anger. It was the emotion that the Army had rendered primary. The first two weeks back in England I spent distracting myself from life. I wanted things to go back to normal. They never did, whatever caused it, the person I was before Afghanistan never returned to me, I never found that missing piece to the puzzle, perhaps I will forever be incomplete or possibly indifferent all the same.

On returning to camp after leave, I sunk slightly lower because I was now completely aware of the fact I had returned to England alone. While I was at home, I at least had the illusion of novelty. The illusion was dismantled once I was in my room back at camp unpacking my kit, mine was the only room out of the entire block of forty-eight that had a bed made. Mine was the only TV that made noise and gave light in the darkness. Places that were once full of life were now empty, my room was on the top floor so each empty step had to be climbed before I could close my door to escape the quiet. Pointless though as I could not hide from the emptiness I felt inside. The time at camp was terrible, every time I walked into my room and closed the door, it felt as if someone had put their hand in my stomach, then turned it upside down. I did everything I could to keep myself out of that room, I would go to visit Ron with the rest of A company. I would linger around dreading the moment I would have to leave. I would play film after film in my room, staring through the screen just to escape silence. I was too scared to sleep in the dark, but the main light was too bright, so I developed this habit of having to keep the TV playing. I would sometimes wake in the middle of the night to the dull noise of the DVD menu with the theme tune ticking over repeating itself.

I can't even count the number of times I laid in bed crying, I would just lay there holding my pillow, darkening the tone of the fabric cases as my tears rolled from my eyes before finally spilling onto the fibres. I don't know why I cried, I just know that I did, I was overwhelmed by my feelings yet had no understanding as to why, I never questioned my irrational emotions, I just accepted them. 'Maybe this is just what happens after war?' I thought to myself. I wouldn't let anyone know, I acted completely fine until I was alone, I felt safe to cry alone. I wasn't embarrassed in front of myself, I would sometimes be still for hours sobbing into my pillow before I could fall asleep, escape reality, avoid the silence. My sleep was often as disturbed as the dreams that came with it. They would not soothe me, and I could not be distracted by counting sheep. The Taliban would enter my head once the silence had left. The catch twenty-two was that I was plagued in both the realm of the sleeping and the awake. I did not dream flashbacks of the time spent at war, my dreams were more sadistic, they were of me being tortured metaphorically. I was unable to move in a paralysis of fear, my demons would eat my soul as I slept, connected to my sleeping body they would empty my bladder.

Going back home was the time in which I could hide, no more empty accommodation, the family house was one of distraction. I liked the noise. My little brother would be running around playing, my sister and her girlfriend would be sat around for convenient conversation. My mum was there for whatever I needed, I would have liked to have spoken to her, the only problem was that I knew neither what to say or how to say it. Quite quickly my inability to release or convey my feelings lead to alcohol once again, when I was drunk I would cry, scream, shout, release all the emotions that would otherwise be backed up like an old hard drive that needs deleting. Once I awoke in the morning, it was like I had been cleansed, apart from the dry mouth and headache of course.

In the early afternoon, I approached the bar in the local weather spoons for a pint of lager. I was asked for ID, which for one reason or the other I did not have, I was refused service. I was old enough to go to war and be blown up yet looked young enough to not be served a pint of lager in my hometown.

Sometime in either September or October the rest of the two companies returned to the UK with their support elements. In the time between me being injured and them coming home we had sustained more casualties. My initial reaction when they were back was that things would go straight back to normal, the complete adverse happened, everyone was different. The first thing we did though was go on a night out, literally the same night they had arrived home. Almost the whole Company went out, all with tanned skin, overgrown hair and clothes that had been packed away for six months. Also coming out with us were bodies that had been wholly detoxed from alcohol. The night was a disaster, before we had even got out of camp the blokes were necking cans of Stella, by the time we had hit town they were ready to kill anyone that came within five meters. It was absolute chaos, I remember 'someone' getting nicked for jumping in the driving seat of a police car. Blokes were running wild, after six months of fighting in Afghanistan, I suppose it's natural that alcohol was going to lead to a bit of a messy caper. Everyone was the enemy, I don't condone this behaviour, it is just an unavoidable occupational hazard. Reading thus far you must have a picture, a step by step guide if you like to how this comes about. Within a week the blokes had gone from fighting for their lives in Afghanistan to a gut full of alcohol in their bloodstreams. This was life at home, alcohol and violence. Perhaps that should be the slogan, welcome to the Infantry, this is how you kill people and here's a bottle of vodka on us.

Once that session was over, we were back home on leave, it was such a quick transition, drop your kit then go, the blokes love it that way as naturally, they want to be home. The trouble is though it's like sending a bunch of attack dogs out in town with no leash on. I had been back in the UK for about a month, so I was used to it, that novelty had worn off, I had spent all my money, was back in my overdraft, so it's not like even spending would occupy me. I was just a kettle of emotion waiting to boil over, even sitting down trying to relax I was restless, something inside me didn't want to sit down, I longed to stand up and smash something. I wasn't massively angry with anyone for any particular reason at all, I was just unsettled, not comfortable in my skin. I thought that it would all change once the boys were back, it didn't, I just felt like I was different to them, I hadn't been there for the last part of the tour. I was stuck at home feeling alienated from my family, from the boys that had returned, to make it worse, I started to take it out on those closest to me. It was like something inside me wasn't letting go, as if I was hiding behind my bravado in order to retain my status as a soldier, apparently I began bullying my little brother.

I was very loud in my behaviour, still just a squad, I was bitter and angry, everything was everyone's fault, but not my own of course. This was ok for now because I was still in the Army, it was my shield to carry on behaving like a squad, still a Rifleman, still one of the blokes. Of course it had to change because I wasn't the same as I was before I left, I started to be treated differently as well and I fucking hated it. I was broken, I was a victim, but I couldn't do what the others bloke did, what kind of a Rifleman can't even fire his fucking rifle? I was the bad apple of the bunch. I had no growth inside of me, I couldn't progress. Instead, I was forced to sit back, watch as the blokes developed as a unit, the fighting force that I was integral to, now didn't need me. That was the hardest thing for me, realising that something I was so invested in, all I ever wanted in my life, something that ran through my blood, something that I was good at, bit by bit it slipped through my fingers until I was nothing more than a spare part. It felt a bit like when you go out with your mates as a child but your mum makes you take your little brother with you, I was the little brother.

My fate was sealed for me, and I was going to get out, I had to. I fucking hated that. I was being pushed out of the family, the blokes would go to the ranges, I would be the one serving out the scoff, in the butts working the targets, distributing ammunition, it was a fucking insult. I now spent my Army career in the med centre avoiding the company because it made me sick to my stomach. It was no ones' fault it was just the natural selection of life, the weak get left behind, I became a problem for them because I was unable to do anything. I was just a headache that they needed a tablet for. Once I had made up my mind though that was it, I spent my life with a sick note in my hand and used every excuse in the world I had to get home. This was sad because I didn't even feel as close to my best friends because I would no longer be Greendog who stayed with the blokes. I was Green who just went home at every opportunity and didn't socialise, I completely isolated myself which was possibly the worst thing I could have done because at that point everyone felt like my enemy.

I pushed at the medical centre for a medical discharge so that I would be able to get out with a War Pension and some compensation. I had to be sent to some Lieutenant Colonel in the medical corps at Tidworth Garrison. I wish I could remember his name so I could name and shame him, the meeting was horrendous, the following story is true. It is the truth about how the feelings for you change once you are of no use to them. I believe that the Brotherhood is a tangible element throughout the Army. However, this expands only as far as the blokes you fight side by side with. Once you reach the higher ranks I believe you are corrupted with politics, budgets and management. This is what I experienced in my appointment with the Lieutenant Colonel that was to decide my fate. He examined me, asked me questions about my injury which I answered. I waited outside while they discussed my case, they being the persons I wish I could name and shame.

I was called back into the room, I was told of my decision, which was a no! They explained that they would not medically discharge me because it would be no benefit. Instead, they would find me employment in either the armoury, handing out weapons, or in the Officers mess where I could serve food. Talk about a kick in the teeth. I argued that, as I had joined up as an Infantryman to fight for my country. They explained that the Army would not pay for me to leave, they elaborated on two other options I had. The first was that as I could no longer do my role, that I could be offered up to the rest of the forces where they may have a use for me. His exact words were:

"To be honest though. No one's going to want to pay to train a one-eyed rifleman with only three years' experience."

That is why I want to name and shame him, in fact at the time I held back kicking his teeth down his smug fucking face. Let that sink in though, read it again if you wish, I had only the year before been blown up on the front line of Afghanistan, now I'm being told that because of my sacrifice no one would want me. The second option was new, 'the PAP 10 process.' It was also called an administrative discharge on medical grounds. What it would allow me to do was leave the Army. I would have to give up my pension and any other entitlements that I had. I could go pretty much straight away because I could no longer fulfil my role.

Like an idiot, I opted for this, I was trying to be grown up about the situation, in 'civvie street' I could maybe make something of myself. If I stayed I would spend my life watching the blokes advance in their careers whilst I rotted in a stale position, stuck between a rock and a hard place. The following process was scarily quick, I had to go and see my regimental career management officer in the battalion headquarters. I asked him for the PAP 10 process, he got me to sign a piece of paper, told me that I had to get it signed by ten people in different positions. This was in July 2010, I got the piece of paper signed that day, I went home that weekend with my car full of all my kit. I had three weeks of summer leave then the 31st August 2010 I was completely discharged. I was nothing to do with the Army, and the Army was nothing to do with me, or so I thought.

Out of the Army, I thought I had it all planned out, my focus was solely on sorting out my life, that all I had to do was get married, have children, get a house and that was it, everything would be normal. I got a job with my mate doing building work, I just sort of dug holes, carried bricks around etc. It was ok because I was able to laugh and do some graft which kept me busy. I started rapping as well, and I don't know why? I've always been into rapping, but now I felt like I had found an identity with it. I had been so used to being affiliated with an outfit. I felt like I needed that belonging and cohesion to something for me to be able to function. Quite embarrassing to be honest looking back, not because of the music, it wasn't brilliant by any standards, but how in depth I took it was. I started talking like Eminem, walking around in shady records red jogging bottoms, I even made a mixtape. I had actual CD cases made up for it then went driving about handing them to people. I called myself Ballistic, which means bomb/bulletproof, I even got it tattooed on myself with music notes. I don't do things by halves, at least I can say that. It's not uncommon for ex-servicemen in my position, perhaps trying to become rappers might be, but searching for that purpose in life is something that happens to everyone. Like football hooligans or gangs, you're searching for a meaning, a family, a brotherhood.

Now I had lost mine I was searching for somewhere else to exist.

Within that year of leaving the Army, I had hit the drink hard, only on the weekends though so it's ok, right? I was aggressive. This was my way of unleashing that aggression. A moron could see that this had manifested from being forced from the institute that I cared for so dearly. Out of anyone I went out with, it had to be me that kicked off, their problems became my problems, as soon as I saw anything going down, I had to get involved straight away. No matter who was arguing I had to be the one to launch and hit someone. I was a disgrace, any excuse I could find to punch someone, I was there, it was that feeling of testosterone, or just the fact that I was so unhappy that if I hit someone, I would feel better about myself.

Aggressiveness aside though I thought I had worked things out, I had got engaged, got myself on the property ladder at the age of twenty-one, also in June 2011 I had found out that I was a successful applicant into the Prison Service. So on the outside looking in I had achieved all my goals that I had set out to get, although because of my attachment to the Army, I could never live up to what I felt I had to prove. Because of the way I felt, I thoroughly resented every single thing that I had outside of that life. I hated going to work, and my relationship was based on arguments and hatred. All I wanted to do to the house was smash it to pieces. Despite this I did what I thought was the right thing, I carried on living that lie, telling myself everything was ok. The number of times I was told that I needed help was ridiculous, I didn't need help I just needed to be left alone that's all. I was, in essence, leading a healthy life, everything that goes up though must come down.

The walls were closing in, metaphorical walls, these walls are not made from breezeblocks, and brick secured by cement and sand. They are glued together by invisible glue created by negative thoughts and stress. They close tighter and constrict my ability to think, my mind races. The more they squeeze the more the mind strives away from a positive thought process. It descends into a spiral of unparalleled confusion, contradiction and miss direction is the path I followed. Bad decisions and snap conclusions are the results. The walls close in, the heart races, the brain lacks clarity and the mouth substitutes for the minds lack of sensible response. My mind in balance has a resemblance to that of a table with a heavy load, supported by unstable legs, legs that are held by the tiniest splint of damaged wood. These pins will never be fully supportive of the amount, there is always a precarious balance between that of the legs of the table and the weight it supports! Very minor incidents out of my routine and these pins will snap enabling the load to uncontrollably tumble around my head with no structure or rational thought. My mind descends into chaos and what would once be thoughts of production, transverse into unhelpful self-destructing sparks which can often fall into panic attacks.

In 2011 I was trying to make a new start, trying to build myself up, but it felt like a lot of things were often one step forward and two steps back. My mind continually battled itself, I pushed everything away that I needed most. Job, house and partner were just too much for me to juggle at once with the vast vortex that is PTSD. The balance became uneven, the legs shook, the table toppled, and I was underneath when it snapped.

PTSD

A frightful desert left behind a young man,
Once was a young boy who got lost in the sand,
Where did my mind go? Many questions I have,

When was I last happy? Why am I so sad?

No matter how much I bathe, the blood remains thick,
I've been to my doctor, yet I remain sick,
I try to be normal but my mind refuses to let me,
I left the war but the war never left me,

It's hard to accept, I am not who I once was,
So much heartache and pain, in this mind that wants love,
When my life at home becomes harder than war,
I find myself wanting to live life no more,

A few years surrounded by thought and regret,
I am proud, I am depressed, I shall never forget,
A thousand voices speak in my head at one time,
Take your life, find love, crack open some wine,

I can't think, I can't sleep, yet still I can cry,
I can't answer your questions so I give no reply,
Please do not ask, which you would not like to know,
Allow me to breathe, I need space to grow,

My mind may have died and many my men,
A cocoon of myself reborn once again,
I try to heal my wounds by closing those doors,
If you don't understand, I died in that war.

- *Gary Green*

Chapter 13
Welcome to the tip of the iceberg

So, from leaving the Army I had become a mess, one that was in denial. I refused to take any acceptance of my behaviour and took complete disregarded to any possibility that the two may be connected. In my fragile state, I had decided that the answer was to keep pushing, that all I had to do was set up a picturesque life for myself, the kind you see on TV, the perfect family unit. This would equal stability and security, thus undoing the unsettlement of leaving my role as a Rifleman. You see the thing was, I hadn't handed in my notice, I wasn't fed up with working overtime or needed more money to support my family. I never had a boss that gave me too much stick, so I had enough and quit my job like an unhappy employee in an office job. That I could handle, that would be a reasonable circumstance. My circumstances were not normal, I never lost a job, I lost my identity. I never wanted to leave, I had to. My choice was that of a mentally tortured family member looking upon an ill relative deciding when to switch off the life support machine. The options were to stay in the Army and live a life of serving the officers their pretentious meals or work in the stores and hand out weapons to the men I had once fought beside. To forever watch them progress through their careers as I gathered dust. My other option was to turn off the life support machine and seek salvation elsewhere, I had to sever the ties to the life I love, to quit, to accept defeat, to admit I was no longer useful to my country.

Moving into the prison service seemed like a logical chess move, keep me institutionalised, keep me in that family orientated organisation, thou shall prevail. I had to go away for training, Rugby I think it was, all went well for the academic side of things, I excelled in my practice, then it came to the leaving do. We were going for a few drinks in the local town to celebrate, the age-old story of me fucking up everything in sight. I just wasn't mentally stable, my humour and behaviour exceeded that of any sane person. When I got back to the academy where our accommodation was, my mind was completely in the state of being Rifleman Green, like I had found my block, my playground. I started kicking the doors of the other trainees, let off a fire extinguisher, finally throwing a bin through someones' open window. I can't possibly remember what was going through my mind, it was just how I acted, that was acceptable where I had come from. I wasn't where I had come from though, I could not distinguish between the two worlds. I have no idea how I got away with it. There were zero repercussions for my actions, I wish this were an isolated incident, it never was, it never will be, for some reason once alcohol touches my lips, I cause chaos.

It's hard to get across how I felt, how I still feel. My problems run far past the fact that I am completely incapable of acting civilised with alcohol. The aggression that came from me over the simplest of things, the tongue that came with it. I could be driving along in the car, not have the right directions so start a full-blown fight with myself until the point I am reduced to tears. Rationally I can see the solution, 'pullover, find the right directions,' at the time though I'm clawing at my face until bleeds, punching the steering wheel. I went to my Mums house to find something I had left there, can't remember what it was, she told me it was under her bed, my mind recalls that much. I was completely sober, I couldn't find it, I flipped her bed, pulled her wardrobe over, kicked the door off the hinges and emptied the contents of her drawers over the floor. This was a lesson for her not to lose something of mine. What a cunt, what person does that? What had I become, what had left the Army or what from Afghanistan hadn't left me? That's not healthy behaviour, I wouldn't do that, contradicting I guess because I did. I don't know why? All I know is at that moment I wanted to do it, even straight afterwards something in my mind goes. "Gaz, shouldn't have done that mate".

If I couldn't find the remote control, the table would get flipped over, the sofa kicked, repeatedly punched until I just sort of slump when my energy zapped. I was tortured entirely, in my rage I would shout things about Afghanistan that made no sense, "fucking Taliban." I would yell as I punched another hole in the door because my shirt wasn't ironed, there was no milk, or I couldn't find my shoes. Anger is a funny emotion for an Infantry Soldier. It' what drives you in the heat of battle. Motivate you to kill the enemy at all costs! This aggression is drilled into you from day one as you have read, transformed into a nemesis to all of Her Majesty's enemies. The Battle Ground is his playing ground, the Battle Ground is where he is designed to be, it's where he needs to be. As I said, anger is a powerful tool. In the wrong environment, it's as counterproductive to progression as sand in a petrol tank. The wrong setting is at home, in a pub, in traffic. The aggression is always here, you never lose the ability to kill someone. Once that attack is installed in you, it continually bubbles under the skin, if not moderated and used appropriately then it can eat at you until it surfaces in the wrong places.

This is how my relationship broke down. My anger was always pushed to the people it shouldn't have, the person who had sent me letters, came to the hospital once I had been blown up. It was nothing more than two people who fell in love at the wrong time. I had no business being in a relationship when I wasn't even mentally or emotionally stable enough to get out of bed in the morning. I was an abusive partner, never physically, I was brought up well enough to know that one of the worst things you could ever do was raise a hand to a woman. Subconsciously without meaning though, my passive aggressiveness was mentally abusive. I was carrying on because I thought it was the right thing to do, I wasn't happy because my situation was a puzzle piece that didn't fit, I was self-destructing without thought. Piece by piece I systematically pulled my life apart, I wasn't trying to, it was just a natural occurrence like metal rusting outside, I was the oxygen that broke down the very fabric of my life.

I must be a ceremonious person because it seems that any event brings out the worst in me, or perhaps I do it on purpose because I don't want to be happy. At a family occasion I pushed my Mum over a car while trying to fight a bouncer, my cousins' girlfriends' birthday I punched her workmate and threw him over a set of drums. Even Christmas, me and my ex-partner argued about something or nothing at all, I took her presents' outside her Mums house and kicked them across the street. The behaviour of a borderline psychopath was normal behaviour for me. First, the mood swings start. I'm quiet, my teeth grind then my head starts to tilt, my eyes widen, if I'm standing, I'll probably twitch on the spot because my body is shaking as my blood boils. This could be started by absolutely anything, the mention of someone's name I don't like, a comment towards me that I've done something wrong, or as simple as somebody not doing the exact thing I want them to. Of course, this escalates into an argument where my tongue shouts things I haven't even thought of yet, the most personal, damaging of insults without remorse or proper rationalisation of the justice or deservingness. Then once this has failed to satisfy my hurt, I destroy something that means something to me, just to top it off with something that will cause me to hate myself when the anger stops. This has been anything from watches, clothes, phones, flowers or Christmas presents. I have to destroy something of value. Then the anger wears off, I'm all very sorry for my behaviour, but all the damage in the world has been done.

How can the celebration of moving into your new home be forever remembered as a dark day? Well, the answer to that question has been repeated through time for people like me, easy! Give me alcohol and chaos will ensue, I was still in denial of any problems, so a celebratory barbeque is going to be washed down with the devils' liquor. The mood in the morning was one full of excitement, an underlying tone of pride as I was about to showcase my life to family and friends.

'Look at what I've done, I own property, I have a new career, yes Gary you have done well since leaving the Army'.

I spent the morning cleaning the house, tending to every detail, tidied the garden making sure I had put enough chairs out, all in excellent order with tables for everyone's food and drinks. I even made sure the tables were spread with everyone's favourite crisps, snacks etc. The BBQ was in a position, so I could cook while socialising, and I had spent money on an oversized selection of meats. I also supplied a ridiculous amount of alcohol that I refrigerated or placed in ice buckets. There was beer for the boys, wine for the girls and spirits for everybody, I wanted it to be perfect, leaving just enough time for a bath washed down with a Corona.

The afternoon started nice, I looked fresh, presentable even. I cooked up the food, and my partner was chatting to her friends, everyone was enjoying themselves. Then after I felt tipsy I cracked open the first bottle of vodka, everyone was hesitant apart from me, "c'mon don't be a fanny it's a party." I practically forced people to drink my exceeding measures of vodka lemonade. That is of course how I start, from this point on I'm a nightmare, everyone feels like they're treading on eggshells in case I lose my temper or take something the wrong way. I'm not a bully by any means. I love taking the mick out of people though, like a swashbuckling swordsman with his blade I'm very precise without delicacy as I thrust my words in an offensive flurry. I think I'm funny. There's no malice with my puncture, I just don't know when to apply the brakes.

With one vodka too many, boys will be boys, one of my mates tripped my little brother up, it was only as a joke, they were play-fighting. Of course, Ashley comes up to me crying. He's a sensitive little soul, well me, I was going to play the part of big brother (not like I had done anything to protect him before - what a joke I am). I started shouting and swearing in front of everyone, embarrassing. For one reason or another I lost it and tried kicking him in the face, I missed, instead my foot connected with his drink like a perfectly placed volley in FIFA sending it flying through the air and smashed. Once again, my heart was in the right place, but my mouth was miscalculated entirely, like my actions. The night only progressed downhill from there, of course, my partner and I started rowing as she called me embarrassing. I didn't know what embarrassing was, I was drunk. By the end of the night I was sat outside in the dark with my sister, two of my cousins were there as well, my mates had gone into town, but I had decided to stay home. My ex was inside with her mates without us, I found this very unsociable, in my drunk state I text her calling her a cunt, followed up with, 'get you and all your cunt mates out of my house'. I then headed off into town. My cousins wouldn't come with me saying it was going to be trouble, of course it fucking was, because they wouldn't go with me I launched an empty pint glass at them as they walked down the road. Shards of glass soaked with more vodka than lemonade spread across the pavement as I climbed into my taxi ready to be transported to the town to reunite myself with people who wanted to drink.

To be honest, I can't remember what happened in town, I'm sure I would've kicked off, but that remains a mystery from my point of view. Also, it bears small significance in light of the events that are to be explained.

I think I received the message in town, it was responsive to the, 'get you and your cunt mates out of my house,' text. It was to tell me that she was leaving me. This wasn't the first time, I had done things like this before, an apology with a slight pass of blame to the alcohol will sort this situation out. Upon return to my castle, I was slightly too wavy to realise the lack of cars that remained outside of the house. Paul and Jay were with me with the intention of carrying on the party. As we clambered through the front door, it was quite clear to see that there had been a burglary, I had been robbed, well after a fashion anyway, the house had been half emptied. It turns out that the text I received wasn't another one of those, 'we need to talk in the morning' kind of texts, it was severe. While I had been in town, they had cleared out the house in their cars. I think this was premeditated because who the fuck drives to a house party? I had visions of them routing through all my stuff, giggling as they were doing it, like naughty school girls skipping class together. I felt like an arrow had been shot straight through my chest. I was somewhere between sick to the stomach in heartbreak and wanting to spit fire in outright anger. As I looked around it was as if time had slowed down, just like the feeling I had when I had been blown up. I was stood in my house, but in my head the bricks from the wall were drifting away, turning into sand as they swarmed around my body in a tornado. I was no longer in reality, I was in a chasm, once again neither living or dead, just existing in my black hole.

Anger very quickly pulled me out of that place, I was stood in my front garden repeatedly ringing the agent of abandonment that had left me in an empty shell. My calls were ignored, accompanied by messages telling me to leave her alone, that it was over, that there was nothing I could do. The only problem is, being told there is nothing I can do, doesn't tend to go down well with me. In my head, I was thinking, 'I need to go there and sort this out.' I'm a bit of a loose cannon like that. I launched my phone against the wall as another one of my calls were rejected, I grabbed my keys. As I headed toward my car Paul tried to stop me, he was in a slightly better state than me, also not corrupted by blind rage. Paul was in the wrong place at the wrong time as I swung multiple punches at his face until he fell to the floor. Jay was the next to try and stop me, I quickly dispatched him over the bonnet of my car then closed the door. Without thought, I drove straight at his last-ditch attempt to stop me driving off drunk out of my face. Looking back, I know this was the wrong move, there's no excuse risking other lives due to my feelings, however, that was not the mind of a reasonable person.

I don't know what was going through my head as I raced through narrow streets, leaving behind a cocktail of an over-revved engine mixed with the stench of stale vodka that leaked from my breath like the exhaust fumes that trailed me. I was hitting speeds of ninety miles per hour as I flew past taxis that were probably dropping off the last of the night crawlers that passed out in the back seats. Bounced over speed bumps without a thought of slowing down. I didn't even know what I was going to do, what I was going to say, I just knew that if I got there in time I could sort this mess out before It got too far. As I pulled up, I thought a little parallel park would be the solution, as I reversed I went straight to the side of one of her mates' cars. In my state, I thought, 'well I've hit it now, I might as well carry on and park behind it.' My wing mirror came off as I scraped the entire length of the car as tried to park behind it. However, another car was there, and I scraped the entire length of that car as well. It made an awful sound as the cars ground together, there was a bang as my alloyed wheel hit the curb. I parked with one wheel on the pavement and the rest of the car facing the road. One of the neighbours heard the commotion, he came running out, he knew me so acted as a neutraliser in the situation, he took my keys and tried to calm me down. I had other plans though. I went banging on the door, the door was answered by her Mum, the whole weight of the situation collapsed on me as I burst into tears. Everyone else had warned me that it was coming, they could see it as clear as a flame in the dark. I had been completely oblivious to what was going on. There were a lot of tears as I sat there, I could finally see the train wreck for what it was, there was no more cover over my eyes, it's as if everything that had happened in my life finally collapsed on top of me.

Needless to say, that all of her mates came to investigate the noise that had woken up the street outside, one of them called the police to report me. At the time I couldn't have given a fuck if they had called the Queen to report the incident, my mind was running at too fast of a pace to realise anything that was going on. I was trying to fix too much at once, I was always taught in the Army that there was still a way out, every problem can be fixed. "Bring me a solution, not a problem." That's what I was trying to do, my head was far too cloudy, the more I tried to solve this broken puzzle the more I wanted to get a loaded gun, swallow the barrel and pull the trigger. For all the thoughts that I had, all that I wanted to say, nothing came from my mouth except the bitter sobbing of a man that had been too strong for too long. Every time I opened my mouth to speak I howled in sobs, her Mum held me for the entire time, until the Police arrived anyway. As they took me outside I was, for lack of better words, greeted by an audience. They were all stood around the cars that I had left looking like they had got in the way of a tank. It was poor timing actually because as I was being escorted to the police car, Paul and Jay had pulled up in a taxi. For some reason, perhaps just real mental illness, I started laughing as I saw them. This painted an even worse portrait of me as one of her mates burst into tears as she screamed, "he's got no remorse." She had no idea what had been going through my head for the two years prior let alone in the last few minutes. I had to have my fingerprints placed on record, my mug shot taken and a statement recorded. As soon as I got inside that cell and put my head on the blue mattress I fell straight to sleep. In the morning I was interviewed again, my head was pounding, I would have admitted to murder if it had got me out of there any quicker. I was released pending a court hearing, I walked home with my tail between my legs. Of all the walk of shames I've done in my time, this was the worst.

It was time to pick up my life, it had been run down, pissed on, kicked in the face a few times and now it had a criminal record. I was convinced that I could sort it out though. As I reached my street I saw the broken glass, not that I needed one, but it was a stark reminder of the night before. My first task was to find my phone, I found it shattered under my kitchen window. It was strange as I had only lived in the house for three months, so I wasn't at home here anyway. It was still chilling how lonely and different it now felt. I felt like a murderer returning to a crime scene, an accidental murderer though, I hadn't committed a crime I meant to commit. A murderer may perhaps want to go back to the crime scene for sexual gratification or out of pride, I didn't want to be here. It was a perfect example of getting kicked while on the floor. Looking at the empty house enabled me to see for the first time clearly, exactly what I had just flushed down the toilet. The previous night I had seen the bricks turn to sand as they flew around my outer body, now the blocks were solid. Half empty wardrobes, the lack of female presence, no remnants of anything 'his and hers' remained in the four walls. Even the paint seemed cold on the walls, for a short period this had been home, it was now nothing more than an object filled with smaller objects.

My ex came to the house, for her it must have been a different feeling, I suppose it was like a prisoner of war returning to the camp that she once stayed captive. As soon as I saw her, my first instinct was to hold on, to try and regain control of the situation. I was broken, instead of trying to fix myself my heart was still trying to rebuild us, something that had long since fallen apart. It's easy for anyone to look in hindsight, make the right decisions all over again, of course, I should have seen everything for what it was and healed myself first. At that time though I was doing what anyone would have done, trying to do what my heart thought it wanted. With this in mind, you can see that we were heading in two completely different directions, I was trying to fix everything, she was trying to walk away, it was the ultimate rejection, I cried, vowed to change and promised the world in exchange for another chance. The more I pushed, the more I begged, the more she told me no, it was harder because I genuinely thought I could fix everything, being told no was soul destroying. It was like one of those dreams where you want to run but your legs won't move. The more she said no, the more my heart was breaking until the very last strand was holding it together, that was cut as she handed back the engagement ring. On that sofa I felt like I had just died, I was sick to my stomach, it felt as though if I tried hard enough, I could puke my heart straight out of my chest. I went into complete breakdown mode, this was the realisation that all was not right. Every memory I had hidden from over the past two years had just snuck up on me, as I turned around to see them they had hit me with a left hook that sent me straight to the floor.

With the weight of the situation coming down on me, I felt the way a nail does as it watches the hammer flying towards it. My floodgates were open, my tears streamed as I sobbed into the oncoming slaughter that my mind played on itself. She left as my Mum got to the house, I laid on the sofa inconsolable, like a baby crying with teething pain, no dummy would soothe me. My Mum held me, we spoke, she intended to let me know that everything would be ok, anyone who has ever felt heartbreak knows that the only cure is time. Not only that though, I was now able to see that I was utterly fucked up. I wasn't just a heart split in two, I was a mind split into a million pieces. In this position the best way to describe my mind-set was hopeless. I saw no way out, no end to the black hole that I found myself in. I think this feeling was the reason I could not stop crying, it wasn't that I now felt lonely, it was because I now felt genuinely empty. The very act I had been playing was swept away from me, and I was nothing. Once again, I found myself feeling like a broken screwdriver, a worn-out tyre pulled from the alloy of a new car tossed onto a burning pile.

Once my panic attack had worn off, I stayed in my pit of self-worthlessness, hidden in my black hole, I don't remember eating or moving for three days. I was hibernating from reality as a hedgehog sleeps from the winter's cold. If I could I would have died on that spot, just given up, "thanks for the memories but that's me done, I'm out, see ya later." The funny thing is I didn't die, I was empty, without a heart, I thought I couldn't survive. How would blood pump through my veins? I remember going to my Nans bungalow, escorted with my Mum who for the short term was not allowed to leave my side, I was borrowing her heart while mine grew back. My mum was holding a leaflet for Combat Stress, the veteran's mental health charity. I called them, they said I had PTSD, from the questions they asked in conjunction with the answers I gave it was pretty much a no-brainer. I was told I had been suffering for a long time, now it was cemented.

I went to see the Doctor in Banbury, he was younger than I expected, he was also a massive prick. I don't use the term lightly either, he was a cock sucking moron with a long face and a shit haircut. I write of him in a non-favourable way because he was as useful as a heater in a desert, I explained to him what had happened over the last three years. His response was along the lines of, 'I don't think you have PTSD because you don't have flashbacks, you're just an angry young man, I will put you on a waiting list for therapy, but that will probably take six months.'

"Angry young man? I will give you angry young man."

In my head I reached over the desk, grabbed him by the hair while I bounced his head off the table five hundred times, then used him as a trampoline, giggling as his blood splattered the walls like a modern art exhibition. I was clinically depressed at this part of my life, neither my Mum or I could believe what he had said, neither of us could afford a taxi either so we walked the two miles back to my Nans bungalow. I could still barely stomach food, I could not go back to my house either, it was too much of a sore reminder, kind of the same way my eye is a reminder of my uselessness. Every time I rub my face, the shrapnel from that explosion stands out like a brail book, the words would be something along the lines of, 'unlucky rubber ducky, you're now a waste of fucking space.' They may not be that harsh. Now they would say, 'well done, keep fighting.' The rough translation of my brail face piece honestly depends on which Gary is reading them.

Once I had spoken to Combat Stress, relayed the Doctors message, I had a sense of hope, they were sympathetic, also they were angry, they explained that PTSD was only just beginning to get any notice for the demon it was. It's an invisible wound, it wasn't as aesthetically evident as a missing leg. They agreed for a care worker to see me, he would take notes on me, asses my well-being, this would give them an idea of the treatment I would need to pull me out of the place I was stuck in. In the meantime, though there was the problem of my house, I couldn't pay the mortgage with my War Pension, I needed to sort it out. I needed to rent it out before I started to miss payments. At this point it would be unfair not to mention my sidekick who I used to rap with, we may not be friends anymore, but I owe him a debt of gratitude as he certainly helped me through this period of my life. He was a good problem solver, he also arranged for work to be done on the house so that I could rent it out for its potential value. As fate would have it, the plasterer who was working on the house needed a place to rent, two plus two equals four in my book. It was a favour for a favour, he rented the house from me without any paperwork or need for anything more to be said, if you know what I mean, also bit by bit he will plaster the house for me for free. I am no David Dickinson, but I know a good deal when I hear one. That night I made five trips back and forth between my Mums house and mine, each trip I moved like a tortoise, not slow, the analogy is used to describe the fact I was carrying my house on my back. Each trip entailed suitcases, holdalls, even carrier bags until I had finished the job of emptying the structure of my memories. They could rent the place as furnished, from the sofa to the bed sheets, even the knife and forks were left behind. At the age of twenty-three or twenty-four, can't remember and can't be bothered to pretend I care about the exact age of myself, the point is I was moving back into my Mums box room in her council house at that age. I felt like shit, not a nice feeling, I hadn't lived with my Mum since I had joined the Army four years previous, yet here I was back in the small room with a single bed and the same wardrobe I had used since I was eleven years old.

With my accommodation squared away, I needed to sort my head out, I did see Combat Stress, once I think, my care worker came to see me, took some notes and instantly referred me for residential rehabilitation. As time went on, I felt ok, with the feeling of stress significantly reduced by moving back in with my Mum, I felt better. I had retracted back to my juvenile state. My Mum had become my source of comfort, I didn't need therapy because instead of facing my fears I now used my Mum to hide from them. I could get used to this life, watching daytime TV, Mum cooking me dinner, watching the soaps at night, it was easy. With the heartbreak there was the odd night I cried myself to sleep, my ex had been secretly meeting up with the person she had left to get with me in the first place only two and half years previous. So, us getting back together kind of went down the pan, all that was left was for me to carry on being a big baby. I thought I was going to be a rapper anyway, so I had no worries, Tim Westwood was going to knock at the door any day now and offer me a record deal, not.

I decided to start doing building again, I got a job back with my mate labouring, this lead to some carpentry work, I'm good with my hands, so it suited me. Also kept me out of trouble during the day and earned me some steady cash that I could give my Mum. It's a sociable job, I also rekindled my friendships from school, we were like a match in a petrol station when we were together though, we loved the drink, every weekend I was filling my emptiness with cheap booze and cheap women. A rough guess would be around one hundred women in the two years that I spent in this cycle, I am not proud of that fact, it's just another piece of collateral damage, another by-product of my condition. Weekend drinking became weekday drinking, instead of going out Friday and Saturday, I would start hitting the town on a Thursday as well. Then they started doing Karaoke on a Wednesday, be rude not to attend, I was spending all my wages on drinking through the week. Not only that I was having days off sick because I was hung-over or turning up to work smelling like I had spent the night sleeping in a bottle of whiskey. I was calling my boss on a Thursday morning asking him to pick me up from random houses where I had chosen to rest my head for the night. One time he even dropped a girl back home in the back of the works van. My escapades were becoming too much, I had pushed slightly too hard and lost my job. I was back to square one, but luckily my Mum was there to cook me dinner. I was jobless, living with my Mum, I also had a very thirsty appetite for alcohol, women and destruction.

Chapter 14

Taking a walk on the wild side

My Mum stuck with me, she was the guardian angel, but I was about to sell my soul to the devil, there was going to be no angel that I would not spit in the face off. A large part of me had been missing since the day I was blown up, I clung on to the rest because I had had my own house, a woman and found a job. With that behind me, I traded the rest of myself in. With a space to fill, I don't believe in mistakes, but I do believe the path I went down was the wrong one to choose, I chose to fill that gap with alcohol and women. Which I suppose wasn't too detrimental except for the bad reputation it gave me, not too surprising due to my actions, but it was what it quickly developed into that was the tragedy of this period in my life. It's no secret me and alcohol have a very chaotic and heavy ongoing relationship, but the relationship I was entering now, was alcohols snow white, heart racing cousin.

Like any seedy story, a dirty scene needs to be set, and mine could be no more uncouth than that of a pub toilet. I was Intoxicated with alcohol, sweating from dancing and had breath smelling like cigarette smoke. As fate would have it in the bathroom at that time was a friend, this friend was savvier in the way of most things seedy than I was, my friendship circles were yet to be expanded into the further field of what a phone call and quick transaction with the right provider could lead you to. I was naïve. This friend offered me a line of cocaine, an experience I was very much a stranger to, the thought bounced around my head, every single event in my life that had changed my way of thinking, sculpted my personality was now making me question the very reaction that would usually be 'NO'. No such reaction surfaced, 'fuck it why not?' My heart was racing, I was nervous. We went into the cubical, and he proceeded to perform the operation perfected with experience. The rock of cocaine comes in a see-through Sealy bag most commonly. Depending on how much you want in each line you crumble off an amount from the rock, you then place a note over the debris using a bank card to crush and rub it into a powder. The note is lifted, the dust is then broken apart and separated into lines. Roll up your currency into a straw, then all that is required is the willing nostril of a lost and confused veteran.

I took hold of the note, 'there's still time to back out,' was the thought racing through my head. 'Fuck it, in for a penny in for a pound,' held my left nostril ran the note across the line of white rocket fuel and snorted up my right like a hoover. The feeling was intense, somewhat instantaneous, my eyes seemed to widen, my mind was racing, my heart was pacing, and my nose was numb. It was an incredible feeling of being in the best mood ever, I wanted to talk to everyone because everyone was a friend. I grabbed my two drinks and went straight to the dance floor, for some reason I just dropped them on the floor, watched them shatter and explode like two mini volcanoes then ran out of the bar and went straight to the club. The rest of the night was a mystery that seemed to happen in ten seconds, adrenaline coursed through every muscle fibre, fired like a cannon into every vein, every atom in my body buzzed alive. That was my first experience with drugs and what catapulted me down a slippery path. The tip of the iceberg had been breached, the snow was falling down the mountain, building up, I was at the centre of the snowball, and I was gathering speed.

Once I had that buzz there was no stopping me, it became a habit if I was drinking I had to have a cheeky line. Otherwise, it was almost as if I wasn't drinking at all. The only thing was that It became more of a daily occurrence rather than a weekend warrior. I wasn't working, I was single, I was depressed but most of all I was bored. I had nothing to occupy my time except drinking. Monday to Sunday. I was Charlie Sheen, only a skint version banging three percent cocaine up his nose, might as well have been snorting baking powder to be honest. There was the odd occasion where you would take something that knocked your socks off. I didn't care though, as soon as I got my war pension, I was out to blow it, three grams for one hundred pounds, that would do me for a night along with a cheap bottle of vodka to ram down my neck while I was waiting for the club to open. I would be the best part of paralytic before I even got there, maybe a line in the park on my way to town just to keep my buzz going. I remember once I put my profile picture of me holding two grams next to my nostrils, felt like a right prick when I saw it the next day, shameful. It was no holds barred as I got inside the club, if I were lucky I would be able to rob a cheap bottle of champers that had been put out for guest list parties. Be the only one on the dance floor in an empty club with what looked like a mint polo hovering around my nostril.

The thing with this lifestyle is that it has to end, the party will stop at some point, the clubs, unfortunately, don't go on for twenty-four hours, and so they close. Once they settle I would still be buzzing, I couldn't go home with that feeling, there had to be an after party, plus I still had a gram tucked into my sock. When you start doing coke, you find lots of other people that do coke. You're all still buzzing so you usually find a house you can all go back to. A bit like football I guess, the best place to play is where there are lots of other players. I won't disclose the names of people or where I used to go, that's not my goal. I will give you one name of someone who was always there, Gary Green, alive with my new identity I would be in every house, flat or crack den I could get to. For about two years I lived in the routine of getting slung out the club, staggering to one of the local, 'establishments' let's call them, with a cheap bottle of vodka in hand. As the wallet drew thinner, the bottle would become three-litre bottles of cider, a few times I had just grabbed whatever bottle was to hand and ran for it. You never quite get the feeling of true disgust until you realise it's a weekday afternoon, you're sat in the same clothes you've been wearing for two days/nights straight, stale with the smell of cigarettes and body odour. Usually, you're too tired even to talk, and lips are chapped and dry from the excess cocaine you've been rubbing into your gums. You look across the smoky room as you're passed a CD case with a slug of white go powder on, you place the note to your nostril, as you attempt to snort a line with both your right, then left nostril you realise they're both blocked. Where the nostrils are blocked you can no longer fit any coke up there, the note just moves the white line out of shape rather than transporting it from case to bloodstream, the coke you're taking now is not to get you high but merely to keep you awake, barely keeping you away from normality. You stick a finger in your nose, pull out a sticky concoction of white powder and snot, no point wasting it, so you rub the paste in your gums then swallow, not quite the picture you imagine in your head when you hear of A-list celebrities taking drugs is it? A couple of years ago I was fighting on the front line of Afghanistan, yet here I sit, desperate to fit in somewhere, so consumed with my lack of identity that I attach myself to the simplest pleasure. As I began to remember my depression, I took another drink. I'm not drunk anymore I'm just in limbo, feeling neither dead or alive. The party had stopped, I had greasy skin, indigestion and a blocked nose, time to carry myself home, lie in bed, cry and wait until I wake up so I can do all it over again.

The nights spent crushing up powder were more numerous than those I never, It started for fun, another buzz that intensified the feeling of freedom than what you gain from necking vodka energy drinks in the club. The euphoria of losing your inhabitations stimulate the neurons in your brain, making you believe that this is the reality, the rest of the world is a lie. As I dance, as I gain sweat pounding the dance floor, manoeuvring my way through the night, I'm released. The hangman's grip feels loose around my neck here, here with the music pounding my eardrums, the voices in my head are silent, anything feels like a small sacrifice for the trip, this vacation from my suicidal mind. The problem is I have no stop button, nothing in my mind can tell me when I have had enough, the drink flows, double, triple, quadruple vodkas fill my stomach, my blood becomes more alcohol than the white and red cells that usually pass through them. The booze begins to best me, a stumble to the bathroom will cure me of this weakness, my phone becomes the platform for my medication, the rolled up note the scalpel for my surgery, the white powder becomes the antibiotic that counteracts my drunken state. Selling my soul to the devil for a few more hours in wonderland, walk on the wild side, take my hand down the rabbit hole as I go to a world where anything is possible. Follow me to a world without PTSD. Well, so I thought, apparently there were many moments of PTSD down the rabbit hole, I just can't remember them as well as those who witnessed them. For instance, my Mum remembers the night she found me outside screaming naked in the snow, crying as I yelled the name Abdul John as my body froze. My Mum remembers a lot, in my worse states where I was blacked out from my mind, I was at home, screaming, smashing up furniture. When I woke up my mind was blank, I quickly grabbed the nearest drink I could find to make sure my memory stayed clear of all that may make me realise that the rabbit hole was not the wonderland I believed it to be. I was convinced I was the smooth Lothario that I imagined I was, I thought I was respectful as I drank myself into a coma. I believed I was funny as I necked pints of vodka, I wasn't, the reality was that as I drank myself into these states, I was leaving behind a trail of disgust, violence and abuse. The alcohol, drugs and smart mouth was keeping me away from reality, but everyone else was right there watching me as I clambered down the steepest holes that you can find yourself in. I was naïve ever to think that I had positioned myself somewhere in life away from my mind, I had merely just forgotten it was there at all. I woke up once and found a knife with blood on it in my room, cuts on my wrist with no explanation, no suicide note, I completely ignored it, things you do when you're drunk right. I had no recollection of this happening, I remember very little from those times, blurred visions of embarrassment remain burned in my skull, I was literally torturing myself.

The anger that flowed through my veins became utterly overwhelming, with the alcohol and drug abuse I was unable to hold onto it. I spent my nights trying to find trouble, you would be a fool to believe that the dance floor was the only place I blew off steam, any excuse for some fisty cuffs and I was there. Once in Northampton, we chased some blokes around for a good half hour before we caught up with them, the lid blew, steam poured from my ears as I screamed, like a Viking going into battle. I clawed, shouted and then laughed as I tore him around, like a deer in headlights he was paralysed by my anger. One mate who I won't mention cried as I screamed and pulled hair from my head in my fit of rage, I yelled at this poor bloke about Afghanistan, something he knew nothing about, I never even hit him, I just screamed, beating myself, grabbing him by the face. I had all but ripped his shirt off him, it was shredded as if a tiger had mauled him, they had started on us to be fair, but for me, it was nothing more than an excuse to release that demon inside of me. I can't explain enough how much of my life this consumed, night after night I was fuelled with a mix of alcohol, cocaine and mental illness, tortured on the outside, exploding on the inside. I had punched more people than I can count, put cigarettes out on people's faces, slept with girls whose names I would never remember, Passed out in gardens, parks, pubs. I had spent more nights per week in a stranger's houses putting more drugs inside my system than I had in my bedroom. Every night I was picking up two to three grams of cocaine, if I had no money, then I was scrounging around mates who would give me some or get myself in debt to make sure I had my gear. I still haven't told you the worst parts of this story, this time in my life was yet to get darker, the truth about what PTSD does to your brain is in the tongue it leaves you with, the spiteful venom that shoots out as you talk. The most embarrassing things I can think off do not compare to the regrets I have when it comes to my Mum. A mother that done nothing more than love her son took the brunt of my hate, I don't know if I was punishing her for loving me or just trying to push her away to hurt myself. I wrote a poem for her that undoes none of the hurt I caused her but will hopefully one day make her understand that the boy that left England on the 9th June 2009 is somewhere still inside of me.

Poem to my Mum

You gave birth to me on the 5th of June,
You comforted me with a softened tune,
Nursed me to sleep with a mothers love,
Stroked my head with an angels touch,

You fed me, clothed me and raised me right with morals,
You taught me brains over brawn would settle my quarrels,
As I grew older, you stayed my mother,
Distance would never, distant each other,

You cried as I left, as they dressed me in green,
You're always my Mum but my oaths to the Queen,
They carved me and trained me and sent me to war,
Mum, I'm your son but your child no more,

Into the desert, I soldier through fear,
A thousand miles away I feel you near,
I stare death in the face one thousand times over,
My face is disfigured my war is over,

A million times I have sat, and I've cried,
Another battle to fight but this one inside,
My enemy and I is one in itself,
The screams in my head so nothing can help,

A cuddle from you can stifle pain for a while,
There's no other bond stronger than mother and child,
I need you now as I needed you then,
Mum, I'm in your arms your child again.

- *Gary Green*

For some reason when I come home I had to pick a fight with her, as I write this I search inside for a reason, to try and somehow justify it but I have no answer. Can't I blame Afghanistan? I do know that when I came home, I was not the same person, the things I have done I know in my heart would not have happened if I had chosen a different path in life. Why have I become a monster? What did that war do to me?

My reputation as a veteran drifted away, the more I drank, the more I became seen as a wreck head, a thug, a druggie, an alcoholic. People told me they were worried about me, people I was drinking with even told me I had a problem. I just laughed it off as I drank more, inside I knew I was suffering from an illness, that it was a matter of time before I had to sober up. Part of me never wanted to though, I wanted to stay drunk until I died so that I never had to face real life. The more I remained hidden from reality, the less and less I wanted to go back, my family were pleading with me, begging me to stop, trying to remind me of the person I once was.

Of course, I never enjoyed being this person, but I preferred being this person than who I would have to be if I faced my demons. I wasn't strong enough, I couldn't mentally cope with having to admit to my faults. Plus I always had some excuse, a way of reasoning that I wasn't out of control, that I'm just young and enjoying the ecstasy of carefree youth. This wasn't the truth at all. I only continued to drink because if I stopped this train, then the carriages carrying my emotional baggage would catch up with me. My financial situation was so bad that I was even blacklisted from having a mobile phone, I spent my life buying top-ups from the garage whenever I could afford one. I had to be connected to WIFI to speak to anyone, which in this day in age, also being twenty-four years old was very embarrassing. My Mum was a carer for my Nan and got very minimal money for her work, yet still, I would be begging her for the last five-pound note from her purse so that I could get a few pints of lager from the local boozer. This way I could meet some people who would feel sorry for my war stories and perhaps buy me a few drinks or give me a free line in the toilets. If this wasn't bad enough, I was receiving a letter after letter from the mortgage company threatening to take me to court because I hadn't paid my mortgage in god knows how long. I had been renting it to a friend, of course, I hadn't been telling him that the second he gave me the rent money I was buying three grams of coke. It wouldn't stay in my hands long at all, by the time I had purchased my gear, paid off another dealer for the last couple of weeks, I had enough for a good night out, maybe two if I was lucky.

The more letters I received from energy companies, mobile phone contractors, banks, bailiffs, council tax etc, the more I thought, "fuck going back to reality," if I go back there I have to sort all this shit out. I owed a lot of money to a lot of people. The problem was I was paying off drug debts before I was paying off my mortgage, my thought process. 'I need to get my priorities right, if I pay the mortgage company they aren't going to give me another house, if I pay my drug dealer he will give me more drugs.' Pay him first then, it's a no-brainer. I was on the verge of losing my house, possibly days away from court I can't remember, I probably rolled the letters up to snort coke with, as is my nature for some unknown reason there is an angel up there watching over me, I tend to be very susceptible to getting lucky. I received a letter through the door from the Armed Forces Compensation Scheme. This letter stated the award system had changed and I was entitled to twenty thousand pounds more compensation that will be getting paid into my account within one week. Once again a get out of jail free card with my name on it, probably ill-deserved to be honest, not for my injuries or my time served under the Queen, but certainly for my behaviour since. Perhaps I deserved to lose my house for a wake-up call, or maybe this was the saving grace to stop me falling entirely over the edge. This money may be the metaphorical hero talking me off the ledge of a building right before I leap. I paid off my debt to the mortgage company, about three and a half thousand pounds if I remember correctly. I paid off my phone bill, my one thousand pound overdraft was cleared and also, I paid off the council tax. That evening I took my mum, sister and little brother out for an Indian, paid off her water bill arrears and got her a new washing machine. I can quite safely say that apart from maybe three hundred pounds that I spent on some new clobber, the rest of that money went on drugs and alcohol. It lasted me about two months, fourteen grand straight down the drain, gone.

I was worse than ever, completely out of control, within two months the money was gone entirely, for that time I paid the mortgage, then it was back to using the money for coke, maybe even a night out. The sad thing or one of the tragic things may be a better way to put it, is that the money was for my injuries in Afghanistan. That money was blood money, perhaps that's why I was angry at having it, guilty or maybe I knew I didn't deserve it. It could have done some good, but instead, I fucked it all up against the wall, what didn't fit up my nose was stuck in a rizzla and shoved down my throat. I did my utmost to burn that money as quick as I could. My Mum recalls me pre-drinking at hers, empty bottles upon empty bottles of vodka laid across my bedroom floor, she would be begging me not to leave as I would call her a cunt, push her out of my way, laugh in her face. Even my mates would be telling me to stop, I would just throw bunches of twenty-pound notes at them, "fuck off meet me at the club," I would shout while I would feel the need to tell my Mum how shit she was. I don't know why I did this, she was the most fantastic Mum in the world, but I had to take this anger out on her. I don't know why? Perhaps I never will? The only person to stand by me no matter what, yet here I was screaming at her, makes no sense, like most of my life since leaving the Army, I hate it, and I don't understand it. For some reason my behaviour got worse as well, I was disrespectful, horrible with my words, became even more violent than I ever had been. Perhaps it was because I realised I had fucked up my only chance of actually doing something decent with my life. Before the money I had PTSD as an excuse for landing me in a bit of a shit situation, now I didn't even have that, that money could have got me back on a level, but with no ones help I drank myself straight back down to the bottom of the pile.

As that compensation money had disappeared, I was back to my old tricks of drinking three-litre bottles of cider at two pounds ninety-nine a pop. I couldn't get coke at forty pounds a gram unless it was war pension day, so I started substituting it with plant food. 'Mkat', or 'meow meow' you might know it as. It's a piss coloured crystal that you crush up into powder and inhale through your nose. When it hits your nostril though it burns for a few seconds. It stinks, no matter where you have stored it you will smell it for weeks. When you pull the crystal bogies from your nose and eat them, it tastes sharp, like a chemical that certainly shouldn't be consumed by humans. Some of the experiences I have had on that scare me, I was once found in a cupboard naked, I was speaking French and thought I was being abducted by aliens. I had no idea where I was or what I was doing. It also has a side effect called T-rex, this is where your arms fold up like a dinosaur, you lose complete control of your motor functions. It's quite scary how easily things can go wrong.

Trust me, if you think drugs are far away from your door, you are mistaken, they're everywhere, and there's always someone who wants your money. I might as well walk into a supermarket, head to the drug section and pick up all the cocaine I can, walk to the checkout scan my nose candy. Rip out my heart and use it as currency, the path I was walking down was sure as hell going to kill me in the end anyway. The gun-toting war stories of my child hood were not found, I didn't feel like a hero, I was the main character in a sad film. I was not happy, I could see no happy ending, I had no red carpet, my journey was one of a short white line that my nostril had lead me down. I know that sounds like the confession of a poorly scripted soap opera, but it was true. My past was glorified in my ramblings, demonstrating fire and manoeuvre tactics with eyes wide open like my eyelids were crawling inside my head, my palms and armpits were sweaty as my heart pounded fast in my chest. The present didn't matter because I didn't know I was in my today, I was adrift in the land of narcotics. They fixed everything.

At this point, I become quite ashamed, not for the drinking or drug abuse, although that in itself is enough to hang ones' head in shame. It becomes shameful because I have to open up apart of myself that I have denied entry for so long, the abuse of my family. The pinnacle of this behaviour or in fact the crest would represent height or top, so perhaps something more insidious. The depths of hell are where this conduct manifested, maybe chasm or a black hole of this behaviour would be even more appropriate. I had, like always returned home at some point with the fire burning inside of myself. Apparently, I had called my Mum some abusive names then wandered upstairs spitting on the floor, swearing to myself as is such custom behaviour, then it went quiet. My Mum had come upstairs to check on me and found me with a pillow over my brothers face, I honestly have no recollection of this what so ever, everyone else involved does remember.

My brother had started becoming closed off. My Mum found him sobbing his heart out in a corner. He shouted, "I'm fat and useless, Gary hates me." This alone is enough for me to want to hang a rope around my throat and jump from a tall building. However, I know that will make nothing better. The resounding answer to his problems came when he was at school. He had many counselling sessions and each time the finger pointed firmly at me. My behaviour was mentally scarring him, and he drew a picture once, the image was a soldier with the words. 'I hate guns and the Army, they should be banned, and everyone should be happy.' Quite humbling that at such a young age he recognised that my behaviour was linked to what I had suffered at war. This gives me minor comfort when I look back at the way I treated him, whether I blamed him for being alive and Abdul John being dead, or whether I was just subconsciously trying to train him, I will never know. All I know is that even writing this a tear makes its way from my eye and follows the shape of my face, an innocent child scarred by war, completely collateral. He is not the first and will not be the last, all I can do is strive to make sure that everyone knows his story, I tell him I love him every day, and try to make him proud. At that time though all I did was ruin his childhood, the time when he should have been most happy.

I don't know the link between PTSD, alcohol or drugs, I wish there were one concrete answer, a sure fix for all that take the same steps I did. No one deserves that misery, I tortured myself for so long, I spent nights inside my room watching footage of Afghanistan with a bottle of vodka in my hand, crying myself to sleep. I crawled the streets at night searching for somewhere to go, wishing time never to end so I would not have to face the disgust that I had for myself. One thing I never wanted to do was look in the mirror, see what I was, see what I had become, Perhaps it was as simple as a distraction technique. It was a vicious circle that kept me from the realisation that I had to let go. It's even hard to say now, Gary Green you are not Greendog anymore, you are not Rifleman Green. 30037006 is not an identity anymore. God even just typing that makes me want to rip someone's throat out and drink their blood.

Whose idea of a sick joke is this?

Who is playing this trick on me?

Why am I not in my green armour defending my country?

Why do I have to get a regular job? Why do I hate myself?

Fuck it rack me up a line in Costa toilets. This writing is bringing up one too many issues, bang and the hurt is gone. Of course, I'm not really in costa toilets with a rolled up note. I'm a pretentious prick these days. I'm sat with my laptop out conversing in the future with the readers of this, with a hazelnut cappuccino, the four tablets I've taken this morning are like a leash on a dog. They yank me back from the urge to do something primal, I will not do drugs again, at least non-prescription ones anyway, I will not kill someone today.

Anyway back to me being a horrendous person, so with the two years of abuse that I had given out to my family, the words that cut like a sharp blade that I will never be able to take back, things had almost come to a head. It wasn't the end as I have never entirely been able to cut the ties with alcohol. Today is January 26th, 2016, I was steaming and caused a lot of trouble in London on Friday night although I have been free from drugs almost two years, silver linings and all that.

Although behaviour and rehabilitation wise things were coming to a head in the summer of 2013, as usual, I was skint. I had stolen some of my little brother Xbox games and taken them to CEX to pawn them, I can't remember what I got for them, but I was at home while my Mum and little brother were on holiday. Important to mention that they were on holiday in England paid for by the government as a break away from me because of my behaviour. It was organised as a result of my little brothers' counselling sessions, this was the first night they were away. I had, with my stolen money, got a cheap litre of vodka, two value packs of lager and a three-litre bottle of cider. I had also got two grams of coke on 'tick' (take now pay later). The day was going swimmingly, the music was blaring out, the drinks were flowing, and the drugs gave me the flying feeling, so I was talking at a million miles per hour, perfect. My sister and her girlfriend were at work. Also, my Mum wasn't coming home. However, my sister comes back from work, I had gone for a ressuply. My mate had passed out on the sofa, so my sister kicked him out. I came home to find my alcohol thrown in the bin, my friend had gone, and my sister was shouting at me. A dangerous combination for someone who was coked off their tits and game for a party. I lost the plot, started smashing the house up, called my sister a fat slag and a dike cunt. Everything in the world that was nasty that you could imagine was flying off my tongue like daggers. Her girlfriend, bless her, had enough of my venom, jumped up and smashed the fruit bowel over my head. I was stunned for a split second before I started screaming with spit flying from my mouth like a crazed lunatic. Subsequently, they left, I racked up a line on the coffee table, got the bottle of vodka from the bin, necked it from the bottle, I smashed their bedroom to pieces and then sat on the sofa laughing to myself. The door knocked, my Aunty had turned up to kick me out, I gave her the same barrage of abuse and pushed her over as she emptied my alcohol into the bin, the police turned up shortly after, I gave them a torrent of abuse. A female officer tried to talk me down, I called her a fat pig as I climbed inside the green wheelie bin to retrieve a can of lager, I cockily asked them if they can arrest me for drinking on my property as I flicked the can lid. It was all an absolute disaster, but the less in control I felt the worse I became.

I lost the battle, possibly also the war, I had to leave the house, so I went to the one place I could count on, the local. I finished off my drugs, I drank the last few pound away that I had in my pocket, and then I rang my Gramp crying asking if I could sleep on his sofa. A twenty-four-year-old veteran sleeping on his grandparents' sofa in the bungalow they live in because my Nan is disabled, I had an empty sealy bag in my pocket and not a penny to my name. This may have been the lowest point in my life. Of course, this had completely ruined my Mum, and little brothers get away as they had received the call that the police were called out. I had assaulted my auntie and reduced my sister to tears. When my Mum got home she was visited by Ashley's care worker along with the police officer that had been called out, the decision was made that if I didn't move out, Ashley would be taken into care. What a man did I feel, I had pushed everyone to such a limit that the decision had to be made that I could not live under the same roof as my brother. My sister and her girlfriend had been living with my Auntie because they hated me. As I had no job, no money, I was going to be homeless, my Mum made my room look like her room, she couldn't see me on the street, so I was living there but in secret. No one could see me; I had to hide when the councillors come round, or Ashley would have been moved to a foster home. This is what I had become, I remained sober so I had to face my demons, I had to admit that this is what my life was, there was no more hiding from anything. I spent a lot of these nights cuddled on the sofa with my Mum crying, explaining my emotions, she knew because I had pretty much done the same every time I drank, she could see how much I was hurting.

This is hard to write for me because of how it makes me look, reading this you would think I was one of the worst people in the world. I get that, I honestly do, even reading this back as I write makes me hate myself. The thing I beg of you to remember is that this person wasn't me, although me in the body, not in mind. It was merely a manifestation of emotions that needed to escape, I was mentally torturing myself every day, by drinking I was stopping myself. Once I was sober I was on a mission, a mission to explore myself without alcohol pulling me away from reality. The sad truth is as I looked in the mirror sober, all I saw staring back at me was unhappiness. Even now two and half years later I only see sadness, although now it's the prescription medication that masks me. What do I need to be happy? I honestly can't answer that, my mind is so active that I only see the possibility of distraction rather than true happiness. I have found those small things that make me happy, when I watch a film or I get lost in or a good book, but that's still not happiness is it? It's just something that shifted my concentration. How can I find happiness without something false that is shielding me from questions I would rather not answer?

A soul that is lost is one that is left to explore, and a soul that is left to explore is one that is lost, such a freedom is often sought after by free spirits, but freedom is not that was found in loneliness for me. I felt no sense of freedom from responsibility but instead found sadness from a lack of purpose. A blunt saw left to rust in a disused toolbox, a rifle with no bullets and a boot with no owner. I was a bird set free but with clipped wings. It is not in the fact that I had no legs to walk my path but the knowledge that my head was caged so for too long my way had been hidden. With a head muddled but a huge heart, I was still able to stumble into my fate. A miracle for which I am eternally grateful, it is the one fact in life that I can take reassurance from, for my knowledge is the power that binds me to my fate. The piece of my head concrete enough in faith for me to know that there is a fight deep in my stomach allowing me not to give up. The clouded storm I once walked through, would have me believe I was destined to continuously sit on a roller coaster in which my carriage were drugs and drink. I can never say I was a junkie, but I was trying to fill a void of excitement left from a life that I no longer lived, and the enthusiasm from war was quickly replaced with substance. For me and especially my family there was a fear that it was never going to end, and that I would become so lost and depressed that I would stay in the cycle until I forgot who I was all together.

Chapter 15
Can I have a line of what you're taking?

I had finally reached my rock bottom, as I looked upon my life I found myself surrounded by water. I was drowning, the longer this had gone on the further under the water I found myself, and I was running out of the air to breathe. As I laid in my bed, It was at that moment, sink or swim. I've been diving so I know that feeling of weightlessness, this was slightly less glorious than diving off the coast of the red sea though. Nevertheless, it's how I picture it in my head, twenty meters below water, floating as if you are in space, that's how I felt. Just floating through my present, laid in my bed around five o'clock at night on a Monday. I hadn't been at work, I had walked through the front door of my Mums house a couple of hours previous, I had been out since Thursday night. I was laid on my bed thinking of all this, half awake, half dead, floating between both words unable to sleep even though I had been awake nearly seventy-two hours. In this space I looked up, above the surface of the water, there was a life I could have, a place where my family was, a life in which I could be proud. Below me was the abyss, it was dark, I couldn't see what was there. To find out I would have to continue further down the road I was going, something told me that if I kept going my air would run out and I would die there. This was the point which I knew I had to find some way of getting to the surface. With all that said though, I had a blocked nose, my head felt like I had once again been punched repeatedly, I needed to sleep before I could start to try and do a climb upward.

This was the time I started writing my book, this book. It's the journey that I have taken that I genuinely hope will help people who read this. I want people to understand my past, to see what I have come through and to realise life exists after the military. There is no solace to be found with alcohol and acceptance means more than a distraction. When I woke up, I felt like I had been awoken from the dead, like an Egyptian tomb disturbed for the first time in a thousand years. (I don't know if that timeline analogy is one hundred percent correct, but you get the picture.) I was like a wrapped corpse, smelt like one as well. I wrote a rough version of that first chapter, and then I wrote the poem to my Mum which I later had published in the anthology of love. At that point I wasn't sure what I wanted, I just knew that my story had to get out so that maybe people who were suffering like me could recognise the behaviour in themselves. Perhaps seek help, my account could help them. I was a long way from the finish line, I knew that, but for some reason, I had chosen to see what could happen to me on the surface, I wasn't looking back.

I had fallen in love shortly after the writing of that chapter, in the August of 2013, for a few months me and Emily had been meeting up. For me it was love at first sight, in a room of ten thousand people she would stand out, glowing like a star in a black sky. I had won my court case against the Army regarding my compensation. For the first time in a long time, I was granted the simplest of pleasures, such as being able to have a contract phone. My driving ban was up, so I purchased a BMW three series convertible, it was destined to be a short trip in this world yet it was one I embraced with open arms. I made sure I had secured some sort of a future for myself, unlike the twenty thousand pounds I had booted up my nose. I made sure I had something to remember this by. I paid off the debt that had built up on my house again, I was in court with my mortgage company as they wanted to repossess my home. I was fortunate enough that I could once again pay it off, I also paid off a chunk in good faith. I was living the high life, although in the back of my mind I knew it was never going to last. Before I could continue I had to sort my head out, if not I was going to crash, I couldn't afford to let that happen.

The twisting never-ending downward spiral had to stop, the only two eventualities were death, either through suicide, overdose or one of the endless possibilities in which my miss-adventures could lead me to. The other eventuality was a new lease at life, to come back stronger, to resolve my issues, learn to live with them rather than covering them up with booze and drug-filled escapades. On the 7th October 2013, I arrived at Tyrwhitt House for residential therapy. The journey there, though it had been a short one, was filled with anxiety, my nerves kicked in the morning before I left while I was packing my bag. These sorts of realisations seem to creep up on you, I had known about this date for a few months, but the months had been filled with falling in love during extravagant trips. Thus, therapy had been far from my thoughts. I had wrapped myself in the soft blanket of Emily's love, we both had issues, so we were each others rock, supporting each other and helping one another to do more, to be free. She helped keep me from drinking, gave me hope and faith in the world again. In turn with her agoraphobia and anxiety I had helped her live her life, do things she thought she would never do again. Love is a potent tool. Hope can help you find a new love, give you a new lease on life. Hope and love are the most significant things to any human being on this planet. Whether you are struggling to pay your bills and having to work two jobs, homeless on the streets, face down in an irrigation ditch under fire or whether you are struggling with PTSD. Love for the people you care about, the love from people who care about you will give you hope. That hope will provide you with the courage to push forward, to keep on going. Cutting that tie for two weeks was a daunting prospect, but I was going to take it with me.

When I arrived, I had that sinking feeling in my stomach, the feeling you get when you're sitting outside the headmasters' office. I wasn't in trouble though, I was just vigilant of the fact that I was mentally about to be broken down, exposed at first then hopefully rewired correctly, I was under no illusion that this was not going to be a quick fix but, I had faith in myself. With the tools in my hand and my future ahead of me I had to make the right decisions. I tell myself I am going to succeed, I will carve my future, this will not beat me. At combat stress I learned about my condition, the strange letters PTSD, the stigma attached to the very title was broken down, it made it less scary because there were no unanswered questions. The flip side of the coin was that I now knew what I was dealing with but only in an academic format, I was told these side effects were mine. I just didn't know why? Does that make sense? Kind of what the Ancient Greeks would have felt like if you went back in time and told them that the world wasn't flat. It wasn't that I didn't have the academic ability to conceive it, it's just that I had processed the information and it still wasn't enough to fulfil my desire to understand everything.

Hypervigilance is the overactive side effect of PTSD, the thousands of thoughts that rush through the mind at one time, the one million outcomes of the slightest idea inside ones' head. This spirals and spirals to the point that sleep or even rest can become non-existent, alcohol becoming the most common solution for the veteran. It's 00:49 and I are more than happy to be sitting at my laptop because thoughts spinning around my head are better converted to words rather than keeping me in a painful contortion of a fruitless attempt to sleep. The thoughts I process are so vivid, too airless to catch, they barely register in my head, there are far too many for myself to comprehend. From the moments that happen day by day to the darkest memories that throw themselves into the mix, a recipe for disaster!

The saying, 'no rest for the wicked,' needs to be used lightly.

Hypervigilance is a by-product of serving in areas such as Afghanistan, as I said earlier in this book, Afghanistan was a three sixty battlefield. For this reason, you were always alert, you had to be on another level of vigilance than you would need to be while walking to the shop or sitting on the sofa watching daytime TV. This is what is defined as hypervigilance, being 'over' alert all of the time. What was that noise? Who was that? What are they looking at? Why are they stood there? All questions you need an answer for in Afghanistan because that person could be watching you to gather information for an attack. Two stones on top of each other could be a sign left to mark an I.E.D. A loud noise could be the initiation of an explosive or a gunshot that is aimed at you. Back home a loud noise could be a car backfiring, fireworks. Rubbish on the floor is part of everyday life, instead of a pressure plate bomb waiting for you to be distracted by the discarded coke can. It's this that fills your head with so many unanswered questions. Everything has to be over analysed until you have wholly tortured yourself.

Once these thoughts have entered your mind, you are then subject to rumination, which means you can't stop thinking about a subject or a feeling. I can only explain this the best way I can which is from my own experience, my ruminating thoughts are predominantly of a cynical nature. For instance, if Emily liked a photo on Facebook I would question it a million times in my head, come up with a bizarre and twisted reason of why this act had the intention to hurt me. Then I would beat myself by thinking of it over and over again until the point that I completely lose my temper. This happens every day because of the world that we live in, bills, work, relationships etc. It's hard to adjust to that once you've been shielded for so long, quite strange to think that a person who can kill someone in the blink of an eye, contemplates suicide because of a bill that comes through the door. The relevance to this is with everything else that continually goes through my head, the everyday things are what push you over the edge. Then add to this that you can't stop thinking about an eight-year-old boy whose legs came off in your hands or the screams of your eighteen-year-old mate who had his legs blown off.

The first week had been one of the fiercest things that I had experienced for a long time, far from the bedroom at my Mums house where I would hide from my anxiety disorder. Clutching onto the bed quilt as a panic attack swarmed over me, poked in the ribs by that dark cloud of depression. Here I was forced to face those demons, educated on what they were, we were given techniques on what we could do to beat them, the anger issues that came with them also. What my problem was, still is to be completely honest, is that there is hypervigilance, then there is me. Being told I was going to be better-meant nothing to me, doing cognitive behaviour therapy wasn't for me. I couldn't talk my way out of a panic attack, I couldn't complete an activity that withdrew the nervous sweat from my armpits. My mind questioned it too much, not in the ignorant way, more in the sense that I needed to know how? Why would this help me? Not just that it would. I felt helpless, to be honest, I had given up all hope. I was more interested in painting, the greenery there is spectacular, there is a tree in the grounds, with the warm sun beaming down, I would prefer to be sat underneath with a book rather than in the classes. Anything that numbed me was what interested me, if I could do anything to escape my mundane existence in the here and now, then I would take it.

Today is the last day of my first week here at combat stress, it's some sixteen minutes past midnight and as usual sleep escapes me. For the past week, I have been forced to face truths, truths about myself, the way I act, the way I feel and the overwhelming knowledge that I am not normal. Normal perhaps not the operative word as we are all individuals, but, I am for all my sins a troubled one. I have had to relive some of the darkest times of my life and have them scrutinised in front of me. I have felt shame, and I have felt weakness in these moments. I am here writing now as my mind has no rest, I am isolated, and I am lonely, the demons inside me battle each other as I try to sleep, vicious memories and a menacing thought process collide leaving me restless. I cannot switch off. There is no simple solution, no reset, this is a simple routine I face most nights, solitude for me is not by myself, as by myself, I fight myself, inside myself.

Ruminating thoughts of bad memories past and present send you down a slippery road of depression, which then forces you to ruminate, making you depressed, once again a vicious circle with no end. The coping mechanisms are too, 'stop thinking!' Very simplistic when written down, but, to me seem somewhat as useful as tissue under water. Instead of not thinking, I seem to do the opposite and think even more. One of the ruminating thoughts that patrol's the back of my mind is suicide, almost all of us have had the idea. It's a thought that surfaces usually in times of hopelessness. Overpowering depressive ruminating feelings drive you to the point that you see no way out, no escape from yourself. I have had these thoughts, but some forty-five minutes ago, I saw myself in my head ending the pain, ending the struggle, giving in.

I put on my coat as the wind is strong this evening, I put my hat on to shield my ears from the cold, my pyjama bottoms are sufficient, but I slip on my Ugg boots to keep my feet warm for my last ever journey. I have never quite thought about where I would acquire the blue rope that is so vivid in my imagination, but it's always in my right coat pocket. I leave my room with only my phone, my bags are packed at the end of the bed. I turn right out of my room through the small corridor and head out of the building. I only have to pass the Occupational Therapy centre which at this time will be empty so I will go entirely unnoticed until the morning. From here on out I have only to cross the dark car park, and I am into the small wood. Less than a hundred meters from where I am now in reality. I find a tree with the appropriate branch which I climb on to, I set my rope and remove my phone from my pocket. I record myself leaving a message to my loved ones, saying how sorry I am for the pain I have caused them over the past years, tell them I love them, that this is the only way I can get rid of all the guilt and pain I have inside me. Once the message is finished I place the phone back inside my coat, I straighten myself up, then I drop, it's over, there is no more problem. It's only a thought, one I would never act upon, it's subconsciously my way of punishing myself. The PTSD inside that haunts me like an insidious poltergeist, poking me closer to the edge, just one more stop then there may be no turning back.

After my time at Combat Stress was over, I wasn't cured, that wasn't their promise, it was just my hope. I kind of thought that after therapy I would be a regular person, it didn't work like that, I can't say I gave it my all, I never. Not out of intent or for any other reason that I can tell you, my mind just subconsciously has to fight anything without logical or scientific evidence. Learning about my condition was brilliant for me, it gave me an understanding of how my behavioural patterns develop, what I couldn't get my head round was them telling me that holding a stone would take these feelings away. I promise you with my hand on my heart that I mean no disrespect with that last statement. It's merely my way of explaining my reaction to the process, what they do is fantastic. With my mind, I didn't find myself susceptible to the treatment, plus my ego doesn't allow me to let anyone in completely. I act up, the mask takes over, and it's as if I have to put myself on an equal level with the person who's talking to me. I can't allow myself to be seen as in need of help.

The best thing to come out of Combat Stress was the 'Christmas Carol' effect, I was like Ebenezer Scrooge being taken by the hand, swept out the window with a gust of wind clinging to the ghost of Christmas future. I was the youngest person there, the men I spoke to were long-term sufferers. Veterans of the early stages of the Northern Ireland conflict, those who had served in the Falklands and the first Gulf war. Their stories were brutal, there was this anxiety disorder that we all had in common, yet we were all different ages. I in my mid-twenties had more in common with a sixty-year-old man than I did anyone else who I had spoken to previously. They had all, but a few, had experiences with domestic abuse, they had mentally (and some physically) abused ex-wives, girlfriends and even their children over the years. I heard stories of those who were once young like me. Although back then there was no such thing as PTSD, they just lived their lives drinking the memories further to the back of their minds. The majority had since lost their families, were not in touch with their children due to their behaviour before they had found any help before they even knew there was a problem. One man had been jailed for beating his wife with a chain, he had never had any history that would have explained this behaviour, just that he could not cope, no excuse I know, but the pattern was phenomenal. With no help these men had all grown into old men living painful lives, carrying the weight of war on their backs like a tortoise carries it shell, slowly moving through time with the weight never lifted. If my path had not diverted, I would be the old man telling the same tails one day, I would grow old never knowing if the grass was any greener on the other side of the fence, they all said the same thing, "please don't end up like me".

My generation of Veterans are lucky, that isn't the right word, to be honest, no one who goes through what we have been through is lucky, to have people who care though is fortunate. I suppose this realisation of what happens is only thanks to how public the war in Iraq and Afghanistan was publicised. Otherwise, I guess we would've come home to picket signs calling us murderers. The twin towers attack was the turning point for recognition for anything to do with the military. No one cared about veterans that came back from war until it was on TV. Until the pictures of eighteen-year-old boys with no legs surfaced in the paper, the young faces of those who had lost their lives were forced in your face on news channels while you were eating your chips on the sofa. It's been going on for years, thousands of veterans have taken their own lives without intervention because war has turned them into monsters, they no longer fit back into their old lifestyles, they may not want to. It's like a piece of paper, once you scrunch it up it will never look the same, you can put it back straight, you can even iron it, but it will never be the same as it was before. What we have now though is awareness, the potency is still underrated, I believe that all those that have served will suffer in some way. Those who have been in prison have it similar, once you are indoctrinated into something so severe, you will never just be able to go back. There is a long process of adjustment, the silver lining to our recent exposure though is that it can now start a lot sooner.

As things were moving so swimmingly with Emily, we decided that we would move into the house together. We renovated the property right down to the last penny, I even had to sell my car to get the flooring done. I knew it made sense, I had set this picture up in my head, I was ready to move from the part of my life that had been hiding from responsibility. I had used PTSD as an excuse at every point in my life, I couldn't work, I could fight in town, I needed a drink, I can't pay my bills, every one of those statements ended with.

'Because I have PTSD.'

This had to stop. I couldn't keep avoiding life, refusing to move forward, allowing myself to be defined by something that I suffer with. As much as I was no longer Rifleman Green, I was now no longer going to be PTSD. All this was good thinking, it was just going to take me a bit longer than I realised to put it all into practice. I did get a job, I will cover that later as we're talking about the rehabilitation side of things at the moment. I had been to therapy, four times I've been there in total, each time doing a two-week residential rehabilitation course for sufferers with PTSD. Although the first time was a taster session which lasted the weekend. This gave me real exposure to how tenacious PTSD can be regarding your quality of life for the future. I knew that I needed to stop drinking if I was going to make any advancement in my life, every time I had been out something terrible had happened. I'll tell you two stories, both of which occurred while I was working, one in October 2014, the first year I had started working, also the last time I had taken drugs, the other was the last time I went into town and got drunk, this was in April 2015.

So, it was a wedding, I was a working man with a beautiful girlfriend, also a French bulldog, he's also my son, Freddie, I'm not the biological father though, we went on Jeremy Kyle and everything. However, even with my new found responsibilities I had not quite managed to stay free of substances, it was a lot less frequent. However, if I had one too many drinks I would relapse by giving in to the temptation. So, at this wedding advertising my lifestyle in an expensive suit, my girlfriend Emily done up to the nines, I was looking the respectable working class man I claimed to be. I had also been to therapy, I was on medication now, so I wasn't mental anymore either. I also had a test at work the following day, this being so, I decided I would only have a couple then we would go home so I would be fresh for the morning. At the evening do, all that changed, a few glasses of champagne, followed by a few beers, followed by a few more, followed by a friendly face being there who I used to do drugs with, found me back in the toilets. I was lying to my girlfriend telling her I needed the bathroom so I could sneak off and snort coke off the toilet seat. This then got me in a state where I threatened to kill the groom because he asked me to calm down. Emily left, I stayed. Naturally, I ended up back at my mates' house until five thirty in the morning, I was once again two hundred pounds in debt through coke that I had got, had work in one hour and a half hours, thoroughly embarrassed myself in front of everyone. The two things that I had done worst of all was let Emily down and let myself down. I spent the next couple of days promising Emily that it would never happen again, that I didn't mean for it all to happen, blah blah blah, the proofs in the pudding and I had come up short smelling of shit once again.

So, I had kicked the drugs, I was a new man, no stopping me, I had been promoted at work as well, I was a leader now so I had even more responsibility. It was Friday, we had a tough week, so I decided to take the two girls who worked for me into the local for a couple of sociable drinks. I had one larger, it felt good to let my hair down, so I drove home, got changed and asked Emily to drop me back off in town. I knew I wanted to get drunk, I was craving that break away from reality, I wanted that feeling of freedom. I lied to her face, I told her that I would be home by ten, I knew I wanted to be out for the night, all I had to do was get out then I could deal with the consequences later. It should have been a lovely occasion. It was at first I suppose, we joked about work, it was pleasant, it was nice to chill out. Then I got a bit louder, and then I started ordering vodka. One of the girls left, so we were down to two of us, we moved bar, by this time I was drunk, they refused to serve me, so I picked up drinks off the bar throwing them down my neck, laughing in their faces. As they went to throw me out, I picked up a pool ball and threw it behind the bar smashing three or four bottles and some glasses. The lady I was with was having a go at me, so of course, I spat on the floor next to her and told her to fuck off. I was banned from town, but there was a pub I could drink in, I stumbled in through the door, got myself a pint, walked up to a group of three men and called them a bunch of cunts. It all kicked off, I ended up getting kicked in the face, I got up and continued to drink my pint laughing until I was politely told, "I think you better leave". I got home about three in the morning with a four hundred pound pair of broken glasses and a black eye, once again wholly letting Emily and myself down, not only that but come Monday I would be making some apologies at work.

I feel like I jumped through those stories pretty quickly, the only relevance to them though is for the below writing. I wanted to give you a picture of myself, in 2012/13 I was a borderline drug addict and alcoholic, I had the same issues in 2014/15 but with a job. Therapy had helped me understand myself, it had given me the strength to go to work, to sort of fit in somewhere in this world, but it was all still there. I was no better off because I still wasn't free from my demons. At this time Emily gave me an ultimatum, I sort myself out, or she was going to leave me. I've done all this before, threw my life down the toilet once, I wasn't going to do it again. I admitted that I was an alcoholic, I didn't need the drink to wake up in the morning, I didn't need it full stop, to be honest. When I did drink though I couldn't control myself, I couldn't stop, and I can not say no. That by default makes me an alcoholic, also the fact that it isn't just recreational, it was a coping mechanism.

"God grant me the serenity to accept the things I cannot change, the strength to change the things I can and the wisdom to know the difference."

– The serenity prayer.

"My name is Gary, and I AM an alcoholic." Tuesday 7th April 2015 and after all the lies, all the hiding my thoughts and feelings and blaming my issues on everyone else I was finally able to admit it. I had never hidden my drinking from people, in fact, I was quite open about it, I had just never been able to curb my problem though. Now here I sat in a small room underneath a church in Banbury, it was a little room and was set out with a semi-circle of eight chairs. Inward facing to a table with various leaflets and place cards brandished with slogans such as, live and let live, take it easy and one step at a time. All rules I had perhaps thought I lived by already. The stone walls and sizeable single pain window disguised little of the outside world, a large bush outside tapped the window every time it was caught by the wind as if it was asking to be let inside, its shadow would become visible as light flickered between the long grey blinds. The rumble of a car going past would remind me that I wasn't in prison or an asylum where I was locked away from society. The faces around the room were happy, I didn't understand that straight away, 'fucking frauds.' I thought to myself, 'why are they fucking happy?' I pondered passive aggressively to myself, but one by one they spoke, and they welcomed me, and the atmosphere became positive. We were a fellowship, we were all here for the same reasons. We were powerless to alcohol and our lives had become unmanageable.

The first lady who due to the anonymity of AA shall remain nameless, a secret inspiration in my eyes, some people in life you are just drawn to. They speak, and you engage. A bit like when you are a child and your favourite cartoon character comes on, if I had been eating a bowl of cereal then like as a child my attention would have been snatched and by the end of her speech my coco pops would be nothing more than soggy remnants of its former molecular structure. She spoke charismatically and intellectually, if I can learn from someone then I absorb his or her words. She revealed her story, the premise of the meeting was, 'how I lived before, what got me here and how I live today.' So in this format, she divulged where she believed her drinking stemmed from, at what point she decided that she needed to stop and how now day by day she remains sober. In her own words she described herself as 'a sophisticated drunk, don't you know.' The ladies words were transferred to me in a way that I could relate, we had lead very different lives, yet there was interconnectivity. She had been a school teacher in a village and was born of wealth and education, I was born and raised in a council house with a single parent and had killed people for a living, yet with those differences aside and in this platform, we were the same. As humans I believe we fail to reach each other on these platforms, perhaps if we did then there would be no wars, I would not suffer from Post Traumatic Stress Disorder, and I would not be sat here. Maybe I would not be an alcoholic?

Once she had spoken to the group, she looked at me and said something to me that made complete and utter sense.

"Inside of these walls, you will learn that day by day you will always be an alcoholic. What you will also learn is that by being sober you will handle situations differently. Before you lose your temper, have a drink or judge people, recite the serenity prayer (above), and you won't go far wrong. It's amazing how much you will need to change to fit back into normal life."

It made me think of myself, something in me needs to give, I do need to change. I need to be sober, and I need to change so that I can become sober. Perhaps with a new perspective, a sober outlook on life, my life can become manageable? The woman had spoken about the aftermath of her recovery, that her day to day tasks that had once been inconceivable was now controlled and managed. She had learnt new things and new experiences, this concept excited me. I had been limited in my life. Take this book, for instance, it took me at least two years to get any weight to it because I couldn't manage myself, perhaps now I would be able to accomplish everything I wanted without the ankle weight of any addiction in my new life.

I have always sought after something, from the Rifleman to the rapper, but I would never have imagined that it would be a god. It wasn't, I went to alcoholics anonymous three times then got bored. This void in which I fill with drink has to be full though, the addiction is there for a reason, no matter how much you drink, shop, take drugs or even watch films or troll social media, the void is still there. Although I didn't continue to attend the classes, by taking a step away from my drinking and the life I was leading I can see that the void cannot be filled with material objects or alcohol. For instance, if you go on a night out for eight hours of frolicking and chasing the dragon, you think you are happy. The happiness that you actually feel is more so in the first few hours, you are in control and talking to your friends and having banter. That communion is the memory you enjoy and remember. The next six hours that you spend snorting coke, arguing with the friends you were previously laughing with, being sick with a kebab you have not eaten, are not enjoyable. The hangover you suffer from the next day is the least pleasurable part because you're scrolling through your phone and cringing at every photo you took and a message that you sent and on top of that, you're skint. I am not here to tell you how to live your life I'm merely reflecting on mine and what has made me suffer so much. I am by no means a preacher swanning around town quoting the bible of a Sunday to innocent passers-by trying to pick up a cheap last-minute chicken from Morrison's for their roast.

The above prayer, the serenity one, is an almost ideal to live by, we all have defects in our characters, I can't be trusted with alcohol, coupled with my PTSD I REALLY can't be trusted. The serenity prayer is something we need to recite in our heads as a gentle reminder of those defects, as a sort of precaution for damage limitation.

I haven't lived my life like an angel since by anyone's standards, even mine, I'm not even entirely functional yet, my mind still wonders from place to place. There are moments at work where I have panic attacks when it all feels a bit real. I don't know why but I have fallen into a world now where I'm not afraid of being me, where I have found a piece of something that has me unwilling to let go. Life outside of the Army seemed impossible at times, it was as if I had attached myself to the very fibre, I was no longer a person I was just a belonging borrowed to the world outside of it. Seeing the faces of the old men that bobbled along at Combat Stress, faces that had died at war whose ghost patrolled the pavement that surrounds us, still had smiles on their faces, alcoholics that had beaten the odds sat in front of me, applauded my willingness to want the change. It struck a chord with me. Perhaps it's why I am now driving towards a new future. I'm not sure, I wish I could bottle up my change, offer it to the world for those who too are struggling to adjust. All who are still searching for the path, look for me, I shall be there to help guide you to the light, it's not easy, you may stumble, but your soul will find the home it once left. As I listened to the stories of strangers that had found sobriety, I found myself wanting a slice of that cake. It's a line that I would be proud of taking.

"Let me have a line of what you're taking."

A new drug has been found, and it's the drug of life, it's something I hope I'm addicted to for a long time.

Chapter 16

To move on, you need to move on

It's 2014, at the moment I am trying to renovate my home and live in the house I almost lost. A sense of normality may be salvaged if I can only pull myself together. A letter I received has snapped one of the brittle supports, one of the table legs that holds me together has broken and I can feel myself spiralling both mentally and physically. My chest is pounding from the increased speed of my heartbeat, my hands are sweaty, and I am struggling to control my breathing. The spiralling in my head is harder to explain, one of the only ways to describe it is to say I am drowning, my head is flooded and by writing it feels like I am flushing some of the water. The letter was to say I wouldn't be receiving the benefits I assumed I would, this incident comes with many emotions, as my initial reaction was to panic. How will I pay my bills? How will I live? What if I lose my house? What will I do now? Shall I get a job? Am I ready to work? Where will I work? Plus, a thousand other questions entering my mind all at once with no answers. That was only my instant reaction, and then the others start pouring in. Shame, guilt, anger, all within the space of two minutes. To most, it may be comprehensible, but to me, my whole world was collapsing from the inside. I feel ashamed to apply for benefits. I despised myself as this was never meant to be an option for me, I used to look down on people who received welfare. The stereotype in my mind would be that 'These people are lazy, dirty and a drag on society.' Now I feel like one of these people, even though my circumstances are different, I still tar myself with the same brush. I started to lose self-confidence and self-worth, I was ashamed.

The most significant step I took in my journey thus far, was getting a job, this was because it's just something I never saw happening. Since I left the Army and even before I joined the Army I vowed that I would never end up in a factory. I would never be in a 'dead-end' job so to speak (that is nothing more than narrow-mindedness which I am glad to have now surpassed, however it is a very common one). With growing up, having needs and responsibilities I ended up working in a factory, I was a temp working for an agency earning £6.50 per hour, about £220 a week after tax. It was enough to cover my bills, still be able to live thanks to the addition of my war pension, otherwise, I would be in my Mums box room for the rest of my life. Believe it or not, I enjoyed it, I hadn't worked for three years yet here I was getting in my uniform with my safety boots. Packing my lunch and going to work, it was a really huge deal for me, I felt like a real grown up. In three months I was offered a full-time contract, six months after that I was promoted to a different department as a deputy team leader running the distribution for clinical trials companies. I was then the acting front line manager for the contract, after a year I moved to work as a despatch process leader for a chicken factory earning double what I had started out on two years previously. Since then I've taken on a team leader role at an automotive company. I've jumped ahead a little bit mentioning all this, but it's something that I'm proud of. Going to work can be a struggle sometimes, there are days when I physically feel like I can't get out of bed. I'm torn between the part of me that tells me I need to move on, but there's a part of me that still feels like a loser for not being who I used to be.

It navigates back to the previous chapter, the hyper vigilance, the ruminating thoughts, self-isolation, all the pieces of the puzzle that make up the mind of someone with PTSD. The realisation I mentioned earlier which was provided to me through therapy was only part of my recovery, the most substantial portion was wanting to change. This allowed me to open up to ideas that before I would not have looked twice at. With any form of recovery, anyone will tell you this, it's a step-by-step, day-by-day process that you have to live with, there's no cure for PTSD, it's not like you can have an operation to change the figuration of your brain. I do take tablets for my condition, and they are mood stabilisers that help my fluctuating emotional pattern. Rather than dramatic lows I just have small dips, rather than ecstatic highs I now get gradually excited. Sounds minor but these help in my day to day life, which is the end goal for us all. I also take tablets for my anxiety, I'm not sure how they work, essentially, they just make me less nervous, in new spaces I can become very anxious, I don't like not knowing my surroundings, these tablets take the edge off. With the five tablets in my system each morning, I'm able to manage all the other little things that crop up that may, in other circumstances head me down a steep gradient. With these five tablets in my system every morning, I'm just about able to be trusted to get up and go to work without killing someone or crying in a corner until I drown in my tears.

In the second chapter you will remember that my father left when I was around two years old, I hadn’t seen him since. That is true up until March twenty-fourteen. Growing up, as a child without a dad is a confusing feeling, as a child there's a lot of questions, does my dad not love me? Mummy why did daddy leave? How comes we don't have a dad mum? All these questions and a lot more were asked during my childhood. There is a general lack of understanding. It's hard to fathom that some children have a father, and some don't. I was always concerned that maybe it was my fault, I suppose it's normal to question yourself when you think someone doesn't want to know you. Perhaps it gave me a slight complex and chip on my shoulder because I became very offensive and conflicted about it. My reaction was very hostile if ever my dad was mentioned. It became natural and reasonable just to ignore the fact, pretend he never existed.

Fifteen years previous to the encounter with my father I am upstairs in my bedroom living out my childhood fantasy with my action figures, I was the hero. They were all set out in my bedroom and one by one my favourite character would have to fight his way to the boss who would have my sisters Barbie held captive. For my age the choreography with the violence was somewhat impressive, my imagination flared, I wasn't in my bedroom, and I wasn't playing with toys. In my head, I was in some far away land battling my way through the enemy stronghold to reclaim my true love. Each man I fought was a long drawn out process in which I would always save the day at the very last second and return home injured. Kind of like my real life to be honest, as I swagger down the road with Emily on my arm. While playing with my toys, I would often wonder about my Dad, because of everything on TV was always family orientated, whom would I take on family fortunes? I remember times I laid in bed crying as a young boy because I had been to my mates' house and he was with his Dad. Or if someone had said something to me at school and I didn't have my Dad to talk about it. I sat there with my toys, I grew up without ever seeing his face, yet as I drive to the pub to meet him, it's as if those years of being without him never existed. So many soldiers come from a similar background, not sure if it's coincidental or not, I know that a lot of my mates come from single-parent homes. I wonder if there is a connection between the two?

I pulled into the car park as we caught eyes, I walked up to his car, it was strange, I think because I wanted it not to be awkward, it was kind of awkward. Kind of like once you argue with your girlfriend then meet her the next day, there's that awkward silence before you start apologising. We went to the pub, when you're meeting your Dad for the first time you have to go to the pub, take the edge off. Also, it's almost guaranteed that he'll get the beers in, which of course he did, we both ordered a Stella, like father like son. As we sat down, all those questions that I had gathered as a little boy just fluttered from my head. There was no explanation because there was no need for one. I was just a boy that missed his Dad, all those times I said. "If I ever saw him I would punch him in the face." Were nowhere to be seen, I was just angry and upset because I missed him, now I was in front of him I just wanted to cuddle him and shout Daddy. He could never have replaced my Gramp, he was my father figure growing up, although at this point in my life I didn't need a father figure. At twenty-five years old I had experienced things that most would never have to suffer in their whole lives, there was not much left for him to teach me. He was my Dad though, and we now have a good relationship. I enjoy spending time with him, it has helped me close a lot of doors that were only left open to hurt me.

Closing those doors meant a lot to me, mainly because I was still hurting from so much. As I walked around I looked like I was okay, I wasn't. I had a lot of wounds that were left open. They were killing me. Invisibly as I walk around I am bleeding to death, no one can see these injuries. The tablets don't help these injuries, I just think they help me ignore them, even today as I write this, I can feel them, they're on my heart, my stomach, my legs. Sometimes it's hard to walk, even though I can see my legs are okay, it's as if there is an extra weight pulling me to the ground. My legs feel heavy, injured, they don't seem to work correctly unless I take my tablets so I can forget they're there altogether. Now and then I look in the mirror, actually, to be honest, I'm quite egotistical, so I'm always looking in the mirror to make sure I'm still handsome. Now and then though when I look, I can see the blood trickling from my eye, I know it's not there, but I can see it pouring. I honestly don't know if this will ever stop, there's no right or wrong, it just is, I just have PTSD, I don't think that will ever change. Will I ever feel proud? The only time I feel proud is when I think of Afghanistan, if I watch a war movie, I can look at Emily and say.

"I did that."

Or I feel proud that I can point out the mistakes.

"You wouldn't go on the ground without a helmet. Their spacing isn't correct, you can't hit someone with a pistol at two hundred meters, you wouldn't fire your rifle from the hip."

But the day-to-day stuff that I should be proud of, just makes me feel like shit. Instead of my brain positively recognising my change, I see the dark side, I should be saying. 'Well done Gary another day without drink or drugs, you went to work so you can live a normal lifestyle, you have paid for your home.' That would be the ideal way for me to think. Instead, my mind goes. 'Another eight hours in this shit hole, can't believe I work in a fucking factory, I'm such a loser because all my mates are moving forward in the Army and I'm stuck here, can't believe all my money has to go on bills.' Every negative thought is a dagger in the side, amongst all my other wounds they just cut that little bit deeper.

One of the things I've been told is that people around me feel like they're walking on eggshells. They don't know what kind of mood I'm going to be in, am I going to be funny, loud and make everyone laugh, or is something going to happen that makes me flip out. Are my mood swings good or bad today? This was indeed the case when I was drinking, more so before I started taking tablets, less frequently now that I take them. I recognise when they say that, I understand it because I walk on those same eggshells, am I going to be happy today? Am I going to want to kill myself? Am I going to be angry today? It's exhausting. Honestly, it is the most precarious feeling. I don't know whom I'm going to be when I wake up. This is what worries me about my future, is every day going to be a battle? Every journey to work I spend trying to find something to smile about, I might as well be travelling with my mortgage provider, the council tax man and my energy providers. All sat in my car with guns to my head, whispering to me.

"Come on Gary go to work, we need you to earn money Gary, come on Gary just a little bit further or we will shoot you in the fucking face."

As they say this to me in their demonic voices, one probably sticks his hand in my pocket. One slips his cock into my ass hole while the other tries making me feel guilty because I spent £2.50 at Costa, although they probably play golf with the person that owns that. These pressures everyone has to face, I just meet them at the same time as already wanting to kill myself, why the fuck do I have to walk around scared? Why do I have to feel like I have impending doom hanging over my head? I was a happy child, I always had a smile on my face as I ran carefree through the estate, now everything I see has a dark tint of negativity cast over it. I feel forced to smile every fucking morning I wake up. I pray that one day I wake up and this has all been a sick dream, I would happily go back to that first week at Catterick when I had that full screw kicking me in my face for being in the wrong place at the wrong time. At least that fear was for something I knew existed, this irrational fear that comes with this anxiety disorder is a death sentence for something I can't even see. Still, at least it's one more day without drink or drugs in my Mums box room, right? I wish these eggshells I walk on would crack beneath my feet, inevitably if my shoulders feel close to the breaking point from the active mind that balances above, the eggshells can't survive much longer?

I climb from my bed at thirty minutes past four in the morning, welcome to another show of the Gary factor, it's a rip off of the krypton factor. This isn't 1977, and we're not in a TV studio with a live audience, we're just in my head. Gordon Burns stands there asking impossible questions, how do you feel today? Do you remember Abdul John? Can you imagine if that was your little brother? Remember when you were in the Army, would that Gary be proud that you work in a chicken factory? They're hard to ignore sometimes, being the only contestant in this impossible quiz show is frustrating. I will never have the answers, they've never slowed either, they never change, and they never become fewer. As flame illuminates my face, I stare mesmerised at the end of my cigarette. Red grows as the fire burns through the tobacco and paper. The embers flicker in the dark morning. It's one of those unfortunate habits I'm still yet to kick. Somewhere in my head I believe it helps me, it distracts me from those questions, that's pretty priceless to be honest, for those first couples of minutes in my day I'm not trying to answer them, I'm just thinking about smoking. The follow up to that breakfast are my tablets, that's a habit now, as much as they may have medicinal value, they have a mental one. Once they ride the watery wave through my mouth, down my larynx, pass my oesophagus I whisper to myself. "I'm ok now." I don't know how I would deteriorate or prosper without them. It's just one of those things, kind of OCD if I don't take them my mind would eat itself. Like a vampire in the sun, I might get to work and burst into flames. These little things help me to function through the day, I'm never going to be cured so to speak, it can't be undone. I have just faced my demons, realised they're not as big as I thought, that hiding from them will only make things worse. I do feel like those American footballers that push against that significant obstacle and run forward. Although my block is mental and I'm going to work not playing in the National Football League.

I believe I have not entirely resolved my feelings yet. I work, of course, but I do not feel brought in to this life at all. I was happier sleeping under the desert stars with my rifle at arms' length than I do in my bed at night with the mortgage wrapped around my throat. That's why I go on these tangents away from the subject I started on, my mind as I warned you about earlier has a strong tendency to freely associate. One minute I'll talk about my healing process, the next moment I have to tell you about how much I hate the government. I do believe it's all relevant though. If I had come out of the Army with PTSD and found myself in a world that was filled with love, I would have had less struggle, of course in a life that is filled with love there would be no need for war in the first place, damn you war hungry swines.

With therapy completed, learning the ins and out of my condition, starting a career, paying my bills, not committing suicide or killing someone. I was, 'on paper,' in the best position

I had ever been. I was still not coping though, I hate the term normal, but I still wasn't normal, I needed some direction in which to move my life in, something positive that I could use as a driving force to keep moving forward. I believe this came in the form of my writing, not the anger diary I was once forced to complete, a document I filled in every time I was angry, why was I angry, what were the repercussions, how would I have done things different etc. Perhaps it's a practical idea for some people, I would never refuse any help. I would never want to discourage anyone from anything either. We're all wired differently so what may work for one will not work for all. Also, what does not work for one may work for everyone else, for me though the angry diary was indeed a miss.

With all my mood swings I would have five hundred and sixty-five million entries throughout the day. I think I filled it in once or twice then threw it in the bin. I'm not committed enough to those forms of help, my mind just honestly doesn't go that way, I need to offload my feelings in a snap second. This is why my book has been such help for me, I can uncandidly write exactly how I feel without any backlash, if I act upon those feelings I upset people, most of all myself. By having my book, I was in turn venting in privacy, every problem I've ever had I could go back and write about it. For instance, that bitch in my selection that said I was a fat bastard, I never told anyone that because I was embarrassed, here I can let off that steam. "Fuck you, you fucking ugly man looking beast." Another example would undoubtedly be my virginity secret, that's something I kept inside for a long time, holding that secret eats away at your soul. I wish that I would have been brave enough to be honest, here's something I've just learned about myself in this second, I don't think I've ever been comfortable in my skin, strange. It's peculiar that I'm not happy because a lot of the time I have fun, I genuinely enjoy myself, I'm always laughing, it's that deep down inner confidence that I lack. I'm happy on the outside, my sense of humour prevails nine out of ten times, underneath though I'm rotting, that invisible illness, I'm a beautiful brand new house, but the foundations are decaying.

From my writing, something beautiful blossomed, a resounding response from people all over the world, people who felt the same, that had not admitted their issues. They spoke to me in confidence, I heard horrific stories, PTSD is most common in combat veterans, this is only because of how highly strung the environment is. As I've explained in this book, from training to the front line is a high octane journey. Although the primary responses were from combat veterans, some friends who I have served with, took very similar to the paths I had made. I also had reactions from police officers, women who had been raped, domestic violence victims, all the symptoms were the same. They believed that my writing had inspired them to be open about their feelings, had helped them realise what they were feeling inside but were ignoring. They were wearing the mask day to day until they got home, once home they felt comfortable enough to take it off, just like me.

From the response I received, I knew I had to do something, I knew I had to help, this is when I had to strike a balance, the problem was I was still suffering. I would be a hypocrite to guide people when I yet didn't know where I needed to go. I was, and am still struggling with my bipolar-like symptoms. I still find it hard to go to work because of those feeling of self-worthlessness, I have to breathe every day slowly while repeating the serenity prayer in my head, I have to count the things I am thankful for, I've mentioned before that I believe in love, positivity and spirit. I think it is the answer to all of our problems if we could all just love each other the world would be a better place. For me it's hard to be positive because of how I feel, then on the news, I see terrorist attacks. Veterans on the street, single mothers struggling to feed their children, the elderly who can't afford to heat their homes. It's tragic that we live in a world where I sit in Costa with a blueberry muffin and a £3.35 coffee, in the same world African babies starve to death, in fact probably less than a mile away in the council estates mothers are taking Ketamine whilst their babies crawl on the floor naked dirty and hungry. Also I definitely know a mile away give or take there are homeless people sat on the streets, it's absurd, in fact I've just made a conscious decision to buy four coffees and go and hand them out on my way home – true story. Once again I've flown off topic, "reign it in Gary for fuck sake." Back to what I was saying about wanting to help the world, yet still being the hot mess that I am, hot mess, what the fuck even is that? Does it mean I'm a bit mental but my outfits on point? Or does it mean I have PTSD, but my hair is on fleek? God, I fucking hate this world 'LOL'. Most importantly it is not ignoring my condition but the acceptance, the serenity prayer is a perfect way to put this into perspective.

God grant me the serenity to accept the things I cannot change –

I can't change the fact that I have PTSD, I cannot change the fact that I will never be able to join the Army again. I cannot change the fact that I will never go back to two thousand and nine and have that lifestyle. By accepting this, I can start to move forward, if I don't agree with these things I will forever stay in the loop of avoidance, avoiding the acceptance, trying to change things that I can't. This is what I was doing with alcohol, I wasn't accepting anything, so I was living in that cycle of trying to forget, if I forget I do not need to accept.

Courage to change the things I can –

I can change my opinion on the situation, I can change the fact that I am using drugs and alcohol as a coping mechanism. I can change the fact that I am living in my Mums box room. I can change the fact that I am mentally abusing my Mum, I can change the fact that my behaviour is hurting my little brothers well being. Once I had accepted the things I cannot change, I could now formulate a plan of how I could move forward. I could start looking at what changes I could make to live in a more positive world. I could stop drinking alcohol, I could stop taking drugs, I could get a job, this does take courage, it takes a lot to admit that you're living negatively, to change those aspects. It takes courage, and it also takes time.

And wisdom to know the difference –

This is where I struggle. I'm a 'run before I can walk' person, in fact, scrap that, I'm a:

'Build a rocket ship, fly to Mars and find a new civilisation, use their advanced technology to solve the renewable energy crisis and world peace before I can walk.'

Kind of person. Once I have an idea in my head I feel like I have to run with it, I have to do it straight away otherwise everything is going to collapse, and I am the only one that can change that. I need to slow down, as my care worker reminds me regularly, things take time, I will only end up hurting myself.

So, to end all the above, the way I take ownership of my day to day life is by listing the things I am thankful for. Reminding myself in the positive ways, I have moved forward. It's basically a silver lining kind of list, by doing this it makes the things I find difficult more accessible. For instance, going to work every morning can be a struggle, there are demons in my head that if visible would be attacking me with axes as I climb from my bed. They would look like skeletons in black robes, hacking at my flesh, cutting my legs apart so I cannot walk, beating me in the head with blunt instruments. The soothing will only come from mind state. There's no other remedy, sadness and anger will feed them. They need to be fought differently, the only way to indeed subdue them is with positivity and rational thought, for me anyway, as I still seek logical reinforcement, it's the only answer. Using my method with the serenity prayer I can rationalise my day to day operations, every day I have to use this technique, even with the tablets, even with cigarettes, I use this. I make sense of things, I accept what is, also what is not within my grasp. This technique is my way of being able to use love against my demons. You have my views on todays' world, how it's made my life more difficult to come to terms, my answer for this now is the serenity prayer. I can't change the world in a day, I can't pay my mortgage anyway other than to go to work, so I tell myself this when I'm finding it difficult to adjust to a situation. My way of life is to use positive thoughts to understand the situations I find myself.

Not too far back I fell into arrears on my mortgage, this time it wasn't because I was buying drugs with the mortgage money at least, it was just because I'm pretty shite with my money. It doesn't hold that much value for me, I'm quite carefree with it, borderline useless if you ask Emily. Because of this, I was being taken to court, again. Safe to say I hit one of my slumps, the world is ending, you can imagine as a PTSD sufferer, or even as an average person what the weight of such a thing would do. The way I used my thinking was to find a sensible solution, what can I change about this situation, of course, the black cloud is telling me to jump in front of a train. "What's everyone gonna say if you lose your house? You're useless? All your compensation money down the drain? Kill yourself, kill yourself."

They're dancing around the black cloud like a dark moment in a Disney film.

"What will you do when your house has been taken,

You're fat, and you're useless or am I mistaken,

Say goodbye to your house,

To your car and your spouse,

Say goodbyeeeeeeeeeee."

Sing that in the voice of Scar from the Lion King, and you'll see where I'm coming from. What I did instead of killing myself, is thought rationally, ok so I owe this money, worst case scenario is that I move back in with my Mum. I won't be dead. I'll just be located in a different place. Best case scenario is that they accept a payment plan. What can I sell? What is the time limit? What are my income and expenditures like? Once I had gone through this process, I realised that there were a lot more options than killing myself. It turned out they accepted a payment plan, without my thinking though I would have tortured myself, completely ignoring and hiding from what was happening until it was entirely out of control. It's a small example but it's a practical one.

When I think about my position in this world I use the same sort of technique. I can't change the fact that I will never be in the Army again, it's something that I will probably never completely get over, it is something I can accept though. So now with this accepted, I think about going to work, if I go to work I get to live in my house with Emily and Freddie, so that's a plus. I do love them both so much, I'm proud to give them a home to live in, I do like the people at work, looking back I never thought I would work. Now I'm working. All these things build a positive force field around me.

Garys' inner dialogue.

"Without working, you wouldn't be able to write, without writing you won't be able to help anyone. Look how beautiful the sky is today, feel the cold air brush your skin, remember that you're alive."

Finding beauty in the small things help remind me that there is hope for the world.

This chapter was supposed to be about what has helped me to move on, I think I have accomplished that even with a bendy road I had to take as I diverged from the topic occasionally. The biggest thing I wanted to get across is quite hypocritical, I wanted to say that it's all about attitude, mind power, belief and willingness. This is quite hypocritical because I still use tablets to keep myself in check, without them I'm not sure how I would react to certain situations. Perhaps one day I will be able to cope without them, I will be able to use the faith I have in humanity to find a central point of peace amongst my very cloudy mind. Anyone can use this process to find life after the Military, I believe my purpose in life now is to raise awareness, to help guide people through the right channels that they need. There's a sea of people that are suffering, lost in drugs and alcohol because they have no purpose, no real reason to get away from that vicious circle. Before healing can start, we need to find these people a goal. Help them find peace and learn to live with PTSD rather than hiding from it. It is a weight that is continuously carried on the shoulders, but it is possible to move, the load can be lightened, we are soldiers after all, without the bravado of carrying on, we are trained to do so. I want to be careful saying this though because we do need to be treated with a cotton blanket like all people in this world, I don't just want to tell you to carry on. That would be very wrong of me, but what I am saying is a bit of robustness to carry the load once you have found your direction, let your love be your light, like once you walked with your rifle, now you need to step with your heart.

Riding a Harley Davidson across Route 66 with Bike Tours for the Wounded - photo taken at the Grand Canyon.

Chapter 17

Where there's a will, there's a way

This chapter is a reflection of what I have achieved since leaving the Army. It's not a very long timeline, what I use this for is to remember in comparison to the down days, it is good. These can sometimes be selfish, I don't think anything you should do should be with selfish intent. However, it's occasionally unavoidable. Also, if it makes you happy, go for it, not to fuck people over or to hurt someone, but, if it's something like a holiday or something to look forward to, use it as a goal. When I'm feeling down, I rationalise my thoughts, I also think of what I have to look forward to, even the weekends, plan something that is nice, whether it's a coffee with your partner or taking your Mum for lunch. That can be your goal to get through the week. It's a way to measure your success. When you leave the Army, you're at a lone standpoint. You're used to being told what to do, once you lose that, there's no management in place for your life. No one helps you either, you just have to find your way in the world, once the demons start taking hold of you, it can feel like there is no way out. Rest assured there are ways to manage this.

One of the men I met on my journey is a senior member of a charity called Deptherapy, he is my primary counsellor at the moment in regard to my PTSD. He has also been a bit of a life coach for me, He's like a conservative Russell Brand. He believes in helping people, but our views differ, I believe in love and he believes in practicality, I believe a balance between the two is the route for success in moving forward with PTSD. As I mentioned in the last chapter I was to fly to the moon before I could walk, He is the man who taught me how to walk, I owe a lot to him and Emily because they have aided me with the structure of my life. As well as a confidant for when I feel close to going off the rails, he also provides that life counselling, for someone with my erratic brain it is invaluable. Sometimes you need to make sure a rickety bridge is stable enough to step on before you cross a canyon. I wish everyone who felt a disconnection from this world had that guidance, which would be my sole aim, to give everyone that bannister as they moved along. One of the best things he said to me was

"Gary you're an idiot."

It started like that, that's the relationship we have, I had probably just called him a fossil in all fairness. He continued -

"You need to look at your life, where you want to go, you're an amazing guy with a heart of gold. Realistically though you can't help the whole world, if you start by aiming that high you are only going to hurt yourself. Start small with the things you can change, how you treat people. You have to go to work, think about how you can make that transition easier before you start trying to think about a world where you no longer have to work".

This is right, I needed to start at my foundations, I'm the living secret in thinking all things positive. Unfortunately, that doesn't always mean I'm good at living my present. This is where the balance of what I have come from, where I am now and where I want to be comes in to play. Without this process you can end up crashing, if you start sprinting in a marathon, you probably won't make the finish line. As I sit here now I have sent a string of messages to Emily in a panic because my tablets have run out. I have hit an erratic state of mind.

It's incredible how much you can achieve when someone believes in you. It helps to have a support network, I suggest that anyone leaving the armed forces has a support network as big as possible, whether that's through your local GP or through various charities that operate through the country.

There are so many times that I have had to search for answers, they are not always written on the wall for you to see, once you dig deep enough you will find a lot of good people out there that want to help you. All you need to do is want change. Even if you don't think you have PTSD, there is still a laborious adjustment process to go through to fit back in. I will never be the person I was before I left my Mums house at the age of eighteen, but I think I'm beginning to find a place where I fit. Since I met Emily in two thousand and thirteen, I have been on an incline upwards, I have seen a life where I am happy, it's literally only got better, it's also the point of my life where I turned my back on drink and drugs.

I don't want you to get the wrong impression, thinking I'm just cured now because I'm not. I've only accepted that this is what my life is, I follow a few simple steps that help keep me on the right path, I try and smile every day and each day I'm thankful that I move forward. I also don't want you to think that I'm trying to be a cheap cliché or act like a smug prick because I'm not, I fall like the rest of us. You would be stupid to think I don't enjoy one or two beers on the very odd occasion. This applies only to a couple, I know my limits, I don't push them. All I'm trying to do is hand a few life lessons over to the generation of soldiers that will be left behind after this war, whatever the reasons of the conflict, we have a duty as humans to comfort the souls of those who have injuries. I could die a happy man if I knew that my book turned the life of even one man around, which he faced his demons with a sword prepared by my words. As I've made my way since the beginning of my recovery I've had to borrow weapons to fight my demons, at some points I've laid on my mothers' chest in tears while she has opposed them for me. My partner Emily has had to be my shield as I have held her. If you are to succeed in life with PTSD, then you need to have a big armoury filled with weapons different to those you had at war. The principles are still the same, but the enemy is the everyday obstacles that you need to face. Your section of men by your side has to be your support network, they will give you the fire support you need as you move forward. Your body armour, your rifle, your ammunition is all your mindset. Depending on how strong-willed you are, will define how effective your shield and weapon is.

I have gone from the extremes, of course, like anything it could have been worse, this for anyone is relative, the worse thing that could always happen is death. In that respect regardless of whether I was pumping my veins with heroin or sniffing coke, it could have ever been worse. What I mean though, is that within the boundaries of where my life has been, with my recovery I have probably hit within the region of the extremes. I suppose it's all a matter of perspective, depending on your journey will have you seeing the water in different ways. If you are sinking, you can only see the current underneath which turns the tide of the turbulent waters. On the boat, you may look down and only see calm water reflecting the bright sun. It's important always to remember that both people are looking at the same thing just from a different angle, I have seen both. Before you can look at both sides though you have to be able to swim above the surface. So to you must have also been beneath the water in the first place. You know when you look at a mountain, it's ginormous, it's the natural skyscraper posing a threat over the world as they stand far beyond anything man-made peeking into the clouds, a single arm reach from outer space. Well, they are huge, they go miles under the ground, even more, significant than they appear on land. That's the perspective you're going to need in this life with PTSD. You're going to have to accept that some people will only ever see Everest in a photo. Some will see the top, some will visit, but only a few will ever understand how far beneath the ground it goes and question what's inside. Some will see your faults, some will just want to know who you have killed, what it feels like to hold a gun, some will want to shake your hand. Some will hate you, they will only see you as a hired gun, some though will want to hold you, will understand that beneath the armour is a human being, some will look beneath Everest, those people are the ones you want to keep close.

Always remember that your journey is individual, like fitness, when you first get to training it's very progressive, your drive may start the same way. You have to work on singular tolerances, and you need to stretch your limbs. Do a warm-up before you run a personal fitness test in under ten minutes (my best mile and a half was just under eight minutes). I don't think I could drive it in that time now. Many times along the way I have failed, sometimes it's felt like I was never going to make it, it's strange because I'm talking about mental health like I'm talking about Afghanistan or training. I feel like Rocky when he's midway through a speech to inspire someone for their next big fight. "You can do this, dig deep inside yourself, you can find the metal to carry on, nothing will hit you harder than life, it's not about how hard you can hit it's about how you can get hit, get back up and keep going." (I was doing my Rocky voice in my head as I wrote that... Adriannnnnn). That is how real it is, that is sometimes what you need to get up in the morning. Find purpose, be thankful for what you have, accept that your life is not what it was, but it's still worth something. You may not be in the Army anymore, but you are still worth something, someone still cares about you and your life still has a meaning.

When it comes to my serving years, there is no one prouder than myself, except maybe my Mum who has a giant canvas of me in my uniform on her living room wall. My Nan and Gramp have Rifles cap badges all over their walls, my Gramp even still wears his Rifles polo top I gave him. That's beside the point anyway, I'm very proud of my years in the Army, if you hear me speaking to the right people you would think I was still serving, especially if I'm conversing with friends who still are. The thing with this pride though is it entirely segregates you from the rest of the world, I believed for a long time that I was born to be in the Army, that it was the only thing I could, even would ever do. That adhesive bond you have with your brothers, that feeling of belonging you get when you're given speech after speech about how glorious you are from your section commanders before you go into an attack. That mixed with the reinforcing talisman from your family and friends when you get home and tell them stories, kind of makes you believe it. Then, of course, you live it, weeks spent away, weekdays spent at camp becoming more and more institutionalised every day, so it literally becomes the only thing you know. You even have your own fucking language. What you must remember though, it was a job, it was not fate, it was not the holy grail, it does not define who you are for the rest of your life. It was a conscious choice you made once upon a time in your life, it was something that you did, you were employed by the MOD.

I must admit I still find that hard to accept, especially days like today, yesterday I had to do a thirteen-hour shift at the chicken factory, yesterday was a Saturday, which sucks man.

I must admit I'm reading this back in 2018 - I can't remember when I wrote the above statement. I haven't worked at the chicken factory for two years - apologies for interrupting you anyway, please carry on.

It is just part of healthy normal boring life though. It's part of growing into this world, every hour I was there I was thinking about my life, longing to be where my friends are. It's important to remember what you are working for, I am working for my future, hopefully to a point in my life where I can help people, until then though I'm just trying to get through life now with a smile on my face. When I left my regiment, came into this alien world, I had no idea that I could be happy. I honestly thought I was going to feel worthless until the day I died, whether that was as an old man or from killing myself. From two thousand and ten until two thousand and thirteen I thought of suicide as an actual answer to my problems. I don't think I would ever have done it, but I thought about it as if it was medicine, a surgical procedure that would cure me, thank god I never made it to any of my appointments.

On my journey of self-discovery, being reborn with hopeful spirit through sobriety and support networks, I genuinely have had the most amazing years. Me Gary Green who has sifted through copper coins in his pocket to buy a bottle of cider, Gary Green who has packed drugs inside of a rizla and swallowed it. Gary Green who used to cry to his mum in drunken states has had the most amazing years of his life since. No money in the world, social status, job title or even position of power can separate us from the common bond that we are all human. We all have the ability to change at any one second, and we'll never be limited to less than that. No matter who you are right now, what you are doing right now, you can do whatever you want tomorrow, the power will always be in your hands. When I decided to change, hit the breaks, turn the car around, (Metaphorical vehicle evidently due to my little incident in two thousand and eleven.) I had no idea of what I was capable of, no idea as to the doors that would open up for me. Once you open your shell, spread your wings like a butterfly as it leaves it cocoon for the first time, breaks through the layers of silk that they produced as a caterpillar, decide not to be enslaved by their own creation anymore, they fly into the fresh air where a more extensive world exists. When you do this, you find that there are so many more people out there, other butterflies, the world is not just full of caterpillars. For the metaphorically challenged what I'm saying is, when you open your world, you open yourself up to the people you can meet. When I was taking drugs, I met a lot of people that took drugs, when I stopped taking drugs, I met a lot of people that didn't take drugs. Both were human, but, those not taking drugs were able to elevate me. Don't get me wrong, I met some brilliant people in my darker years, but they wanted to stay in the dark places, I was fortunate enough to have a mindset that wanted to go above that. The people I have met on my rise have also been brilliant, I believe all people are bright, but if I would have stayed in my dark place, I may never have met them. More people certainly does mean more opportunities.

By opening up about my condition, turning to the light side, I had managed to open the floodgates to people who were genuinely wanting to help people like me. Something I never even knew existed, there are many amazing people out there that genuinely want to make a difference. I'm humbled and inspired by the generosity and compassion. A community exists out of the Army, a neighbourhood full of people who want to help, a society where all is welcome. All that is needed is the willingness to be supported, also a desire to help others if needed.

Like a mythical phoenix rises from the fire, I have risen from the fires of hell, I have genuinely walked beside the devil, I have been burned by the flames of my mind, caged inside my imaginary cell. If you are there, your anxieties are no more than an unbalance in your subconscious, you are governed by your emotions, they can be beaten, you can, and you will get past them. As a reborn me, a stronger advocate of PTSD, I have managed to build my life back, piece by piece, day by day, I am now standing on my own two feet far above where I once was. You too can build above and beyond your current parameters, see your mind as a project, learn about anything that is holding you back, belief in the fact that the only thing irreversible in life is death. A wise woman who also happens to be my future mother in law told me that, it's a saying that I value, the rest of the time she talks shit, that's a joke. It allows me to rationalise any problem, combined with the methodical thinking of an ex-serviceman, I believe it gives me an executive armoury to be able to combat my day-to-day. If you can think that everything can be changed, you should never be stuck, whether it's debt, relationship problems, work or whatever the problem, you have the power to change it, as long as you are not dead you can move forward.

Once I adopted this mentality, this unbeatable, non-shakable belief I was able to adapt to being normal, not my half attempts to diet or to give up smoking. Even when I was addicted to drugs I had periods of trying to give up the drink that usually lasted until the weekend, this was different though. I wasn't lying to myself anymore or even lying to social media for a few likes. I was genuinely just standing up and walking forward. With each step I took, I grew stronger, the muscles in my legs were able to carry me further, the winds pushed against my body, the chains of my mind pulled me to the ground. I was strong though, the links broke, the winds felt weaker against my body, I'm still not in a position to run, but each day I understand that as long as I move forward, I will not have to be kept down, no matter how shit my day gets.

As I said before, work was my milestone, it wasn't the finish line though, it was undoubtedly a huge part of my development, it added normality to my life, grounded me slightly, gave me a reason to get up in the morning. The next was the conscious decision not to drink, to avoid situations that may lead me to abandon my rational thought, I don't believe you can reach your goals in life if you abuse alcohol or drugs. From the financial aspect right up to the lack of productivity, nothing good comes from drinking. Drugs are an obvious one. I had to break away from this, also, unfortunately, break away from the people that associated with them. Not because of them, but because of the temptation, I honestly don't believe I am sharp enough ever to cut that tie completely. If I put myself around them, I know I could slip face first into a pint of vodka and an ounce of cocaine at any moment. I still can't be trusted, and that's my fault. To the friends I distanced myself from, one day I may be strong enough to see you again correctly.

Each day I grew a little bit stronger, every day at work I felt myself pull an inch beyond that part of me that was stuck in Afghanistan, that shell I was living as filled up with each alarm that went off at 05:00. It's so strange writing this, something that is everyday life to me now was once an alien existence. Even driving to work is impressive for me, now I'm here I want to enjoy it, smile at the hangovers I don't have now. There have been things I have done now as this new me that would never have been possible. I have worked my way up the civilian corporate ladder, gone from working in the factory to a leader, felt the pride in that achievement, the satisfaction of having my abilities as a person appreciated and recognised. In the years that have followed my progression into everyday life, I have skydived, driven a Lamborghini Gallardo, ran the London Marathon, travelled Route66 on the back of a Harley Davidson and scuba dived off the coast of Egypt. I owe all of the mentioned accomplishments to nothing more than a positive mindset, saying no to PTSD, acknowledging the wrong that I was doing, most importantly just deciding to take the necessary steps in my life to move forward. Open your minds, find the right people out there that you need in your life, cling to those that will elevate you, accept the legs up, deny those who wish to drag you down.

The reason I have chosen those, '*accomplishments*.' (I put that word in italic because they are hardly accomplishments, they are just experiences. However, they are positive.) Is because they are also things I thought I would never get to experience in my life, it was just by opening my mind I was able to seek out the opportunity to be able to do those amazing experiences. I will talk about the less superficial things I have accomplished as well. These are just relevant for this part of the chapter. The skydiving became available through work, it was an annual event that a group of people from work go and do. It's a big day with a BBQ afterwards. If I would never have started working, I would never have come across the opportunity. I felt part of something, I felt accepted, to be invited into this social event, I felt elevated in spirit, also I must add you never feel quite as alive as you do when you are falling from 15,000ft above the earth.

The Lamborghini one is a bit of a cheat. It's not like I even put it in there because it was a big success or anything. It was paid for by my girlfriend, it was a fantastic experience because driving a Lamborghini is cool as fuck. That's not the context it's here for, this isn't a Jeremy Clarkson book, I am not the Stig. I put this in here because it's a prominent symbol of my relationship in a way. It's normal being a couple where you share experiences with each other, Emily has been my rock, she has helped me at my weakness and shared the pride of me at my most successful. Driving the sports car was cool, it was the fabric of it as a present that was the symbol, being appreciated by someone so much that they want to spend the rest of their life with you, that was the accomplishment. The driving experience was a small representation of that, something that I would never have experienced if I hadn't changed, opened up my heart to someone who has taught me how to love again, hugs over drugs – cheap cliché.

The London Marathon was the first time I was able to give something back, I ran it for a forces charity. I looked obese in the vest they sent me, like playdoh squeezed into a bottle cap, horrendous. You know when you used to see people trying to make sausages on game shows, they put the mixture into the skin too fast, so it bubbled up, yeah? That's what I looked like, never mind though. It was a surreal experience, well to be perfectly honest it was traumatic. I hadn't trained nearly enough, I entered the Banbury 15, which is a fifteen-mile cross-country run, I couldn't even finish that, near the end I hid in a cemetery and had a cigarette as I watched pensioners run past, shameful. The event itself had the most glorious atmosphere, a real coming together of every culture that exists in London, all for the common purpose of raising money through sacrifice. For charities with all different agenda. I managed to collect just over £1000 for the charity. When I crossed that finish line my legs were shaking, each time my feet had touched the ground after the sixteenth mile, it was as if my shins were being pelted by a rock and the road I was stepping on was made from nails. To finish that in the name of charity was humbling, to be supported on the way round by people who never even knew me was touching for the soul. If I had never opened up my heart to the idea of help, seen the benefit in charity and accepted support from those willing, the graciousness in being able to give back, I would never have known the humbleness of victory in the name of others.

Riding a Harley Davidson across Route 66, now that was special, it indeed was an eye-opening experience. Also, it was something that someone in my position could only ever have dreamed of. People who grew up on council estates as I did, didn't go to America, let alone on a Harley Davidson. That trip I will have forever embroiled in my skin, we went to Las Vegas, Los Angeles, Saint Monica Pier, the Grand Canyon, just an absolute host of things I had only ever seen in the movies. Not only was I living out a childhood fantasy, but I also had a ten-day break from life. Ten days without having the worries that continually smash against my brain, that was the actual gift of that trip. Flying down high ways and long roads with the wind in my hair, the sun glowing on my face, I was in love with the whole experience. I was surrounded by fellow injured soldiers. Whether you have served together or not, you still share that common bond that ties you together, moulds you into an instantaneous unit of men. This was a charity, they take injured veterans on bike tours around the world, for the more physically injured this could provide a sense of accomplishment. For the mentally scarred like myself, it offered a respite from the daily struggle. This would not have been possible had I not started the long road to recovery. Charity is only afforded for the deserving, seek and ye shall find or so the saying goes anyway. These things are available in life, with or without charity, these experiences exist, if you elevate yourself beyond your own demons, you will discover a life with more flavour. Looking back at what I could have missed out on had I refused to move forward makes me think of what I missed out on while I was stuck in limbo. Maybe it's too late for reflection, perhaps that's null in void, without those years spent trapped I would have nothing to write about for a start. The long and short of it is, stop hiding away from PTSD, stop using it as an excuse not to live, seek help and you may be able to go to America, bing bang bosh.

I also believe fate has a part to play, like, with Emily, there are a lot of things that have made me think we are meant for each other, even down to the timing. Perhaps if my life had inclined before I met her, we would never have found each other. Also by being in America at that time, I met Chris, he is a double amputee that was injured in Afghanistan, we grew a strong friendship straight away, I love the geezer I really do. To be honest, his high spirit makes me ashamed to be so fucking depressed, that's not strictly true, everyone suffers in different ways, rarely will you see a bloke with no legs always have such a smile on their face though. We both donned our motorbike vests as we walked around different parts of the states. You would have thought it was a camp version of Sons of Anarchy the way we cut about, being loud with our exaggerated British accents and combed over hair. It is that brotherhood that makes all your problems drift away, I never feel as safe as I do when I'm with my brothers, brothers in arms, brothers for life. I've diverted again as I usually do, the reason it's important, the reason it is like fate is that Chris was an ambassador for Deptherapy.

From where I had been in my life, the day to day struggle to move forward with my mind strangling me, I had reached a point in my life where I could say I was happy, could even say I felt safe. I wasn't going to let my life be controlled by my mind. I wasn't going to let anyone tell me I would be PTSD for the rest of my life, I wasn't going to be limited by anyone or anything. If being blown up in Afghanistan taught me one thing, it was that life is short, too short to spend it laid in my bed with a blocked nose, too short to fear my life for the rest of my life.

Me deep sea diving in the Red Sea with Deptherapy. Helping a double amputee under water.

Chapter 18
No more free trips

So, with the fate of meeting Chris on the Route 66 trip, I am aware that I am yet to tell you why it was fateful, hold your horses I am getting to that bit. I just had to close off the previous chapter, the importance of moving forward. Otherwise, it was just some dickhead telling you about how he did some things once, the emphasis is why he was able to do them. So, I met Chris, I opened up to him about a lot of my issues, how I had been struggling to adjust back to life since leaving the Army. We also shared stories of how we were double hard squaddies because that's what you do. We didn't talk much about the charity he was working for, also I took it as lip service, not to be rude. When you meet an old friend you don't speak to anymore, and you close the momentary reunion with, "we'll have to meet up sometime." You mean it as you say it, but, you never see them again. That's how I took it, however, a few weeks after the trip, I received a message. Chris had been speaking about me with Rich, not hard to believe because I'm awesome. He had told him about how I was struggling, he had described my journey. Everything we had exchanged in the natural context of conservation, it's effortless to open up with other veterans because you just know they will understand, you need no mask, you need no guard up.

They were keen to get me involved with the charity, they truly believed they could help me. Richard believed in me from day one, he read my writing, he spoke to me, and he listened. The first few correspondences were through messages, I think he wanted to gauge me, make sure I wanted the help, also make sure that I was ready for it. It's easy to say you want help while you're feeling down, just because you want to feel better, like when you're hung-over, as soon as the hangover goes though you're happy to carry on. The other thing is, you get a lot of bull shitters, people who jump on the bandwagon of PTSD.

Especially since there have been a few programmes about it, now anyone who's been in the armed services which are having a shit day, automatically say it's PTSD. These sorts of people are just attention seekers, they waste charity money though, that's where I don't agree. People give their money in the hope of helping someone in need, it should not be wasted on people who are looking for a sympathy vote.

I was coping at work better, I was pushing to move forward rather than dwelling on the fact that I may be forever stuck. I think my dreams make me doomed to be unsatisfied, whatever I accomplish, no matter how many times I'm promoted if it is not the end game then I feel like my appetite has not been absolute. Perhaps mildly wetted by a slight pay rise. I have this thing where I am consumed by the idea of being a writer and work is almost a chore. As if it's unfair that I am pulled from my calling to work in a blue-collar dress, besides from sitting in Costa with my laptop, I have a career. I have a five-year plan, but because it's not writing, I feel like it's redundant, that I've failed again in life if I have to settle with it, how arrogant. Richard is the Nemesis to this arrogance I have, arrogance is slightly unfair I suppose. It's a subconscious feeling, I feel hurt by it rather than actively yearning to feel unfulfilled. Regardless of the reasoning for my undying terror of living a healthy life, my knight in shining armour swoops down with a swift blow of realisation to make me aware of the fact that, life sucks. It's a simple answer to a lot of my problems, the point is that in this life not many people enjoy their job. If you're honest with yourself if your employer stopped paying you, would you turn up tomorrow? Probably not, but unfortunately we all need those little notes in our bank accounts. So, I put it in the most straightforward term 'until you are a writer, you need to go to work otherwise you will have no house, unarguably a real but shite fact.'

The charity was organising a December trip to Egypt, a place called Roots, which sat on the coast of the Red Sea. I was put forward for the trip, Richard believed that from speaking to me, scuba diving was going to help me. I was sceptical, to say the least, I love the water though, so out of all the therapy I have had over the years, this was one I was keen to try. Richard and I spoke frequent, after reading more of my writing, hearing how much I wanted to help people, he talked to the board members of the charity. They unanimously decided to make me an ambassador of the foundation, I was the first person to become an ambassador before going on the diving trip. As an ambassador, it was my job to speak to veterans who may be struggling. I was already trying to do this through my writing. I am continually searching for veterans who may be struggling, to work and guide them through whatever it is they are having problems with. I honestly believe if you can help someone or just make someone smile each day, then that is not a day wasted.

Feeling inspired by my new position, I decided to make a video to raise awareness for those who have PTSD, perhaps for those who can't see the symptoms yet, even for families who just need to recognise the signs. I followed the theme for a day in the life of me, it starts with a workout, then getting in the bath, trying to hold my head beneath the water. Then once out I'm looking through Afghan photos and drinking alcohol. I go to take my tablets but then end up throwing them across the kitchen. There are a few scenes like this all leading up to the point where I write a letter to my Mum and then hang myself. The whole thing is silent with me providing a voice over of my poem, the end scene as I step of my stand with my regimental tie wrapped around my neck is haunted with an echo of the last sentence of my poem. "I died in that war." I am aware of the fact I made that sound as painful as a fart in an elevator. However, if you watch the video, it's honestly really good.

On social media the video had over 250,000 views, on its YouTube post it had over 3,500, it is a staggering number of people to reach. I only hope to ever achieve more though through my writing and hopefully through TV/film in the future. It was undoubtedly a step in the right direction though, it also gained a lot of interest from veterans who began contacting me. This was from all over the world. People were asking for my help, telling me it was the first time they had seen something that truly captured how they felt. I had helped people. The below is a message I received from a mother of a US veteran.

"Hello, I'm across the pond in these not so United States of America. (Love your posts and enthusiasm, positivity, joy & belief in humanity.)

But I just Needed to tell you that a year ago today you posted a poem on PTSD, well I read & reread that poem every time I'm about to see or talk to my son, U.S. army vet injured in Baghdad, the only survivor of his squad in Sadyr city, 2007. His PTSD keeps him locked up inside himself, every suicide attempt grows more lethal... your words and my refusal to give up, well, I want to humbly thank you...on the anniversary of the attack I wasn't all mushy or needy, I simply wrote "son, I'm texting to acknowledge the somberness of this day, all that you lost. Please do whatever you need to do this day, to grieve, to honor what you've given, the brothers you lost. I will never say I understand, for I never will, as you will never understand my own hell, waiting, terrified I wouldn't remember your voice, but I'm okay, and I'm hugging you and all your fellow infantrymen in my heart. Now I leave you to honor this day in your own way, honor your grief, for the fallen and the falling. Just know I am and always will be here if ever you should need me."

~ Mr. Green, my tormented son responded IMMEDIATELY w/. "Momma, your words, giving me space & room to be alone, I know how hard that it is for you & why it means so much to me, you made me want to open up for the First time... Thank you momma, you probably cried texting me those words, that was incredibly brave of you.... I love you."

~ Sorry so wordy, but from the depth of my soul, I honor you, your work, your passion. That poem you wrote may have saved

his life that killing season (March/April '07).

Respectfully, one soldiers lucky momma.... bless you & yours...."

Being able to help people feels like a calling, a reason to be, a reason to get up in the morning. As well as having to go to work, I do feel a sense of employment through my promotion of all that is PTSD. It's a feeling that gifts more than anything that money can purchase, a reward for helping someone is a warm glow on the inside, it can't be seen, it can be interpreted through a smile that never leaves my face. No financial sum in the world could replace the feeling I have now, the feeling of being able to help, to inspire people out of the darkest places. If I could I would genuinely invest every second of my time into people that need it, I have a deep pain in my heart for all those that suffer. I sincerely believe that if we all unite, if we find that which brings us together stronger than that which tears us apart, we could genuinely all be happy. I'm not in a position to save the world, maybe one day I will, at this point I would just like my face to be used as a MEME for positive inspiration. So world peace is in the future, a pipeline goal lets say. At the moment I am lucky enough to be able to help a few people, whether it's through my writing or my video. I can raise awareness and make a difference, through my position in Deptherapy I hope that I can only do more.

I wish I were more spiritual. I would love to be one of those green eaters, only eat vegetables. Yoga at six In the morning, drink gallons of water per week, clean soul stuff. It's just not me. It's not in my genetic makeup, I love coffee, I like pork pies, burgers and chocolate, especially when all that American gear started coming over, selling Twinkies in the pound shop was genius. I'm no slob don't get me wrong, I'm not a couch potato, I'm not even that fond of TV, I have been known to get addicted to the odd series, especially if it sparks my imagination. When Breaking Bad hit the screens I was absent from work for a week with a multi-pack of crisps ramming salt and vinegar down my neck, I'm surprised Gary Linekar didn't bust through the living room window. I am trying to encourage myself somewhat to be slightly more health conscious. Especially the cigarettes, it seems to be my only vice though, plus I think I look like a badass when I smoke, what a knob eh? I think we all need to do it, mass diet for the nation, join Jamie Olivers' bandwagon, I was a bit gutted when he said no to Turkey Twizzlers though. Get rid of the chips, I agree with you, but potato smiley faces? C'mon they look so happy. The only reason I've said all the above is because of the mindset we're all stuck in. Now I see things from a different point of view. Perhaps rather than Turkey Twizzlers being the friend of the smiley potato faces in my school life nostalgia, maybe they were part of the problem why I can't now diet as easy as I want to? I think advertising warped a lot of our perceptions. If the potato faces weren't smiling, we wouldn't have eaten them. If the Army weren't portrayed as glamorous, I wouldn't have joined, and perhaps if PTSD weren't so invisible it would have more recognition?

Excuse the above I was just rambling on, as usual I know. As the video grew popularity, I networked throughout the dive community, the reception was incredible. There is a tremendous amount of support for our armed forces. This was refreshing. I just wish to replicate through the entire world, not only for soldiers, for all humanity, compassion for all, from all. People suffer for all reasons, it isn't just soldiers who face daily struggles, everyone does, you should never look down on someone. We may be on different levels but we're all certainly on the same boat, if it all comes crashing down, everyone will need everyone's help, digressing again but that's just my nature, perhaps I care too much? Is that possible?

In December I went on the trip to Egypt, it got off to a bad start, on the plane I was handed a scalding hot coffee at the same time we hit a slight turbulence. The beverage landed on my foot, I only had a pair of trainers on, the gym kind that has breathable material, they worked perfectly in absorbing the scalding liquid, so just the right amount got my foot. Of course, I acted double hard like it never bothered me, two minutes later I felt my skin flame up as if someone had a flamethrower on me, it's no exaggeration either, I was in agony. Stuck however high in the air with a hot foot is not lovely. Can't go and run it under a cold tap, it was absolutely horrific. The skin had gone elasticised, it moulded to whatever shape you put it in. Richard had a walking stick on him, it was a fold up one, he has terrible hips but the walking stick was extended to me. As we made our way through the airport I had my walking stick, next to me was a paratrooper who had lost his leg in Afghanistan, he walked on a prosthetic leg, I felt like a royal prick walking next to him limping because of a cup of coffee. At least I fitted in more with the crowd, thank god no one asked me what was up, I would have had to said I was hit with a grenade. Maybe I'll write another book, 'Coffee For Breakfast - the dangers of a beverage at 30,000ft.' The Taliban need to do away with I.E.D's. They should be running around with kettles and a pot of coffee. "Look out lads he's got an espresso machine on rapid fire – fucking hell it's a Kenko grenade aghhhhh."

My partner read all the above writing, I like her to read through what I've written, it makes me proud, it also boosts my ego a little bit, everyone needs that reassurance don't they? She was honest with the first part of the chapter. She said it wasn't as gripping as the rest, a bit harsh because I thought the Jamie Oliver and Tetley grenade bit was funny? I hope that's not true, if you're bored I apologise, I'm just trying to walk you through my journey. I didn't want it to be all guns blazing though, I could write one book on what happened in Afghanistan but I just find it quite repetitive, the same with the drugs and the abuse to my family. What I want to give you is the full picture, the three sixty of my life, the journey of a man that managed to find himself after being lost. Every word has been necessary, every second I have spent in a recovery of PTSD has been a battle. Every person who has held that hand out to me has been a lifeline. At no point have I tried to find page fillers, my emotion runs through every page of this book, it is with tears, sweat and blood that my story becomes a full circle. I have written this with the intention that one day someone says to me that because of my book they found the strength to turn their life around.

Anyway all that explaining of my battered ego aside, I arrived in Egypt with a gammy foot, long hair held back with my adventurous hair band, (that I had bought in the duty-free at Heathrow) and my carton of Marlborough Gold. It was amazing. I love being in other countries, I enjoy other cultures. On the bus to the dive centre we were in the pitch black, we had met up with our dive instructors, as soon as we were on that bus, the banter started flying around. It was like back in the day on our way to the ranges, if someone had stuck their willy in my mouth while I was asleep I would have felt right at home. Just for your information, I'm not homosexual it's just that in the Army, someone putting their willy in your mouth was a punishment of falling asleep.

The actual ins and out of that trip are not necessary, this isn't a tourist book, it isn't a diary of an idiot abroad either, there is real substance within the journey. For the first two days we were in the pool, basically learning how to scuba dive, it was cool being under the water and being able to breathe, quite the sensation. We had to simulate every eventuality that could happen while in the sea. It's a lot less forgiving than a pool but believe me, the feeling of having no air or just your regulator popping out of your mouth is terrifying. It was more severe than I had imagined, naively I figured you grabbed your tank and jumped in the water, there was indeed a lot more to it than that. I enjoyed the regimental structure of learning the drills and skills that could save my life. I felt like I was back in Catterick, back with the boys, I was a part of something again. It was refreshing to have that feeling.

Once we had completed the skill set in the pool, it was time to head out into the sea. This was what I had been waiting for. When I entered that water for the first time my heart was pounding, there's something quite unnatural about going under water, your mind sort of knows that it isn't right, but once your head goes under the mind shuts off. I was talking to myself in my head, but I wasn't thinking if that makes sense, or maybe that's how I should feel all the time, only focussing on the now. I was saying the drills to myself, and I was looking forward and behind to make sure my buddies were ok. I was checking my gas, I was reading my depth, but I had no other thoughts in my head, I wasn't torturing myself, I had no anxieties. I was just gliding through the sea with ignorance of anything that was happening above the surface of my freedom.

As we entered the reef, we were briefed that we were to follow a line that would get us from the shores current to the sea that waited further afield. Even those first few moments being under water, pulling ourselves across the guide ropes was such an adventure, something I had only ever seen in movies. Something I never knew could be experienced in the real world. My eyes were wide open, more open than I had ever known them to be, I was fixated on every detail that this alien world had to offer. I was mesmerised by the way the sand floated as it was disturbed to the way I was able to drift in time, feel weightless. I was a jet in this underwater airspace. I was able to operate with no withdrawal, I conducted myself like a soldier again, using my kit to its full capacity, my compressed mind did not minimise me. I felt as if the further I went the less pressure was on my mind, I was captivated in the moment. If I could feel like I had at that moment for the rest of my life, I would never have to worry again, I felt reborn in the sea, like a seal that had burst its mothers' womb in the ocean and began to swim. I was at one with myself I flew through the water, I found happiness, true happiness, the kind that makes you smile on the inside and the outside.

I found a secret in the water, I am Poseidon, I am the god of liquid, I am the unshuttering master of my own feelings. I can decide whether I am happy or sad. I have only been placed in another place so how can my feelings change? How can I be satisfied in one place but not another? Surely if I can be happy in one, I can be content in another? If I hold a potato in one side of the room, then walk to the other, it will still be a potato. So, if I'm happy here, then I go home, I should be happy there? It makes sense to me. I can't take the sea with me, but if I could just capture this contentment I have in the water, if I can somehow dope myself with this at home I would have slain all my demons. If I could bottle this feeling, I would sell it and become a millionaire. It's all just a reflection on what I learnt from it, in the water I was too busy being mystified by my surroundings to contemplate what anything meant. I was in love with this world. If you have been diving, then you probably know what I mean. If I could live there I would, what a simple existence, all you have to do is smile and keep your eyes open. In the water though, everything can change in a second. Over a large piece of the reef I saw Dickie swimming holding on to Danny, one of the other lads on the trip. He was holding onto his gas tank, which had come loose, I could see the panic on his face, rightly so as well, there are no second chances to be had. Literally, under the water, you get it right, or you die. Maybe it was this excitement, this endearing danger that made me feel alive again. That's why I was so content here. The fear kept me interacting. The story isn't that exciting, to be honest, all I did was hold Dannys' hand while Dickie and Andy strapped his tank back to his BCD, (Buoyancy Control Device.) In my head it was far more dramatic though, I joked for the rest of the trip that I saved his life. Danny if you are reading this, then honestly don't worry mate anyone would have done the same, don't mention it, haha.

It would be an overstatement, to say that diving cured my PTSD, I am not healed, I am perhaps forever broken. Yes the statement that diving cured me is far too bold. What diving offered me was the chance to see that there is a world in which I can live where PTSD does not. That, believe or not I can unlock my savage cage, I can bask in the glory of normality, there is a place where I am equal, a life where I am not subservient to my mind. That was reassuring, it gave me hope, I was in the best position that I had been in life. I was working, I had a home, I had a partner, my French bulldog, I had my driving license back, but I was still missing something that was not covered. I was hollow, I was heading for another fall, I could feel it, I was scared of it, the anxiety alone was eating away at me, the hope I got from diving kept my head above the water. In a metaphorical sense anyway, in reality, I was twenty meters below. That precious realisation of salvation gave me another reason to fight, another bullet in the gun that was no longer held at my own head. I was just able to see the light, that there was an end to the tunnel, that I won't have to be afraid for the rest of my life. If there is anything in that world that can give you that feeling, then reach out with both hands, find anything that can help you break what you know. Find something that restores faith in yourself, belief in the impossible. The whole time I've been writing this book all I've wanted you to think is, 'well if he can do it, I can.' I'm just a man who had a good family, a good support network, and I was lucky enough that the people I needed gravitated towards me. It's the power of attraction, belief in yourself. You can pull yourself from wherever you are. Diving for me was a revelation, it was the revealing of myself, the birth of another confidence, another boost up the mountain, in life you need to use the things that help you, like a big game of snakes and ladders.

After the trip I had to return home, back to the fires of day-to-day life, the existence that made me feel like I was walking on nails, each day I have to wrap my feet up and start again. Back to the tablets every day, back to saying the serenity prayer when I'm hit with belts of depression. I have to use my strength every day to stop me falling, our lives can't be perfect, they can be happy though. That's what I aim for every day, no matter how shite I feel about myself, I try to do something different, something that puts a smile on an otherwise sad face. It was great being an ambassador for the charity, even though I was home, I was still involved, now I could pay it forward as well, offer the realisation to other people that may need it. On a daily basis, I was communicating with other people who had PTSD, helping them get through the day, sharing my experiences with them. Help others make the journey I did. There's no one I can't mention, because all in some way helped me get to where I am now, whether that was directly through helping me or just teaching me a lesson, no one helped more than the other.

I was asked to give a talk at a fundraiser. Apparently, I was chosen because of the realisation I had had and because my words as well. Hopefully, I'm as talented at this writing malarkey as I think I am, if not then I guess I will have to take up another hobby. There's not many I haven't tried. My head got slightly bigger as I walked into the fundraiser, I had my Mum with me, we were clapped into the hall with a standing ovation as we were guided to our seats. It was very emotional to be celebrated, a strange feeling, to be honest, I wasn't used to it. Very humbling that people would go out of their way to organise such an event, to donate their own money, then clap you into the hall as well. We had dinner, thank god as it gave me a chance to pluck up some courage before having to speak to a very educated, upper-class audience. To warm up the crowd before I talked to them my video was played. At the end of the video I stood up to a round of applauds, I could see people in the audience with tears running down their faces, men and women. It made it more important, but harder, it brought home the importance of what I was doing. I feel like that added more pressure to me. I was shaking as I stood in front of everyone, just like at my passing out parade all those years ago, the twitching leg was still there.

What I learnt from this is that charity is right, it can provide a source of funded income that would otherwise not exist. I realised that I was more supported by Deptherapy outside of the trip than when I was on it. The funding that is raised in my opinion needs to be centred on this support. It's no good sending injured troops on luxurious trips. Anyone can go on holiday. There is still life to live before and after that trip though. What's the point sending forces' skiing, skydiving, surfing or whatever else there is out there? That doesn't help with the life that they live in the real world. I wouldn't just want the publics' money to be spent on holidays. It needs to be focused on rehabilitation and reintegration. The lads might not agree with me when faced with the option of skydiving in California or a CV course, but I can guarantee the CV course will do more good. There should be no more free trips! If you want a holiday, then go to work and pay for one. The charity should be there to help you get to a point where you can pay for one. Life coaching and career support. Daily help and reinforcement, not a free trip to take some nice photos then fuck you off back into a world you don't understand. It's a waste of money and waste of resource.

From this I propelled, and I am now a PADI Ambassadiver for the UK. I have been made a board member and trustee of the charity. I am making a difference. I have completed my Rescue Diver, Dry Suit Diver and Wreck Diver courses. I am now a trainee PADI Dive Master; this is all working for me being able to teach disabled veterans (mentally and physically) how to dive and free them from their demons. Last year, 2017, just before Christmas I had the pleasure of being able to fulfil a dying mans wish through this new gift I have received. The below two paragraphs explain this.

The cold metal of the bolt on my shed stung my bare skin as I pulled it from the lock. My knuckles turned white as I pulled the stubborn pin free. Inside my shed my diving gear was stowed away, protected from the elements, I sorted through the various tools that I would not need, the diving knife, the boots for my dry suit and the Halo dive torch presented to me by John W (Otter Dry suits) all placed back in its housing. My Apecs regulators, fins and BCD were set inside my travel pack. The temperature must have been below zero degrees as I filled my car boot in the early morning frost. The remnants of the previous weeks' snow had mostly been washed away by the rain. Pieces of ice were still present on my driveway, it occurred to me had quickly things could change, a week ago my car was completely snowed in. I started the car to free the windshield from the condensation smothering the glass. I looked down at my legs, I may have made a mistake wearing the shorts I was going to dive in. The hairs on the bare skin stood up as if saluting the cold air as the engine ticked over forcing cold air through the vents. I held my body waiting for the cold air to turn warm.

Cars rushed around me, a light rain bashed against the window, wipers swiped left and right giving a second of clear sight until reinforcements replaced them. Then swipe, swipe, again the droplets were smashed away and forced off the car. The cars in front threw up dirty water from the road, trailing their movement creating a slipstream of mist behind them. I was in no rush, I wasn't going to be involved in a car accident, what would be the point? Just how quickly the snow had gone, filled the roads only to be washed away by a more powerful mother nature, the man I was going to meet knows how quickly things can change. I was not going to waste whatever life I have been granted by rushing in the rain filled road. The man, Colin C has brain cancer, not long ago he was healthy, he spent around 600 hours underwater diving, clearing the Thailand Sea from plastics and fishing wire. Then just like how quickly the snow had disappeared, so too did his health. Only this information and realisation has forced me to see my mortality, as my car hit a patch of water snatching the traction from my wheels, I realised I was not in control. Nothing is a given, life is fragile, so as I watched cars speed passed me I couldn't help questioning their decision. It would only take a second for everything to change, I slowed down and decided that anything that was in my control, I would take, I was not going to crash on the motorway for being ignorant, Colin's story had taught me that. I took him diving in a pool near Sandhurst, it was his dying Christmas wish, to see him smiling as his head came up above the pool water made my journey in life, let alone across the motorway, worthwhile. He died three months after that dive, I had the gift of meeting him and being able to make a difference, no matter how big or small.

We all need a purpose in life, it must be more than a materialistic one, it must be one that gives you a warm fuzzy feeling inside, mine comes from the emotions I make people feel through my story. I hope it helps provide people that understanding. Compassion is necessary, I think we all need it. I don't want my children or my children's children to live in a world where we find it ok to hurt each other. War is not the answer, the only people that think war is the answer is those who make money from it. The only people who think war is glorious is those who have never had to go.

Divers

A band of brothers all in suit, some with fins, some no boot,

Wet suits tailored to cover limb, battling currents battering him,

A band of brothers strong together, on land, in water, in any weather,

We stick as one side-by-side, in the desert or highest tide,

No missing limb could stop him dive, the feeling keeping him alive,

Whether swimming arms or kicking feet, not one man admits defeat,

They were once soldiers, now are survivors,
They are now veterans, now are divers.
- *Gary Green*

Me, my Mum and my little brother Ashley - this photo was taken late 2009 at the 4 Rifles Medals Parade.

Chapter 19
Straight from the horse's mouth

Before typing the following account up, I first had to read what my Mum had to say about all this, the twenty-eight-year rollercoaster. It was probably as hard for me to read, as it had been for her to write it. The below is her account, she has been the closest person to me while I have been through each of these emotions, especially the downward spiral that followed my tragic injury. You have read my story. Hopefully, it has helped you in some way, whether that was recognising your demons or merely the knowledge that there is always a light at the end of the tunnel. If it was just understanding that you needed, then I hope you reclaimed which you sought. If for any reason there is any need for reinforcement, then I hope my Mums input will solidly concrete your need for her desperate words. Please read with a sympathetic heart from the broken one from which these words came forth. Below is my biggest supporter, the person I treated the worst, the person I love the most, my Mum.

Well, it all began on the 5th June. I woke to labour pains about 7.30am, pretty strong may I add. I took my daughter Kylie to my Mums. She was 14 months old at the time, I was so excited, I had always wanted my children to be close in age. I hoped they would grow up together, be close friends, I was not wrong, as that's what happened. My labour grew harder and faster. I was pushing from two in the afternoon until nine o'clock at night, that's when Gary finally made his appearance. There he was, my beautiful baby boy, my family was complete. Well, not really, my marriage was already soured, but I had two children now and had to protect them. So life went on, so did the fights. In the end, as a mother my instinct was to protect them, I had to keep them safe no matter what the cost, so I filed for divorce and started my life alone with my children, which I continue to do right to this very day.

As a child Gary was very much a mummies boy, he would cry when I left the room or put him down. He was a good boy, straight to sleep when I put him to bed, always up between four and five, yes he was an early baby. I would have all my housework done by eight in the morning, congrats to me. Gary and Kylie loved each other, even to this day I get scared when they get their heads together because it always means trouble for me, they were mischievous together from day one. We would spend hours down the park having picnics, even if it were raining I would say, “right that’s it grab your coats and wellies, we are going on an adventure." So off we went to a wet and gloomy park, but we always had fun. I never liked my babies being at school, I missed them and wanted them close to me. I would help at the school as much as I could, and I loved it. I never lost a parents evening or a school play, even when Gary had to play the troll under the bridge bless him.

The school was not a good time for Gary, don't get me wrong he had plenty of friends, but he would much rather be with me at home. So he would cry a lot, he would even have to be pulled off me. There is nothing worse than having to see and leave your crying child at school (see mummies boy). His schoolwork was right, he never got bottom marks, but he never got top marks either. Maths was his best subject. The big school took a long time for Gaz to get used to. He hated it and even got my sister to take him because he just used to cry, I could not get him there alone, I would give in. It was bloody awful. When Gary’s baby brother was born, oh my gosh Kylie and Gary were so excited to have this beautiful baby. They welcomed him with their arms and their hearts. I remember walking through the park, Gary’s friend came up to us and said.

"Is this the baby?" Gary said "yes." The lad looked into the pram and said "well done Gaz" and walked off as if he was Gary’s baby. I had to laugh.

I did not want my children to be jealous in any way of their new baby brother. I waited for the little money I would get to come through, and I would spend it straight on them. We would even go for dinner, not very exciting but we never really had much, we were like four best friends. They would bring all their friends to see Ashley. They were so excited, I really had nothing to worry about. They loved him so much and were very protective of him.

As the years went by, the children got older. Kylie would hang out with friends. Gary watched Ultimate Force with Ross Kemp. He was obsessed with the violence, the heroism. He would watch them over and over again, and the boy even built a base camp down the garden behind the shed. Gary finally finished school. He still had his job at Littlewoods, I was so very proud of him, such a hard worker, everybody there loved him. He was polite and helpful, he knew just how to act in front of the right people, such a good boy. Back to the Ultimate Force, this was what he wanted to do with his life, lead men, his troops, his followers in the battle. He wanted to wear that gear with pride, so he came to me and said he's going to the Army's Career Office. As a mum I was scared, but at the same time I was so proud! My soldier boy all dressed up so smart. Everyone was so happy, excited, thrilled as Gary went off to make his two-day selection. By this time I had a five-year-old son Ashley, who loved his brother very much. We all missed him so much, but, of course, when he came home he had passed with flying colours, as he always did.

As a mum, you go through so many emotions. It's not been easy bringing them up alone. He's my little army base boy who used to tie his sister's dolls to the fire guard and shoot them before their heads would melt, stood in front of me ready for the army.

After Gary's selection he went out drinking with his friends for the first time, I waited up for him as you do. When the door knocked, a policeman stood there and said, "does this belong to you" while holding up my son. I wanted to say no but of course I never. The policeman said they didn't want to arrest him as he said he was joining the army. I said thank you for bringing him home safe. They laughed saying something like 'we think you will do more damage than us.' The next day Gary said that he hated being that drunk, that it was not what he wanted to do with his life. I said, "thank god for that, you have to set a good example for your little brother, someone to be proud of, and someone he can look up to."

Off went Gary for his six months training, there was not a dry eye in the house. In those six months, I only saw Gary a handful of times. He spoke about his training, and it was terrible to hear. When he sent me a text, I would cry. He told me about the gas chamber, how they punched him in the stomach so he would breathe in the gas, how he was sick afterwards. All the running he had to do, then be sick again. He hated heights but was even managing them, I don't know how but he was handling the whole of it well, he was having the time of his life. We went to visit him after the first six weeks were up, it was terrific. They were all so young. Just babyfaces in green clothes. I had never felt so cold, I've never felt cold like it. Even my bones were frozen, but as I said, Gary loved it. I have heard rumours about Catterick, so I was worried. I kept asking him if he was ok but his face and his grin said it all! I missed him, but soon the big day was here, it had finally arrived. My baby boy had passed, he had got through and completed his six months training. Not only had he finished, but he also got Best Recruit, my son! My god, I was so proud. We had a t-shirt made for Ashley and his cousin with the soldiers' picture on saying, 'good luck boys.' Ashley's little face was a picture, his big brother was going to be a soldier. We hired a van that day, and a few of us went. It was wonderful watching my son march across the courtyard. We all cheered when they said, "the best recruit." There he was, stood in his uniform, that proud smile stayed with me for a long time. Gary came home for a while. He was going to choose 1st battalion, but for some reason, he decided, the fourth Battalion the rifles. Wow, what a smart name. I must have told everyone I bumped into, my son, the rifleman, how proud am I? I think most of the family had put Gary's photo wearing his uniform in the local paper. I think at that time I wanted the world to know.

He still had a very close relationship with his sister just like I wanted they had grown up very close, and I'm sure they will always remain best friends. He left Catterick, and he became Rifleman Green 30037006 of Quiwi barracks, Salisbury. He was so excited, it was what he wanted, what he had dreamed of for a good while now. His fellow soldiers came to stay at weekends, what a good bunch they were. They liked drinking, but they never brought trouble back to my house, the police never had to knock my door. They respected me, my house and the others that were staying here, Ashley, Kylie, and kylies partner. In fact, for a good while things were excellent, when my son Gary would see his uncles or granddad he would shake their hand and call them sir. Whenever I left the house, I would come home to all the housework having been done. The washing up in the drainer, the laundry hung out to dry. I would be thinking. 'Who's this? What have you done to my real son?'

Wow, I liked the army, it's made a man out of my son. But then that moment I had been dreading came, the one thing I never wanted to happen. Gary had his date for Afghanistan, the 9th June 2009. This could not be, please no, not my son. I had been watching it on TV, I was terrified, his friend, a soldier also from Banbury, had been telling him all about Afghanistan. At one point he said he didn't want to go, but soon he was telling me how excited he was and how he vowed to stand by his brothers' sides. See by then it was all about his brothers, they were his family, there was nothing he would not do for them, their bond was so powerful. He loved them, It was lovely to see, they thought the world of Gary, I often thought it was true what they say, brothers for life.

The weekend before departure soon came, it was Gary's birthday on Friday the fifth June, so his mates came down for a birthday and farewell drink, I was going on a holiday Saturday sixth June, so we all went out together. I was so nervous, I was petrified of him going, this might be the last time I see my son alive, maybe the last time I see him with all his body parts. My sister saw how upset I was, we were supposed to be having fun, but it was more of a nightmare for me. I stayed up waiting for the boys, I was leaving for Yarmouth but Gary was passed out, I tried so bloody hard to wake him. I wanted to hug him, say bye, I needed him to know how much I loved him, how much I would miss him but he did not wake. The other three did and said goodbye on his behalf, but it was not the same. I got in the minibus with my family and cried the whole way, Gaz phoned me from the airport, but the phone cut off. I found a café and sat alone in silence for quite a while, little did I know I would not be ok and that things were going to change forever, If only I knew.

He would ring me from Afghanistan. Sometimes he would sound upset, scared. Sometimes I could hear gunfire in the background. I would send, well the whole family would mail him, and his mates' parcels. Even the man in the post office said, "blimey he eats better than me" and laughed. Little did I know that Gary never received many of them. I would often cry myself to sleep if I had a call from him. Sometimes I stayed awake all night. The worry would be crushing my head, making me feel sick. I could not get him out of my mind. I tried to get on with normal things but how could I? My child was out there in that awful place, every time you turned the TV on another soldier was dead. You would feel awful because you were happy it was not your child, then realise my god its someone else's child. I had a phone call from Gary, I was always so relieved to hear his voice. He was alive and safe, but this was different, he kept talking about a child, Abdul john. They brought him to the gate, he was so upset to see the child in a wheelbarrow unconscious wrapped up in clothing. Gary grabbed him, picked him up and his legs fell off, this was just too much for Gaz. He was crying on the phone, repeating himself over and over. "There was nothing I could do. He's dead." Over and over again. When he finally put the phone down, I fell to the kitchen floor and sobbed for ages, my god that phone call was horrific.

My mum and I had arranged to go out for the day with my cousin Mary, I started putting washing out as it was a sunny day. I was looking forward to a day, but I said to my neighbour that I didn't feel well. I have no idea where those words came from I just said that I didn't feel right. On the journey there I shouted, "please stop the car, I need to get out!" Mary pulled over. "I just don't feel right. I feel sick. Something is wrong". I know at that point my phone had rung, I looked at it and couldn't answer. I handed it to Mary and walked away then just stared at her face. I watched her expression change, and I knew, I just knew. "Its Gary isn't it?" my whole world collapsed. I've never felt anything like it, I sat in the car silent, I could hear nothing, I did not speak for a long time.

We went back to Marys' house where the padre phoned me, he let me know that Gary's face was quite messed up, but he was chatting up the nurses. The next day we drove to Solihull, it seemed to take forever, they sat us in the family room when we got there. Through the glass I could see Gary, he came into the room, but I could already see he was different, I held him in my arms for a while but he did not hold me back, he just said. "What are you doing here, don't be silly." It was awful, so strange. There was nothing I could say or do, even his uncle tried to talk to him. Gary just laughed and said odd things, and then he said with a louder voice.

"I couldn't help him. There was nothing I could do, he just died."

I said, "I know love." I tried to reassure him, and then he snapped back at me.

"I know, why are you talking about him, there is nothing I can do."

So we sat in silence for a while, my brother and I just looked at each other. Later on, we went back to the hotel. We were so quiet, we got a drink and sat in the garden, we looked at each other, I said to Martin, "that's not my Gary," he said, "I know Lou" we both just sat there and sobbed for ages. We had a few beers but we felt nothing, I think we were hoping to feel something, anything, but nothing. It was like we were looking through a window, looking at a family going through this awful thing but in reality, it was us. The sad truth is, it had happened to my son, and we had to get him through this no matter what it took. Ash came up to see Gaz in hospital, he got scared, he would not allow Gaz to pick him up, I could see this upset him. Poor Thomas came, he almost passed out, he was so upset he nearly fainted, he swiftly had to leave as the sight of Gary and the other injured troops was just too much, so many young faces without legs or arms. We kept seeing soldier after soldier being brought in by ambulance, It was so upsetting to see them, their poor parents. For me this was the worse thing in my life, seeing these poor lads, but all they could talk about was getting back out there, they all had this guilt because they were still alive and not out there helping their brothers. They were so dominant with that band, yet so weak with what had happened to them. The band of brothers made them fearless, if they would of let them go back in their wheelchairs, they would of, I swear to god. I still think about their faces often.

We took Gary into town shopping, he wanted to buy a watch before heading back to Banbury. I said I was going into a shop "what about me?" he snapped, then it dawned on me, he didn't want to be on his own, he just kept looking around, it was like he was on his guard. I could see he was scared, he could not sit still, he would constantly roll his fingers, his nerves had gone. My little boy was scared of everything for quite some time. We come home but he did not come in, he went to town, I think he had to prove he could do it. My sister commented on his behaviour, how a different person had returned, once again I cried. I could see that he had changed so much, there was nothing I could do, my son had gone to war but a ghost had returned in his place. His auntie got upset when she took him for a walk, he stopped dead in the street. Looked at her then said, "that's what you've got to look for," she said she was confused, a group of men was going in their house, he pointed at them "together, like that. You've got to be careful!" This upset her, she told me he was genuinely cautious about them, she said his hands were twitching.

The army was not kind to him when he went back, in fact saying to him, what use is a one-eyed soldier, he was devastated, he was a rifleman that could not shoot a rifle, he felt useless. The others were still in Afghan, so Gary felt so alone, he described the barracks as empty and ghostly. He came home as much as he could, but by this time he was getting drunk quite a lot so home time was more like, come back to get pissed time. When he stayed at the barracks, he would spend the whole weekend drinking by himself. He seemed cockier, like he thought nothing could touch him, let's face it, if two I.E.D's could not kill him then what could? I did not think much to this new Gary. This made him unique, a someone, not only was he drinking a lot, he was loud, arrogant, he thought he was better than anyone, anything. He tried to be the boss of the house, telling us what to do, by this time I could see his then-girlfriend seemed to be scared of him and his drinking. It was getting worse, I remember one night not long after he got blown up he went out drinking, he came back banging on the door, I let him in, he stood on the landing screaming and crying, then he laid on his bed and screamed and screamed and cried and cried so loud. I did not go to him, I just sat on my bed and cried, I cried for him. I could not help him, what could I do? There were many nights like this in the end, but this was the first for me, scary it was.

Gary's friend Cas came to stay, also from the army, they had got drunk on Friday night, they had been arrested in town, by this time I was getting so worried about Gary. His welfare officer came to the house, I had called them to express my concern, and he told them to behave. Like they were going to listen? That night they went out, I waited up as I mostly did. They came in shouting and laughing, punching the air, covered in blood. They laughed, they said not to worry, most of it wasn't theirs, then I could hear them whispering, laughing. His then partner worked at the hospital, she saw the lads they had beaten up, one had a punctured lung, a broken jaw, both their faces smashed to pieces. I was gutted, so ashamed, I couldn't believe that my child could do this, what sort of a monster had he become. Another drunken night he came home and pretended to eat his brothers' goldfish, but tripped and killed it. Ashley was so upset Gary had not shown any feelings, he just laughed! This was worrying. I thought about Afghanistan, what had he done out there? What had made him so numb to these emotions? Or was this just what he had to be?

Eventually, in August 2010, he left the army. They said he could hand out the new uniform to the new soldiers, how could he do that after being a rifleman. I would sit listening to him screaming in his bedroom after drunken nights, "you fucking deserved that, I punched ya, I knocked your fucking head off, ill kill you, you wanker!" These words were disturbing. He had a row with his then partner, he came home and smashed his watch up, broke things in the house, terrorised the family puppy, she wet herself as he punched a hole in my cupboard door. I tried so hard to calm him down, not a chance, by this time we were all scared of him, especially his little brother who was only 7. All day, every day. One day Ashley got a certificate from school, he was so excited to show Gary. He laughed and said, "what did you get that for? A pie eating competition?" Ashley's little face, I can still see it now. His head just went down. I was never sure if Gary was this way because he wanted to turn him into what he was, toughen him up, or maybe he was guilty because of what happened Abdul John, I will never really know.

Gary started drinking during the week, I would sit on my bed waiting. I could always hear him coming up the street, shouting, swearing and screaming. Either down the phone or just in the sky! Every night he crashed through the door, there would be a row, he would shout the most horrible things at the whole family. One night I said sobbing to my neighbour that I couldn't put Ashley through this anymore I've got to take our lives. I begged her to help me and tell Kylie how sorry I was. I even got the tablets ready, just like twenty years previous though I just couldn't do it. The only thing is though I could not protect all my children. I just couldn't take anymore. Many times my friend would sit with me in the house or garden until it got light, I was dying inside, and it was Gary who was slowly killing us.

Finally, he got his own home. I smiled on the outside but inside I knew he needed help, his finger was on the self-destruct button, yet he added more pressure on himself. That dreaded night came when things changed for the worse, if they could get any worse, but believe me, they did. Gary had a BBQ to celebrate his new home, I said to his sister, he should not as it was on the anniversary of his friend's death, big mistake. Later that night I received a phone call, he had been arrested. Due to his behaviour, his partner had packed her things and left while he was out drinking, on the way to her mums she text him. He went home, got in his car drunk and drove to her house crashing into her friends' cars. In one night he had lost everything through drink. I was there to pick up the pieces once again. He was diagnosed with PTSD that weekend, it was as if the whole world he knew had just crumbled at his feet, he promised to get help but when it came he denied the fact that he needed it. Once again he just tried to carry on.

Gary hated living alone, he was scared and admitted this to

me, which was brave in my eyes. He asked if he could move back home, of course, I said yes. Maybe this had opened his eyes and made him see he needed help. Could this be the wake-up call he needs to start a new life? Afraid not, this is where the abuse and drinking got worse. The real terror had now begun. Ashley was excited about having his big brother moving home. So that Gary could have his room, Ashley gave up his bedroom, he gave away hundreds of pounds worth of toys, gave them to charity shops, he said he wanted to make people smile. What a kind-hearted child he is, especially with everything that had happened. Anyway, Gary moved in.

We soon realised we were frightened of him. He would just turn the TV over, and we would sit there and say nothing. I would say stuff or shout, but Gary would just shut me down. Eventually, Ashley would learn to look at me, and I would shake my head, say nothing, do nothing, how wrong is that?

He wasn't working, he had a few little jobs with his friends' building etc. He always lost them through drink though, turning up for work drunk, sometimes not even sleeping. He would always be asking for money to drink, of course, I would say yes. For two reasons, so he would go out and leave us alone, and because I did not want to fight. One night he wanted money, I remember throwing the penny pot over his head, I was scared the second I did it. He put his fist to my face and pushed my head to the ground to the money and said I was no mother and that I was a fucking bitch. As always, he would come home, get me out of bed. "Sit down, fucking sit down," he would shout. "You should have seen this blokes face, I fucking punched him, and punched him and punched him! Stay there, fucking stay there." He would be shouting at the carpet, mimicking the violence. If I moved he would follow me, "see mum, this is me. This is who I am, I do what I want, when I want". I believed this, in the end, there was no stopping him. I just sobbed then went to bed to cradle my youngest child. My worse fear was family parties, I knew he would get drunk and start a fight. He screamed at me once at my nephews' partners' birthday, all her friends were watching as he pushed me into a car. He walked back in as though nothing had happened, I walked home crying because in front of all these people he had been screaming in my face. As usual the next day the word sorry would come out.

I was beginning to realise at this point that Gary was now on drugs, my worst fears. My worst nightmare had become a reality. I had found cocaine in his bedroom, I could not stop crying, I was somewhere between distressed for him and ashamed. By this time his friends had nicknamed him 'Charlie sheen' who could be proud of this name? Only my son. I become convinced that someone was watching my house, my daughter would find me staring out my bedroom window all hours of the night. I was having terrible nightmares about Gary so I couldn't sleep. The thought of him out doing drugs terrified me, the people he could be mixing with, the things that could happen to him. Every night he would come crashing into my bedroom, he would pull my arm and downstairs we would go again. "You don't know what its like, you don't know what I've been through, you know fuck all, nothing, you cant tell me what to do, do you hear me." I would say Gary you are killing yourself. He would just say "good, you stupid cow, don't you get it, I don't care, don't you think when I have a bath I just want to put my head under so it's all over." These nights were tough because sometimes we would hold each other and I would say, please let me help you, please let me call somebody. But being honest, I had already called god knows how many people, but unless Gary called himself then there was nothing they could do. I started dragging the chest of draws to the door, I was scared of my son. In the summer he would drink in the garden with friends. On the way back from school I could hear music, shouting, swearing. I would ask him to leave, but he would just yell at me. He would always go off in the end to town drinking anyway. I was terrified because he was scared of nothing. He would just have drug binges for the whole weekend. I was sure he was going to be found dead.

The school had noticed a change in Ashley. He had become withdrawn and was not himself. Ashley's teacher knew the family as she was Kylie and Gary's teacher years before. She asked me if there was anything going on at home that she may need to know about. I broke down and could not stop crying, I repeated over and over again, he hates us and I don't understand why. It took me a few minutes before I could adequately get my words out. I would often find Ashley in the corner crying, saying he was ugly, fat, useless and could not do his homework. I tried so hard to make him realise this was not true, that his big brother was ill and did not mean the things he had said. By now, Kylie was also beginning to lock her bedroom door. We were continually checking Facebook to see the state he would be in and if we should be ready for a fight. I would try to get ash to sleep first hoping that he would not be disturbed, that he would not have to hear the fighting. The whole family was now living in fear, scared of a son, scared of a brother. The nights were spent waiting for him to come home or the police to knock the door or if he would even come back at all. I heard a strange noise in the front garden, it was frightening. Then I listened to the screaming, I opened the door, there laid my son naked in the snow. I dragged him into the house, I tried to get him upstairs, all the while he was screaming. He stood at the top of the stairs shouting, I just cried and didn't know what to do anymore. He was my son, my responsibility, I wanted to be the one to pull him out of this nightmare. I should have realised he was beyond my help, all it did was drag the family into this awful life.

It was now beyond my control, the school got involved very quickly even though I only let the teacher know half of what was going on. The thought of losing my child made me want to take my own life. By this time there were vodka bottles all over the house, I had to go home and bin them most days. Lads would be drinking in his room, or in the garden. I would just have to wait until the storm was over or until they went to a friend's house or town. I was at the end of my rope, there were holes in all my doors where Gary had punched them. I was so tired of getting no sleep, at school the teachers would cuddle me and say. "I'm so sorry I can see things are no better." It was almost embarrassing that everyone knew my son was terrorising us. If a friend would ask how I was, I would often just break down. I was now prescribed antidepressants and sleep tablets, not that they worked.

The school decided Ashley, and I needed a break. A holiday away from everything, they funded a trip. Ashley was so excited, I, on the other hand, was more worried about leaving Kylie and her partner alone in the house with Gary, but for Ashley's sake, we went away. The first night was beautiful, I looked at Ashley's smiling face and knew we had done the right thing, just like Gary's face when we went away when he was only my little boy. Before the PTSD, I had little money now as I did then, but something about the British beach makes you smile. He could sleep peacefully, not waking to the sound of the door being kicked through. The silence was terrific, but at the back of my mind, I was worried. I received a phone call the following night. Gary was drunk and his friend was passed out. My daughter was sobbing on the phone to me. As usual, he had kicked off and her partner had thrown a fruit bowl at his head. He went upstairs and smashed her room to pieces. The police were called but Gary had just shouted at the officers, even grabbing beers from the wheelie bin when they told him to stop drinking. By the end of the night he had to stay on his Nan and Gramps sofa. Neither his sister or auntie will say much of what was said that night, I guess something's are better left unsaid. Our holiday was ruined. I was sobbing down the phone to my daughter, she could take no more and who could blame her? She had been through so much, too much abuse. Ashley was crying saying what has Gary done mummy. What has happened? All week I just wanted to come home. When I finally did, it was horrible. No one to greet us, just an empty, lonely house.

People must be reading this and thinking why? Why did you put your family through this? The answer is easy, because he was my son trapped inside PTSD. My son would never have treated us like this, he would never have said those things. War had destroyed my son, made him hate himself from the inside out. I could see what was happening, a bomb was waiting to go off, I was going to be there to shield him. He was self-destructing, he wanted to die, time and time again he would tell me, “don't you get it, Mum? I don't care, I want to die!” Those words haunted me, I was not about to let that happen. He wasn't the boy that went away, but sometimes I could see that somewhere behind this awful mask was my son. He would say to his mates before going out, "say hello to my mum." If they walked out the door he would say, “oi get back in here say hi to my mum, don’t disrespect my mum." It was not always bad, many nights he would sit and chat to me for hours, until the very early hours of the morning saying “mum I don’t want to be like this anymore, I don't want to take drugs or drink." We would both sit and cry together. He would mostly be like this off his head or drunk but sometimes sober. I knew he wanted help, but if I told him I had spoken to someone, he would explode and tell me to mind my own business.

It all got too much one night, Gary had stumbled upstairs drunk, I could hear him talking to Ashley and his cousin, then it went quiet, I ran upstairs and could see his cousin looking terrified. Gary had the pillow over Ashley’s face, I screamed and dragged him off. My poor little boy took a deep breath then yelled, Gary, laughed, spat all over the floor then rubbed it in with his shoe. He went into his room punching the doors and walls. I held Ashley for a long time trying to make him feel safe, he was shaking. We could not carry on like this, but what could I do? I believe if I had let Gary live alone he would not be here today to tell his story. The whole family had had enough of it, it was hurtful to hear them speak poorly of my boy, a man they once had respected and been so proud. They kept saying that I had to get the police involved and teach him a lesson. So one night he came home and started shouting, being abusive. I called the police but by the time they had called back, Gary was asleep. They came in the morning but little did I know, they would call social services because there was a minor in the house. I was petrified, I had a tidy house, food in the cupboards, and a fridge full, but of course that was not enough, we had to talk about Gary and the safety of Ashley.

Gary was my child, he also needed my help, I had to think of Ashley though. Gary was angry he did not want these people interfering with his life, to him these people were scum. I knew they were just doing their job, they said no drink in the house also that Gary was not to enter the premises while under the influence. I was sure if I did not stand by this I would lose my son. The height of this period was when Gary came home, I told him he had to leave. It was a red flag to a bull, he went mental, I have never heard such vile abuse. He spat, he wanted to fight, he kept pushing, poking me. It was like he hated me, he said he's never had a life, never been brought up, he was dragged up, I was a useless fat whore, such a sick mum, I should have had my kids took off me. Kylie was shouting, trying to make him stop, he just cried, "come on then, come on I fucking dare you, make the first move, just try you bitch" over and over again. I phoned Emily, Gary's new girlfriend and told her to come and get him. I sat on the wall, his sister blocked the door, I could hear him screaming, he wanted to get to me, Emily came and cuddled me while I was sobbing. He opened the door and saw Emily then he shouted at me for calling Emily, we were screaming at each other down the road, I begged him to stop. I went home and he yelled at me that I was dead to him. He pushed past me and tried climbing the stairs. I dragged him back down, he couldn't be there else I would have lost Ashley. I shouted to Emily, he is your problem now and I slammed the front door shut on him. I was sobbing until 6 am, I had to be up at 7 am for a meeting at Ashley's school with his head of year and social services, I was in no fit state but I went, Gary never turned up.

I somehow managed to speak to combat stress. I begged Gary to talk to the lady on the phone, he did. Was this the start of things to come? The man would meet Gary, he was not drinking as much, I was beginning to feel hopeful again. I could see the light at the end of the tunnel, but it was going to be a long road to get there. The drinking had all but finally stopped, the drugs had stopped entirely, I believe this has a lot to do with his girlfriend, Emily. They moved into their house together, got a dog, Gary has started to work, he has even been promoted a number of times. To see my son at a point where he was going to commit suicide, to a man that has faced his demons, has been the hardest thing but I would do it all over again.

Gary's feelings for Emily grew very strong. He was and is devoted to Emily, also their dog Freddie, we could see that he was trying. I was feeling the pride for my son beginning to come back. I never fully relax, I know he can slip at any moment, but he's strong now, much stronger than I've ever known him. He got involved in a charity called Deptherapy. We went to a charity event in aid of Deptherapy, Gary told his story in front of the whole crowd, it was lovely, and this time I cried but it was tears of pride. I'm so glad I stuck by my son, as you have read, it sure was not easy. I was broken many times, almost lost my family. I even realise I have left bits out, but Gary is not a monster. He just needed the right help, guidance from the right people. I love my children with all my heart. I'm so very proud of each one of them. Gary, you have walked through hell, got burnt along the way but my son, you have made it out the other side. I'm so proud to call you my son. Keep fighting and never give up. Your loving mum, always and forever.

So, the above account was my Mums story, I asked her to write a chapter that would enable the reader to understand what it's like to love someone with PTSD, to live with them every day. She wrote fifty-four pages all handwritten, after her busy days of looking after my Nan she would stay up to the early hours with her notebook and pen. In two days after me requesting it, she gave me the pages, it was quite a howling job to sift through the abusive pages, it's certainly a stark reminder of a life to which I never want to return. It reminds me just how vital my little rituals are to keep me going on the right track. Also, it makes me thankful that I had such a supportive family that I so nearly lost. I will forever be in my families debt for what I put them through, I just hope one day I make them all proud, show them the reasons that it was worth sticking by me.

Me and my fiancé Emily at our home in Banbury. The lady who taught me how to love again.

Chapter 20
A Time for Reflection

So, I guess now you know my story, the story of thousands that have fought in wars, in conflicts, those that have felt the chaos and heartache of a soldier that cannot adjust back into normal life. Now you know this story, the truth, it may be easier to understand the actions of those like me and know when someone has a problem with which they reflect in their behaviour. Recognise that someone is trying to self-destruct his or her own life repeatedly may be through deep anger and pain. My life will continue, and I'm in the process of learning to adapt to my problems, as the saying goes:

'It's not the most intelligent or fittest of people that will survive. It is, in fact, those ablest to adapt.'

I have learned to accept that PTSD is not something I can lose, it's not something I can just take medicine for. It's a part of me. It co-exists in my mind. It is me, and it is a part of every decision I make. It will be an ongoing battle for the rest of my life. I am lucky enough to have a loving family that will continue to support me. A fiance that understands my situation. The important thing for all those to realise that whatever your past, whatever your position, that there is always a light at the end. There will still be someone there to love you, we all have a cloud that sits above our head that is dark but fuck that cloud and smile. The critical thing to remember is that it is never the end, there will always be things you need to fight for, something you need to live for and when you find that you will see that the most significant thing you need to live for is yourself. Maybe I live in the past sometimes, but that doesn't exactly have to be a bad thing, I try not to dwell on my mistakes but to learn from them. I always enjoy my writing and will peruse a career in it. But now I work as well and have adjusted to the real life, but finally and maybe the most important thing is that I am still proud to have served in the army. I no longer live on that reputation, I have learned lessons, and I have moved on.

My fuel was my family, without intentional actions I was ruining their lives, I knew I had to change for them, and in realising that and having some of the fog removed, I saw I wanted to change for myself. After Afghanistan and leaving the Army I hated my life, I felt like I was useless, there was never going to be anything I could do that was going to bring that pride back. I have to live with that for the rest of my life, those things I saw and done out there are imprinted on me. They are what shape me, but no longer will I let those things define me. I granted thoughts and memories to hold me back. I tried drinking those memories away. I tried doing drugs and partying my life away to redefine my character. All I did was purposely self-destruct over and over again because I hated myself. I see now that the person I was becoming was a far worse person. A person who had no respect, a person that had no self-respect, an embarrassment to my former self, where was that respectful, fresh-faced, kind-hearted young man that everybody loved? I know he is still inside me, but I will never be that same person again. I know I can be a better person for myself, my family and in the future for my wife and children.

A wise old bird, Emily's Mum, she will kill me for saying old, said another saying to me that I love, it again helps me keep a balanced mind in times of adversity, no matter how big or small. She said to me, "just remember, it's a bad day, not a bad life." That's so true. Of all the shit things I went through, no matter how bad things seemed at the time, I have come out the other side, I have made it to the happy place. I believe that everyone can, no matter your vice or reasons, it is just a bad day. I love those videos that people post about how awesome people are, if you're ever down just watch those, people are amazing, no matter how hopeless a situation they will always restore your faith in humanity. I know it can be hard sometimes when you feel down, you are worn down easier, small problems can seem dominant on top of your already facing fears, anxieties. The trick is to remember. It is not a bad life, think of your happy place, think of all that is possible. If your job is that bad, quit, fuck it, life is too short. There are a lot of things in this world that will make you sad, don't let something in your control be one of them. It's a bad day, not a bad life.

The more I have written in this book, the more I have pondered with the final chapter, is there going to be a big revealing, will there be a speech or a secret? There is neither. I wish there were, but I've been sincere through this book so there would be no point making something up at this point, there is no secret I'm afraid. There is only progress, time. Life is just a journey, we are all on separate paths, we all react to things differently, the one thing that we all have in common though is hope. From the man with PTSD with a gun in his mouth about to pull the trigger hoping for a reason not to, to the homeless man that sits outside the local shops hoping for someone to throw a penny in his hat. We are all human, we all need the same treatment, everyone has a long journey behind them, there is only a split second that separates us, and you can be on the top as quickly as you can be at the bottom. If you learn one thing from this entire account, I hope that it is that the word impossible does not exist. There is always an answer, you can always find solutions if you look hard enough, or have a few hands pointing you in the right direction, remember a problem shared is a problem halved.

I am just a boy, a boy who became focused so fearlessly on a dream, when the fruition left me outside of the world I had resided in, I could not cope. I think we can all relate to this, remember the hopes and dreams you had as a child, are you following them now? Are you satisfied with your life? Would the child you once were, be happy with the life you have now? Would you have tried harder? Pushed your dreams further? It is never too late to turn back the clock, to decide that you are no longer going to be unsatisfied, it is never too late to have a dream. Even now as you have read this I am sorely unimpressed with my life, but not my progression. I would be a liar to say I'm not grateful for my progress from the drug houses I spent so much time. However, I still know that my appetite has not been fulfilled. The power is in all of us. We hold the key to all doors, all you need to do is seek for what you want. It's like a smoker with cigarettes in their pocket saying they have no money, and I'm the same. I always find the money to smoke, so theoretically I should be able to find the money for anything?

I wish we had equality in this life, not just for race but circumstance, if the rich get hooked on drugs they would have the investment that could turn their lives around, they could then accomplish things. When I was on drugs all I had was my family, they were the sole supporter and barrier between me being a frequent drug user to me being on the streets in a sleeping bag, I would have become another statistic. Here I sit now though as someone who may be able to make a genuine difference in peoples lives, in fact someone who has already, should we all not be allowed that opportunity? No one is helpless, the right time and investment in someone could be all that is required, just to be shown what is possible. No one in this life is too far gone in any direction, remember the only thing irreversible in life is death. It's what I would like to accomplish with PTSD, your issues are only small bumps, they do not have to define you. They will forever be a part of you, your name shall be forever carved in the sand or dirt where you have fought, but your mind is allowed to come home. Take it from someone who has been lost.

I don't quite understand this thing I have, I have learned a lot about it, I know I have it because I can feel it. When did this invisible demon attach itself to my soul? Why must I now forever feel so different, so alien in all aspects of this world I now live? To whom do I seek help from? No one is the answer. Like a weighted day sack that sits upon my shoulders, this curse now holds me down a little further every time I drop my guard. Every thought I have is now present with a little whisper of doubt. It's hard to explain, how do you explain something you don't fully understand? I guess the answer to that question is to write a book. I'm sick of all the stigma that is attached to it. I'm sick of those who tell their stories with strokes of heroism and GI Joe arrogance. I have seen war, I have lived with the demons that have since attacked me, but never have I called myself a hero, never have I lied about circumstance. I consider myself a human being with an anxiety disorder, a human being that was stretched a little bit too far. A person like all others that now struggle to live in this world that has been limited by social status and bank balance.

The suicide rate for US veterans are twenty-two per day, how crazy is that? How sad that we live in a society that veterans feel so trapped they would instead take their own lives than try to seek help. That isn't including other groups of society that take their own lives. I had a search on the internet to try and find some statistics on UK veterans. Unfortunately, there wasn't many that were available. I found one source in the BBC that stated in 2012 more soldiers died through suicide than had in combat. How disturbing is that? I mean it's a good thing for the war, I'm happy that our soldiers had a low death rate. I wish it were zero, and I also wish zero veterans had wanted to commit suicide. One is too many. There is a big world out there, and the possibilities are endless, no one should feel confined to anything smaller than the whole world. Whether you are a veteran or not, no one deserves to feel that life is not worth living. Mental illness is curable. No one should be left hopeless. Everyone can be helped, every person is a human being that deserves respect, mental illness is nothing more than a bi-product of the world we have created. For that reason, it is everyone's responsibility to pull together to make everyone feel loved, to make everyone feel wanted.

The best outcome for this world is a unity that we can all pull together. I loved my job, I loved the Army, in the grand scheme of things though it honestly isn't the answer. I'm proud of my service, the adrenaline is something that appeals to all males, it's that animalistic feeling of testosterone. I get that I do, but no matter how you dress it up, how good the mollie grip pouches look, violence is not the answer. Whether terrorism is nothing more than an invention of government to control the population through fear to launch illegal wars, or even if it is a real threat to our society, there are better ways to deal with it. I do believe that if we all came together to fight for world peace, to use our joint efforts for good instead of segregation and wealth, that we wouldn't need an army, there would be no wars. I'm not stupid, I know we need to protect our national security, I know we need soldiers to do the dirty work, I just hope one day my children never have to know war, that they will have peace. I do believe the only people that want war are those who can benefit from it, I never profited from the fight, I'm thankful for my journey, I never made millions from it though, I wasn't selling arms to the government. A rapper, Akala from London say's a brilliant line in one of his tracks.

'A pawn is on the frontline with minimal movement. The game was fixed from the start.'

What I think he's trying to say there is that people like me who were on the frontline have no choice in how the game is played. It was just pick up your weapon and go there. Those who decided to go to war, those who choose on how to utilise our billion-dollar/pound weapon, don't get hurt. They are doing nothing more than weighing up the balance of expenditure and profit. How much can they make from the war? What do they have to spend? The last thing they worry about is how to sell it to the country. How do we tweak the minds of all the little Rifleman Greens out there? How do we convince them to risk their lives? Easily is the answer. Institutionalize them, the one thing people will always fight for is the people they love, give them a purpose and they will provide you with their lives. That was me. They made me part of that gang, I believed in that gang with my whole heart, I gave them my all for that reason. I was brainwashed, I was moulded as a young man to do whatever they wanted me to do, we all were, it's just a legal version of the Mafia that's all. If someone isn't paying up, send in the heavies.

I've grown now, in the literal and metaphorical sense. I'm not the person that was so easily manipulated as I was back then. I will no longer be lead so blindly by those who dangle carrots. My primary objective is that the day I die, I can say that I tried to do something to stop it. I tried to make the world a better place, I stood by my brothers before, during and after a war. I suppose it takes seeing something to believe it, what I have seen is a system that has left me hanging, who from the world that I once gave all to was there to stop me hanging myself? Who from that world wanted to protect my families' welfare and mine once I had returned from war? All I had was my family, those civilians that I was made to believe I was better than, at least those civilians loved me, at least those civilians held me up until I was able to stand by myself. The weird thing about all this, I would probably do it all over again, just through some undying commitment that I still feel. If I could go back, I believe the voices in my head will stop talking, maybe because it's true that ignorance is bliss? When I see those videos of Islamic state pop up on TV, I instantly wait for the racial reaction over social media. It's crazy, whoever creates this stuff must be sitting in their chair with a smile and one hell of a spoon. I believe that the country as it stands at the minute would be ready to vote for war wherever they said it was, no matter what the cost. It all started recently with this drift of migrants from Syria, I too was annoyed, my heart melted for these poor people that were leaving their homes, but financially it was always going to be a disaster. If we can't already keep our economy stable, how can we then justify allowing such an influx? If we have drones in every area of this world, how did they not see them coming? I can find my Patrol

Base in Afghanistan on my phone in Google maps, so how can the government not see thousands of people marching across Europe? Also, who thought it was a good idea to just split them across Europe like cake at a fucking birthday party? Surely it would have been more productive to help them build up their own country, help them to rebuild a sustainable and peaceful land rather than begin dropping £500,000 bombs on to their homes? Am I thick or am I missing something? If your boiler breaks, you call a plumber and get a new boiler. You don't pack up all your things, move in with your neighbour and then chuck a petrol bomb through your window. If this world continues the way it is, there will only be more wars, more veterans, more injured, more dead, more side effects that come with it, more PTSD and more serviceman and women that will take their own lives.

As I look back over the past few years, I can salvage a small amount of hope. I can recognise that I can keep moving forward. Of all people, I know that no matter how gloomy the situation looks, there is always a move to be played. I have to look into the sky, see the sun that is shining down on a spring morning, remember the miracles that are happening every day. Remember that the sun is the perfect distance from the earth so that we do not freeze or burn to death, everything else is irrelevant surely? Veterans are taking their own lives. Soldiers are living on the streets. They have the same mental health problems I have, while there is blood running through my veins I must remain grateful. We must all remember that compassion is a medication. If you can look at others in a less fortunate position than yourself, recognise what you have is what they need, then you should never feel out of control. If you spend your life looking at those with more than you, envious, then you will always feel out of control. PTSD can be viewed in the same way. If you continually look at people who are doing better than you, you will never feel like you're moving forward. If every time I have a down day I dwell on it, I will never feel as if I have stepped ahead. Whereas if I look at it as a glass half full case, I will feel positive.

"I hate that I'm having a down day, but at least I know it won't last forever, last year I was in a worse position. I should be thankful that I'm not still there, imagine where I could be next year."

With this mentality I can block out the negative thoughts, at least I can try anyway as if I'm Luke Skywalker.

"Come on young Jedi use the force."

"Thank you, Obi-Wan Kenobi great words of wisdom as always."

"PTSD you have, stay positive you must."

"Ok, Yoda sounds like a plan mate."

Although the problem with that is, like anything, it's a lot easier to say than it is to put into practice. If I were a Jedi, it would be a lot easier. Knowing my luck though if I were to be a Star Wars character, I would end up being Jar Jar Binks. For those not familiar with Star Wars, Jar Jar Binks is a very clumsy creature that ends up messing everything up. He does have a heart of gold though, so perhaps there are underlying comparisons between the loveable idiot and me. Jar Jar Binks would be the one to end up feeling insulted though.

"Me sir no stupid as Gary Green."

That is to be read in a Jar Jar Binks accent, and I hope I haven't revealed too much of my geeky side. Perhaps we should kick back and trade Pokémon analogies for the rest of this concluding chapter? I suppose it's easy to find any parallel that works with PTSD because it is so diverse. It affects everyone in different ways. Not too different, I have seen that most people share common symptoms, the anger and hypervigilance are the most frequent. Especially those from the more recent theatres of war, alcohol and drugs are unfortunately the most common coping mechanisms used by the veterans I have spoken to. It makes me feel so sad because it's such a dishonest mask.

With all that has been spoken through this book you know me

now, you know almost everything about me. Why I am the way I am, why the way so many veterans are the way they are. I do think since the end of the Afghanistan campaign they've been forgotten about.

"The job is done now, quick sweep this mess under the carpet, tell these veterans to keep quiet. Nobody wants to hear about suicide and PTSD. It will put people off their dinner."

Everyone wanted to hear the heroic stories, they wanted to know our boys were doing a good job, maybe it made their consciences feel better about all wanting to go to war. It's easy when you think it's as glamorous as it appears on the news or the way it's portrayed in film and TV. You don't just pick up a fucking rifle and go shooting bad guys though. You don't just put that rifle down afterwards and continue normal life either. It's nothing like you can imagine, my book doesn't do it full justice, you need to go and experience it. Go and pick up some child's legs that's just been hit with an I.E.D, trust me it's not clean. When you have to look into his eyes and know that I.E.D was meant for you. Some eight-year-old child just lost his life for no reason. Maybe if you had to do that, you might have chosen a different way to vote. It's a sad realisation that you were nothing more than a pawn, I made no difference in Afghanistan, to be honest, what did I do? What did any of us do? I went somewhere with a rifle, I shot in the direction I was supposed to, I was injured when I was supposed to, I do not see how I made a difference to that country? I don't see how anything changed. If anything, it felt like a bit of a tear up and nothing else. Our CO may as well have been Danny Dyer.

"Alright boys I'm the facking guvna, this is England away, we're playing Afghanistan. When we get there, we're gonna turn em over like the facking mugs they are. Then we're gonna come home sink some larger and cause some trouble, real facking naughty like."

That's basically what happened, we went out there, had a tear up and came home. Now nobody wants to talk about it, it was never justified, no one ever told us what objectives we accomplished.

All there is to do now is move on for ourselves, that's all we can do. We need to make sure that our past benefits our futures rather than holding us back. No matter what we feel for what we have done, if it doesn't serve us now, then we have to be able to move forward without it. We can't let negative experience rule our lives. Otherwise, the outlook will always be negative. We signed up to fight, and we fought when and where we were told to, now we need to fight for something that means something, our futures. We need to find peace; there's a new generation that we're going to bring into this world. We need to be the difference, and we need to be the ones to say enough is enough. There's a saying that is so true.

'Rich mans' war, poor mans' blood.'

How true is that? We're the sorry morons that go out there and fight their fight, why? I would fight for my boys any day of this week, but why the fuck was I out there risking my life for someone I don't even know? Whoever this fucking person was they didn't even come and say thank you for putting my life on the line for them. They certainly don't care about how my life has turned out now.

I guess this is time for me to sign off, to say goodbye for now but not forever. I feel quite emotional actually because this has been a focus of mine for so long, now I will need to find a new one. Trust me though you haven't heard the last of me. From those who gave me free drugs to those who taught me how to live, you were all part of my healing process. Helping me to express myself in one way or another, I thank you all, to those who are still supporting me, bare with me, I'm worth it.

"Creativity is the product of imagination but when the reality is more intriguing, write that and give that to the uninformed market of consciousness, the truth." – Gary Green.

Acknowledgements

I'm guilty of failing in 9/10 cases to read the acknowledgements of most books that I have read. If you're reading this then thank you, you have found more persistence with books than I. I hope you enjoyed my story and the way in which I conveyed it to you all. Although I have mentioned certain associations and people throughout, it would be unfair for me not to have an acknowledgements section for those directly involved in my development and my book.

Firstly, Emily Potter, my fiancé, my true love and the most beautiful person. We fell in love back in 2013, four years and seven months ago currently. An awful drag I must say. I would like to think at one point in my life I may have sorted myself out if it wasn't for her, but that is something I will never need to know as she was the catalyst for my transition. My abstinence of substance since is almost thanks to this woman entirely, because you are never truly rich until you find something money can't buy and you never want to lose something as much as something you can't live without.

As you now know I work a full-time job, as time has gone on and I've progressed, the work has become more challenging and full of worthwhile responsibilities. During the editing of the final manuscript, I was working a three-shift pattern, mornings, lates and nights. It was hard to find the motivation to wake up and begin editing over 100,000 words after finishing work at 07:00 in the morning. Thank you, Emily, for being there at every turn to help me, for reading every word I wrote back to me, for my 5am coffees, running my baths after work and starting my car on cold mornings. Thank you basically for making sure I never had to worry about anything when I felt like I had everything to worry about.

My Mum, Louise Green, who I think we can all agree we have heard far too much from already, slandering my good name and such. Something I left out of this book is that before I was born, the doctor said I was going to be born disabled during one of my scans, he offered my Mum a termination which she refused, she was going to give birth to me and love me no matter what. It turns out it was a misdiagnosis, but my mothers' selfless love was not and never has been. Since a child I have seen my Mum take care of the whole family at one point or another, she has never stopped, a born carer, a sensitive woman and a real angel reincarnated. You never gave up on me, from the potential disabled son to what must have been the biggest burden on your shoulders. Thank you.

To Leona Potter, a small mention but a deserved one for your intellectual discussions, your lent ear, your sound advice and for introducing me to theatre. I will never agree with you on Maggie Thatcher though.

Richard Cullen, I mentioned Deptherapy but I did not mention you specifically. I would like to thank you for the hard work you selflessly pump into the charity. On a personal note I would like to thank you for the times you've given me advice and continually supported my diving and my helping others.

There's an unsung hero, or two in fact in this. One is Elizabeth and one is a fellow Rifleman but a very long time ago, he's also an author, Ronald Cove. Elizabeth had read one of my Facebook posts at a time when I was thinking of giving up my dream of being a writer. She put me in touch with Ronald who reignited my desire and put me in touch with MTP Agency, thank you both.

To my whole family, there are so many isolated reasons in which I could mention you individually, but there honestly wouldn't be enough pages. Tim for coming to bail me out of drunken states from Oxford to Birmingham, Sue for the horseshoe token. I simply couldn't list them all, but I think each of you must hold a special capacity for love and forgiveness. I am truly sorry for the pain I caused you, thank you for not giving up on me, I love all of you the same amount and for individual reasons. I have to give a special mention to two of the family that had to live with me, Kylie and Ashley, I love you both to the moon and back.

To everyone else, those who are out there in this uncertain world helping people selflessly and unsung, I thank you, from those that dedicate their lives to helping those less fortunate to those that deposit their change in a charity box.

Please remember that it's easier to turn the other cheek, but it's more valuable to do the right thing. To smile at your neighbour, to hold the door open, to choose forgiveness. Choose love, choose the right thing for our children and our childrens' children.

About Gary Green

Name: Gary Christopher Peter Green

D.O.B: 05th June 1989

Gary Green joined the British Army as an Infantryman in the winter of 2007, he finished his Infantry training top of his platoon and was awarded the honour of Best Recruit being presented with the Baker Rifle.

He joined his battalion in 2008 facing challenging training to prepare him for war. In the summer of 2009 he deployed to Afghanistan to fight on the front line. There he faced the true horrors of war dealing with injured civilians and colleagues as well as daily fire fights with the enemy until he himself was blown up by two I.E.D's.

Being left blind in his right eye from war and medically discharged from the armed services in 2010. In 2011 he was diagnosed with post-traumatic stress disorder and battled with drug and drink addictions until conquering them in late 2013.

In 2014 he had his poem PTSD published in the anthology of love, following that in 2015 he produced a video of the poem that reached over 250,000 people on social media. He completed his first book, Bombs For Breakfast in 2016.

He is now a Trustee and Board member of the charity Deptherapy, where he plays a part in rehabilitating veterans who have life changing physical and mental injuries. He is also a Padi Ambassadiver for the UK and ran the Virgin London Marathon in 2015 for Tickets for Troops.

In 2017 he was part of a documentary 'Amazing Humans' with BBC3, this was viewed by over 5.6 million people. He published his first book Bomb's for Breakfast in 2018 and is currently working on his first novel. He currently resides in Banbury with his fiancé.

36315664R00199

Printed in Great Britain
by Amazon